Mac OS X for Java™ Geeks

Related titles from O'Reilly

Mac OS X for Java™ Geeks

Will Iverson

O'REILLY®
Beijing · Cambridge · Farnham · Köln · Paris · Sebastopol · Taipei · Tokyo

Mac OS X for Java™ Geeks
by Will Iverson

Published by O'Reilly & Associates, Inc., 1005 Gravenstein Highway North,
Sebastopol, CA 95472.

O'Reilly & Associates books may be purchased for educational, business, or sales pro-
motional use. Online editions are also available for most titles (*safari.oreilly.com*). For
more information, contact our corporate/institutional sales department: (800) 998-9938
or *corporate@oreilly.com*.

Editor:	Brett McLaughlin
Production Editor:	Emily Quill
Cover Designer:	Hanna Dyer
Interior Designer:	Bret Kerr

Printing History:

April 2003:   First Edition.

ISBN: 0-596-00400-1
[C]

Table of Contents

Preface

This was a surprisingly difficult book to write. It was difficult not because of the topic's technical complexity—after all, I've been working with Java™ since before the release of JDK 1.0 and developing on the Mac for over a decade. No, the hard part was deciding what should actually go into a book called *Mac OS X for Java Geeks*.

The unknown element of this book is the skill set possessed by the reader. If you're an expert on Swing looking for tips on how to build a Java application, you won't want to slog through pages of duplicated content explaining how to build such an application. The same goes for readers interested in JSP™, EJB™, SQL, and everything else related to the Java platform.

In the end, I relied on two main guides. First, I leaned on conversations with other developers (particularly developers who were unfamiliar with Mac OS X and interested in switching platforms). Second, much time was spent with the broad array of excellent existing Java development texts. If you've never developed an application in Swing, this text won't teach you everything you need to know, but it will teach you how to transfer that application to Mac OS X, package it, and generally make it behave in a first-class manner while maintaining cross-platform compatibility. If you really have never built an application in Swing, this book provides an annotated working example.

If you're just beginning to develop applications in Java on the Mac OS X platform, you'll find an excellent survey of Java development by installing and working your way through the examples in this text, following the suggestions for further reading when appropriate. Fortunately, O'Reilly provides an excellent library from which to choose.

This book, then, is meant to supplement the Java programmer's library. If you're a Java developer and want to see what Mac OS X can do, or are just getting into Java and want to ensure that Mac OS X is a viable development platform, I think you'll find your answers in this work. Enjoy!

Organization

This book provides a learning path for a Java developer new to the Mac OS X platform. It assumes a basic working familiarity with Java.

Chapter 1, *Getting Oriented*
Covers the history of Mac OS X and provides a preliminary introduction to the platform.

Chapter 2, *Apple's Java Platform*
Explores the technical underpinnings of the Mac OS X Java implementation, including the layout, classpath, and additions to the standard Java environment.

Chapter 3, *Java Tools*
Explores the pragmatics of Java development, including how to set up your development environment, and an overview of available tools.

Chapter 4, *GUI Applications*
Builds a local desktop application in Swing and examines how to extend this application while still retaining cross-platform capability.

Chapter 5, *Apple Extensions*
Discusses and gives examples of Apple's various additions to the Java platform.

Chapter 6, *Cross-Platform Programming*
Looks at the potential pitfalls of developing applications that are intended for multiple platforms and examines how to mitigate them.

Chapter 7, *Standalone Applications*
Describes how to package and deliver an application to end users that looks and behaves like a native Mac OS X application.

Chapter 8, *Web-Delivered Applications*
Examines how to build client applications that are delivered via the Web, including applets and Web Start applications.

Chapter 9, *The Mac OS X Speech Framework*
Discusses how to make an application generate human speech and respond to your speech.

Chapter 10, *QuickTime for Java*
Examines an application that provides support for rich multimedia.

Chapter 11, *The Mac OS X Spelling Framework*
Adds real-time support and interactive spellchecking to an application.

Chapter 12, *Databases*
Provides basic information on installation, setup, and usage of the popular MySQL and PostgreSQL databases.

Chapter 13, *Servlets, JSP, and Tomcat*
> Builds and debugs a web application using standard Java presentation technologies.

Chapter 14, *EJB and JBoss*
> Examines the development process for creating Enterprise JavaBeans™ on Mac OS X, and details installation of the JBoss application server.

Chapter 15, *Web Services*
> Builds XML-RPC and SOAP web services and communicates with these services by using Apple's AppleScript scripting package.

Conventions Used in This Book

The following font conventions are used in this book:

- *Italic* is used forUnix pathnames, filenames, and program names; for Internet addresses, such as domain names and URLs; and for new terms where they are defined.

- `Constant Width` is used for command lines and options that should be typed verbatim; and for names and keywords in Java programs, including method names, variable names, and class names.

- **`Constant Width Bold`** is used occasionally for emphasis in code.

 Indicates a tip, suggestion, or general note.

 Indicates a warning or caution.

Comments and Questions

Please address comments and questions concerning this book to the publisher:

O'Reilly & Associates, Inc.
1005 Gravenstein Highway North
Sebastopol, CA 95472
(800) 998-9938 (in the United States or Canada)
(707) 829-0515 (international or local)
(707) 829-0104 (fax)

There is a web page for this book, which lists errata, examples, or any additional information. You can access this page at:

http://www.oreilly.com/catalog/macxjvgks

To comment or ask technical questions about this book, send email to:

bookquestions@oreilly.com

For more information about books, conferences, Resource Centers, and the O'Reilly Network, see the O'Reilly web site at:

http://www.oreilly.com/

Acknowledgments

One person can write a book, but alone, one person cannot write a book like the one you hold in your hand. I send my appreciation to the oft-unseen engine behind the production, marketing, and sales of this book. I know you're there and appreciate all of your effort.

This book wouldn't be what it is without the valiant efforts of my editor, Brett McLaughlin. His tireless effort has made it a far better work than it might have been.

Thanks to Michael Loukides for entertaining and supporting the idea behind this book, and for making it possible to work with Brett.

Thanks to Tim O'Reilly for all the fine tomes that grace my bookshelf, and for allowing me to add my own title to O'Reilly's great library.

For their time, feedback and enthusiasm, I would like to thank James Duncan Davidson and Daniel Steinberg. Both could have written this book with their eyes shut—I just got lucky, I guess.

Thanks to Allen Denison for his support and enthusiasm; Bodhi for taking the time to provide feedback; the MRJ-Dev mailing list for asking and answering all my questions before I even knew to articulate them; and everyone at Apple Computer—many long hours go into building your beautiful software.

On a personal note, thanks to the entire B-night crew, the Anagamin players, and the LJ crowd.

And finally, thanks to Mom, Diane, and Cynthia. You are simply amazing.

## CHAPTER 1

Getting Oriented

Mac OS X is, in many ways, a new paint job on a 30-year-old operating system. BSD (the Berkeley Software Distribution), the Unix root of Mac OS X, has been around since the 1960s. The Mach kernel was developed in the 1990s, and the underlying user interface was created in early 1980s along with Lisa (Apple's ill-fated precursor to the Macintosh). In other words, everything old is new again.

Mac OS X doesn't feel like a 30-year-old clunker, though, but the culmination of countless hours of experimentation and refinement in desktop and workstation operating systems. To a Unix expert, Mac OS X is much like a solid distribution of a classic BSD system with the most egregiously beautiful window manager you've ever seen. For the Windows veteran, it is a simplified beast—a pure workhorse of modern productivity stripped of decades of anachronisms and distilled until it has an almost Zen-like simplicity. For the Mac OS 9 user, it represents an even more significant change. Nasty crashes and ridiculous extension conflicts are now a thing of the past, while Aqua, Mac OS X's new user interface, is clearly the look of the future.

Most importantly, though, Mac OS X is finally a developer's platform. With the melding of BSD, a killer user interface, and unprecedented stability, code can finally be written on the Mac OS X platform and deployed to Windows, Linux, Unix, or other Mac OS X servers. This book was written with the Java developer in mind. It assumes some degree of Java experience and familiarity with basic Unix commands such as cd, ls, and pwd. Maybe you are interested in porting an existing Java application to Mac OS X (perhaps because your customers asked for a Mac OS X version). Or maybe Linux is your development platform, but you are interested in moving to Mac OS X to access powerful graphics applications such as Adobe Photoshop. Maybe you're a bored Windows user, or are philosophically opposed to the Microsoft hegemony.

Your degree of experience really doesn't matter; Mac OS X is a great Java development platform for people of all programming and operating system backgrounds.

All Those Confusing Names

Mac OS X has, at different times, been associated with several different names. At one point it was called Rhapsody. Prior to that, it was NeXT's OpenStep and NeXTStep platform. The underlying Unix guts were also released as an open source project, Darwin, which includes BSD and the Mach kernel. With that in mind, explaining where Mac OS X started and where it is now will contextualize Mac OS X in its current incarnation.

Mac OS X 10.0

Mac OS X 10.0 was the first commercial release of Mac OS X. That release, however, wasn't particularly usable.

Convincing a large body of developers to embrace a new platform is not easy. You can release developer seeds, betas, and prereleases all you want, but at the end of the day, major operating system vendors have to release something that can be called a 1.0 product (or, in the case of Mac OS X, a 10.0 product). Releasing this product lets users know that you're transitioning from testing to "prime time."

The commercial release of Mac OS X 10.0 was just that: it was Apple's way of telling developers that the system was ready to go and that they should get on board. At this point, Apple began shipping Mac OS X 10.0 with their hardware, but didn't make it the default operating system. The release was lacking in quality, features, and supported applications, and everyone knew that the product needed more work.

Mac OS X 10.1

Mac OS X 10.1 marks what most people consider the first usable version of Mac OS X. Developers fixed a lot of important bugs, addressed performance issues, and added missing features.

Even more significant, however, was an Apple announcement at Macworld in January 2002. During one of the conference's keynote addresses, Steve Jobs announced that Apple would begin shipping Mac OS X as the default operating system. Users could still switch back to Mac OS 9 if they wanted, but when someone took that shiny new iMac out of the box, Mac OS X's Aqua greeted them. Apple's commitment to Mac OS X as their default platform was a clear message—developers and users both were assured of Apple's commitment to Mac OS X as an operating system for mainstream use.

Mac OS X 10.1.x

A few patches quickly followed the 10.1 release. Mac OS X 10.1.1 became Mac OS X 10.1.4. More importantly, a large number of critical applications became available, such as Microsoft Office and Adobe Photoshop. For developers, a large number of open source projects started to make regular binary builds available for the Mac OS X platform. Are you interested in MySQL, Apache, PHP, or Tomcat? All are now available, prebuilt specifically for Mac OS X. Some open source projects (such as PostgreSQL) that weren't even available for Windows have become available for Mac OS X.

Then Macromedia announced that their MX line (products like Flash, Dreamweaver, and Fireworks) were to be made Mac OS X–native via Carbon. Suddenly, the best platform for Unix and web application development started to resemble Mac OS X. Furthermore, several Java applications became available for Mac OS X. Many were server applications or developer products, but their appearance started to convince users that Mac OS X was becoming a friendly platform for developers.

Mac OS X 10.2 (Jaguar)

This release, despite being the first major release to not offer upgrade pricing, was in many ways a major infrastructural improvement. Much of the technology included in this release, such as Rendezvous (Mac OS X's auto-configurable networking), had a distinctly infrastructural feel. Most significantly, this release included several low-level improvements required for Apple's JDK 1.4 implementation. Although Jaguar shipped with a JDK 1.3 implementation, JDK 1.4 can be installed on Jaguar.

 Chapter 2 details the installation of both 1.3 and 1.4 JDK runtimes.

Beyond Mac OS X 10.2

Future releases of Mac OS X will ship with JDK 1.4 support (or whatever the latest JDK version is at release time). As of this writing, the contents of the J2SE 1.5 release are already under discussion for inclusion in Panther, the code name for what will most likely be Mac OS X 10.3.

Why Now?

Apple has shipped Macintosh computers since 1984, but my tale of the Mac OS begins with Mac OS X. Describing all of the prior releases and their features is beyond the scope of this book, but all "Classic Mac" operating systems share a common set of weaknesses, including:

- A lack of memory protection
- Explicit shared memory for important structures
- An overburdened, fragile, and inadequate system-extending mechanism
- A lack of true multiprocessing
- An amazing legacy of cruft, including the Motorola 680x0 emulator and various other obsolete or cancelled technologies

The list could go on. Every Mac OS X installation includes a complete working copy of this Classic Mac OS, and when you launch an old-style Classic Mac OS application, you actually launch a complete working copy of this environment as a process for Mac OS X.

However, with the release of Mac OS X, Java development is finally a reality, rather than a marketing ploy or an Apple employee's pipe dream. So let's dive right into Java development on the Mac.

Apple's Java Platform

With a basic understanding of the Mac OS X platform, you're ready to get down to some bits and bytes...well, almost. First, you need to make sure you've got your Java compiler running properly, your environment variables set, and all program directories in the right place. We'll deal with all of that in this chapter.

Apple JVM Basics

First, make sure you have a Java Virtual Machine (JVM). Open up the Terminal application, type java -version, and you'll see the following message (or something similar):

```
java version "1.3.1"
Java(TM) 2 Runtime Environment,
    Standard Edition (build 1.3.1-root-020219-20:07)
Java HotSpot(TM) Client VM (build 1.3.1, mixed mode)
```

This message indicates that your JVM is set up and working, and that may seem like all you need to know. However, there is much more to a JVM than the ability to fire up a Java process. For starters, Apple preinstalls the JVM in a specific location, automatically including a number of additional classes. These classes number in the hundreds and add Apple-specific functionality to the core Java distributions.

 In this section we'll look at Apple's JDK 1.3.1 installation, which is included with all Mac OS X 10.1 systems and beyond. The JDK 1.4.1 release is available for download via Apple's Software Update feature or *http://www.apple.com/ macosx/downloads*. It will install only on Mac OS X Version 10.2.3 or later.

The Swing settings are also unique to the Apple JVM: the default look and feel corresponds to the Aqua user interface, which has quite an effect on your graphical applications. Apple also added hardware acceleration (for JDK 1.3) and implemented a shared memory model for reducing the overhead of running multiple Java applications. Although you've got the same basic JVM as on a Unix, Linux, or Windows platform, you should pay attention to some additions and differences.

Apple's JVM Directory Layout

Even if you're an experienced Java developer, it can be a bit difficult to understand exactly where and how the Apple JVM is installed and configured. Apple has carefully hidden some of its files and libraries to keep users from accidentally wiping out their data and to manage the complexity of upgrading the Mac OS X operating system.

 Although its philosophy is unlike that of Windows, Mac OS X tries to maintain a high level of integration between the OS and the programs that run on it. Java is no exception, and the Apple JVM was created with integration and ease of upgrade in mind.

Begin your system tour by opening the Terminal application and going to your hard drive's root directory (or folder). The quickest way to get there is to open a new Finder window and click Computer in the toolbar, and then double-click on the Hard Drive icon. This is the Mac OS X "root" location, which is what you would see from the terminal by typing cd / and then ls:

```
[Wills-Laptop:/] wiverson% ls
AppleShare PDS          SimpleClass.java        etc
Applications            System                  mach
Desktop DB              TheVolumeSettingsFolder  mach.sym
Desktop DF              Trash                   mach_kernel
Desktop Folder          Users                   private
Developer               Volumes                 sbin
IE Install Log File     automount               tmp
Library                 bin                     usr
Network                 cores                   var
Office X SR1 Updater Log dev
[Wills-Laptop:/] wiverson%
```

Libraries

You'll find a folder called *Library* immediately inside the root directory. This folder contains several default directories. When you install Mac OS X, these directories are created automatically so that the applications will have appropriate default directories available to them.

 For Unix users, Mac OS X's default directory structure is similar to having /usr/local and /usr/local/bin created by default rather than forcing make or a *configure* script to handle the task.

Each user will also have a *Library* directory in their home directory. Items in the root *Library* directory are shared between users, whereas items in the users' *Library* directories are specific to each user.

Immediately inside the root *Library* directory, you will find a *Java* directory. Inside this directory, you'll find two folders: a *Home* directory (which is really an alias to another location) and an *Extensions* folder (which *is* a real directory).

Extensions

The *Extensions* directory is empty, and is one of several locations where you can drop JAR files that you want to make universally accessible. There is only one systemwide JVM, however; you may not want to make a library (for example, an XML parser) broadly accessible, as doing so might cause versioning conflicts with application expectations.

The core JVM

Inside the *Home* directory, you'll see a familiar layout if you've worked with other Java distributions. The *bin* directory contains all standard Java tools, such as javac and jar. You'll need to drop out to the Terminal to use these tools effectively. Double-clicking on these tools from the Finder won't give you anything but a strange error message.

 If you're paying attention to the file descriptions, you may notice that the *bin* directory is a sham: all items in the directory actually point to files in a different location. To see these links, use the command ls -1 from the Terminal.

The JavaVM.framework Directory

Navigate back to the root directory, and this time go to the */System/Library/Frameworks* directory. Inside, you'll see many folders. For now, navigate inside the *JavaVM.framework* folder.

This directory might be listed just as *JavaVM* if you've turned off file extensions.

Now you'll see what appears to be yet another directory mostly filled with symbolic links (again, use ls -l to see the links). You may start to wonder when this house of mirrors will actually end, but all of this redirection is important to ensure the proper flexibility when the system JVM is updated. By setting up this structure, Mac OS X applications can be assigned preset locations for finding things, which simplifies operating system updates and upgrades.

Inside the */System/Library/Frameworks/JavaVM.framework/Versions* directory, you'll find a link to the *CurrentJDK* directory, as well as a real folder (one that isn't a symbolic link) labeled *1.3.1* (as well as *1.2* and *1.3*). By the time you read this book, you may have a different operating system update installed and see a different version of Java, such as *1.4* or even *1.5*. The *CurrentJDK* directory will point to the currently used JVM, generally the latest version folder.

The "real" files

Open the */System/Library/Frameworks/JavaVM.framework/Versions/CurrentJDK* directory. Now things will get more interesting. Instead of a *JRE* directory or a *lib* directory with *rt.jar*, you will find:

- A *Classes* directory containing a few JAR files
- A *Libraries* directory containing some Mac OS X native libraries
- A *Commands* directory containing the actual files for the items traditionally inside the Java *bin* directory (e.g., appletviewer, jar, java, javac, or javadoc)

Missing items

You'll notice that the traditional *lib* directory is missing, as are the property files you would typically expect to find.

To find the "missing" *lib* directory and property files, look in the JDK *Home* directory (*/System/Library/Frameworks/JavaVM.framework/Versions/1.3.1/Home*). You'll see a *lib* subdirectory, with all the files you would expect. Also notice that the items in the *bin* subdirectory point back to the */System/Library/Frameworks/JavaVM.framework/Versions/1.3.1/Commands* directory. While you don't need to distinguish between real files and symbolic links in your programming, understanding the Mac OS X directory structure aids in getting the most out of Apple's JDK.

The Big Picture

You may want to explore JAR files and directories in different locations to better understand how the pieces fit together. Figure 2-1 shows this entire layout in pictorial form.

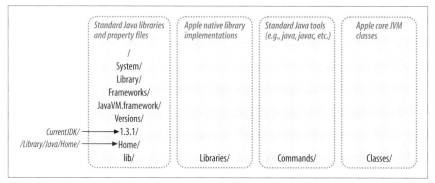

Figure 2-1. Apple's JVM layout

 Another good way to understand the JVM directory layout is to use the JavaBrowser utility included in the Apple Developer Tools, as described in Chapter 3.

Apple's JVM layout may seem confusing, but it simplifies the use of the JDK. For example, by including the core java JVM executable on the path, you don't have to install it or worry about which version you have. You can just rely on the presence of certain paths (such as */Library/Java/Home/*). Conversely, if you want multiple JVMs on your machine (for example, if you use a beta version of a future JDK), the default system JVM will be available in a pristine state. You can also point the *CurrentJDK* directory to another version and easily change the system's JDK.

 For this very reason, I strongly advise you not to throw lots of directories into your system JVM classpath. Instead, consider application-specific scripts that set the classpath.

Handling Classpath Issues

For Java libraries that you wish to place on the classpath for all users, Apple recommends the */Library/Java/Extensions/* directory. If you wish to place the library only on a specific user's classpath, put the file in the ~/*Library/Java/Extensions/* directory. This directory may not exist, so you or your software's installation program may need to create the directory before installing files within it.

Per the Apple documentation, the Java library search order is as follows:

1. User's home directory (~/*Library/Java/Extensions/*)
2. Local domain (/*Library/Java/Extensions/*)
3. Network domain (/*Network/Library/Java/Extensions/*)
4. System domain (/*System/Library/Java/Extensions/*)
5. $JAVA_HOME/*lib/ext*   (/*System/Library/Frameworks/JavaVM.framework/Versions/CurrentJDK/Home/lib/ext/*)

You'll note that the user's home directory takes precedence over the other locations; this helps a developer working on a system to easily share a machine with other users and avoid classpath difficulties.

Additional APIs and Services

The Mac OS X Java installation includes several additional APIs and services besides the default JDK installations available from Sun for Unix and Windows. In theory, you could build applications for the Mac OS X Java platform that won't run on other platforms. Purists may argue that Apple's JVM is therefore no different from the infamous Microsoft JVM and its incompatibilities. It is very different, however.

Apple hasn't removed anything from their JVM implementation. All the expected services, including the politically contentious RMI, are available on the Mac OS X Java platform. If you build your application against normal J2SE APIs, you will have no problem porting your applications to other platforms. For more information on cross-platform compatibility, check out Chapter 9.

However, Apple provides many features in addition to the core Java APIs. Spelling, integration with QuickTime, and the Apple look and feel, for example, are specific to the Macintosh, and you will have trouble porting applications that use them to another platform unless you're willing to change some of your application's code. However, this book will help you recognize what is Mac-specific, and you'll soon avoid these APIs or adjust them for use on other platforms when cross-platform compatibility is a concern.

Later chapters cover many additional services, such as the Java Speech and Spelling Frameworks and application bundling. For now, though, here's a summary of what the Mac OS X JVM adds to the standard Java bundle:

- Support for Aqua, the translucent, swooshing, pulsing user interface Apple introduced with Mac OS X (as well as Metal, the default Java look and feel)
- External BSD tool support (significant if you need man, ifconfig, or other unusual BSD tools)
- Java interfaces to QuickTime, for multimedia support
- Java interfaces to OpenGL, for sophisticated 3D graphics
- Java APIs for the Foundation and Application Kit frameworks in Cocoa
- Some J2EE packages, including RMI over IIOP, JNDI, JDBC, and JSSE
- Java threads implemented as native Mach threads, which provides free symmetric multiprocessing
- Automatic sharing of Java class data and HotSpot-compiled code across instances, which dramatically reduces overhead for running multiple Java applications (reducing memory and increasing performance)
- Automatic double-buffering of all windows
- Hardware acceleration availability for Swing applications
- MRJAppBuilder support, allowing you to create a seamless integration with the Mac OS X Finder GUI shell
- Integrated support for XML-RPC and SOAP

If you're already a Java developer, most of your standard cross-platform development efforts will remain unchanged. If you're building Swing applications, you'll continue to develop them the way you always have. If you're building server-based applications (for example, with Apache Tomcat), you'll use the same commands and the same packages. The most significant changes will apply to configuring and installing, as well as deciding which Apple-specific features will be easy to add and will provide real value for your users and customers. You should be concerned about cross-platform techniques only when using Mac-specific features, like those in the list above.

However, many of these technologies are already cross-platform, despite their nonstandard functionality. For example, you might add QuickTime support for Java first on Mac OS X, and then decide to make that support available for your Windows users. The rule, then, is not to avoid these extensions like the plague, but to be aware of when you use them. Learning more about these features will help you decide when to use them.

Hardware Acceleration

One interesting feature of the Mac OS X Java implementation is its support for hardware acceleration. When you work with a release prior to JDK 1.4, you'll want to manually enable hardware acceleration. On more current versions of the Mac OS X JDK, though, this support is turned on by default.

Multiple Mouse Buttons

The hardware Apple ships includes only mice with a single button. This limitation is unfortunate, as the second mouse button has become an important GUI standard on most platforms.

On non-Mac platforms, icons often serve as "nouns," and right-clicking typically activates a pop-up menu that provides a list of "verbs" or actions that can be performed on that noun. In many ways, this approach is more intuitive than clicking an object to select it and then traveling to a distant menu bar to actually perform the action.

In any event, you may want to buy an inexpensive two-button USB mouse to use with your Mac OS X machine, especially if you plan to use the popular Java-based IDEs. Although two-button mice are not Mac standards, Mac OS X ships with support for two-button mice, as well as mice with scroll wheels.

 If you are unwilling or unable to use a two-button mouse (for example, on your iBook or PowerBook when traveling), you can simulate the second mouse button by holding down the Control button while you click.

An application could be written for another platform that actually maps a Control-click with the single button to one action and clicking with the second button to a different action. This situation would be unusual, but you should be able to check the configuration options for that application to set different modifiers (and write a note to the application's developer asking for a more manageable control mechanism).

Java on Classic (MRJ)

Java isn't new to the Mac OS platform; the previous version, now dubbed Classic, included a Java Virtual Machine. To distinguish from other JVMs, the Classic Mac OS implementation was called the Mac OS Runtime for Java (MRJ). That JVM never progressed beyond support for JDK 1.1, even though the MRJ version number eventually crept up to 2.2.5. Because every

Mac OS X machine includes Classic, each Mac OS X machine technically includes two JVMs: the JDK 1.3.1 (or later) version running native on Mac OS X and the JDK 1.1.8 JVM running in the Mac OS 9 Classic environment.

If you are new to the Mac OS X environment, Mac OS Classic might seem bizarre. Open the Apple Applet Runner, located in */Applications (Mac OS 9)/ Apple Extras/Mac OS Runtime for Java/Apple Applet Runner*.

 If you have Mac OS 9 installed on another partition or hard drive, you will need to change to that volume or click on the appropriate hard drive icon in the Finder.

If Classic isn't already running, you will see a dialog noting that the Classic environment is starting. Click on the "Show Mac OS 9 desktop window" triangle, and you will see the old Mac OS 9 boot screen with a series of extensions marching across the bottom, as shown in Figure 2-2. Congratulations! You've just booted an entire alternate operating system as a process in Mac OS X.

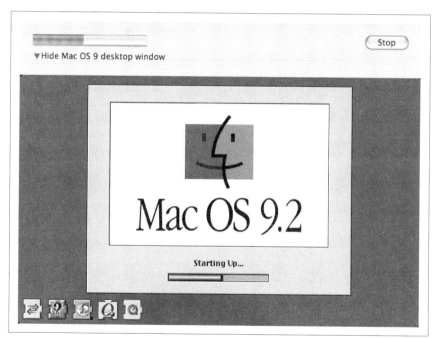

Figure 2-2. Launching Classic

This environment is known as True Blue (TruBlueEnvironment in the process viewer). Eventually, the Classic Mac OS will finish booting and the Applet

Viewer will appear in the Dock. Its appearance is the first sign of a set of interesting hacks that Apple has made to make the visual appearance of the two environments coexist more peacefully. Clicking on the Applet Viewer Dock icon, however, reveals a radically different menu bar (visually and in terms of the layout) from the standard Mac OS X menus.

From the Applet Viewer, click on the Applets menu, and select "Lightweight Gauge → example1".

As shown in Figure 2-3, you'll see a series of shifting bars over the face of a colorful coworker (er, primate). When you click on a menu item in the Applet Runner, the bars stop moving; simply clicking a menu item blocks the environment.

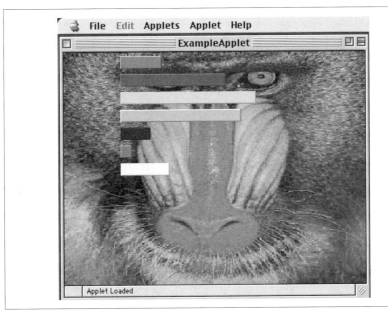

Figure 2-3. Applet Viewer

The Mac OS X equivalent to the Apple Applet Runner is called Applet Launcher, and you can find it in */Applications/Utilities/Java*. To run the Lightweight Gauge demo, as shown in Figure 2-4, you'll need to open the following URL (you can navigate to it using the "Open..." button):

```
file:///Applications (Mac OS 9)/Apple Extras/Mac OS Runtime For Java/Apple
Applet Runner/Applets/Lightweight Gauge/example1.html
```

In comparison to the Classic MRJ, clicking on the menu bar in a native Mac OS X applet will show off both Mac OS X's slightly translucent windows and its multithreaded nature. The bars continue to move, and no blocking occurs.

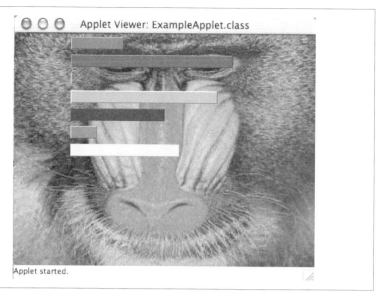

Figure 2-4. Mac OS X Applet Viewer

You can also find an MRJ SDK at *http://developer.apple.com/java/text/download.html*. It includes a variety of tools, including a wrapper mechanism for launching command-line-based tools. MRJ has some interesting features, including a JAR caching mechanism for improving network performance of applets, which may be a required environment for legacy system support.

Ultimately, there is little reason to invest a lot of time and energy in the Mac OS Classic environment. It's a very difficult environment, since it runs an obsolete version of the JDK. Apple has clearly stated that the future direction of the Macintosh platform is Mac OS X, and unless you have significant development and testing resources, you probably shouldn't spend time or money on what even Apple considers a dead platform.

Going Forward

Now you've explored the basic foundations of the Mac OS X Java platform. The next few chapters cover different aspects of Java development, from IDEs and tools, rich desktop application GUIs, and application packaging to Apple-specific technologies such as QuickTime and the Speech Framework.

If you are interested in desktop (also known as client-side) development, start with Chapters 4 and 5, which cover GUI applications and Apple extensions. From there, you may want to move on to standalone applications in

Chapter 7. Then you might benefit from exploring other Apple technologies, such as Speech, QuickTime, and Spelling.

There is also a lot to be said about Mac OS X's enterprise support for Java. If you are primarily interested in web-delivered client applications, look at Chapter 8. If you want to learn more about web application development, concentrate on Chapters 12 through 15.

No matter what sort of application you're building, if maintaining cross-platform compatibility is important, be sure to review the material in Chapter 6.

## CHAPTER 3

Java Tools

One of the nicest things about Mac OS X is its very broad range of tools. The Classic Mac OS platform had many software development tools, of which the most popular and flexible was Metrowerks CodeWarrior. The release of Mac OS X, however, has broadened the range of available tools tremendously, and a large set of Java- and Unix-based tools is now available. Mac OS X also ships with Project Builder, an integrated desktop environment for programming in several languages, including Java.

It's worth taking the time to review the various tools. If you're an old *emacs* or *vi* hand, you'll be able to access those tools (just fire up the Terminal). Even if you're an *emacs* or *vi* addict, you still might want to browse through the tools just to get an idea of what folks are talking about.

Terminal

The revolutionary thing about Mac OS X for a developer is a single, boring window with a blinking cursor. Double-click on the main icon for your computer on the desktop, navigate into the *Applications* directory, and then into *Utilities*. Inside this folder, you'll see a Terminal icon. Double-click on this icon to open the application.

You'll then see a "Welcome to Darwin!" message and a localhost prompt. The shell is the Unix standard tcsh, which stands for "Tenex csh." csh was the default shell for BSD Unix through the 1980s (and Mac OS X is based on BSD Unix). tcsh is an upward-compatible enhancement of csh, which includes "command completion" borrowed from an early 1970s experimental operating system called Tenex.

If you're an *emacs* user, turn on emulation of the Meta (alt) key in the "Terminal → Preferences... → Emulation" screen (or by selecting "Shell → Inspector... → Emulation" for a per-window modification).

Basic Terminal Commands

Learning to use the Terminal is far beyond the scope of this text, but a few basic commands are required for basic system navigation. These common commands are listed here:

cd
    Change directory.

ls
    List the contents of the current working directory.

pwd
    Print the current working directory.

man
    Enter the manual (documentation) system.

more
    Format output to display a page at a time.

When you first launch the Terminal, you are presented with a blinking cursor. Type pwd and press return. You will have started in your specific user's home directory (for example, my username is *wiverson*, so my Terminal starts in */Users/wiverson*).

Now type ls. This will print a directory listing to your screen. Then type cd Desktop and hit return. Type pwd, and you will see that you have changed your current working directory to */Users/[username]/Desktop*. Type ls and you will see files on your Desktop. Type cd ~ (on many English QWERTY keyboards, this is the shifted version of the key to the left of the number "1"). This command will return you to the home directory.

A Simple Java Class

Now enter pico HelloWorld.java. This command launches the pico application, a simple terminal-based text editor. The editor is now ready to work on a file called *HelloWorld.java*. Enter the text shown in Example 3-1.

Example 3-1. A simple HelloWorld class

```
class HelloWorld
{
```

Example 3-1. A simple HelloWorld class (continued)

```
public static void main(String[] args)
{
    System.out.println("Hello World!");
}
}
```

Press Control-O to save the file (or "WriteOut", as the command is labeled). Then use Control-X to quit pico.

Type javac *.java at the command line and hit return. It may take a moment, but assuming there are no errors, the *HelloWorld.java* file will compile and a *HelloWorld.class* file will appear (use ls to confirm the new file in your working directory). If you have problems, type pico HelloWorld. java again to open the file and make changes.

 If you've installed JDK 1.4.1, the system will have updated the command-line tools to point to the JDK 1.4.1 versions of the tools such as javac. If you want to use the JDK 1.3.1 tools after you've installed JDK 1.4.1, you'll need to refer to them using their full path in */System/Library/Frameworks/JavaVM. framework/Versions/1.3.1/Commands.*

Once the file compiles, type java HelloWorld from the command line (don't add the *.class* extension). It should now print out "Hello World!" You can take this *HelloWorld.class* file, and any computer that has a Java Virtual Machine should be able to run it.

This section has reviewed a very basic set of operations. If you need more information, consult one of several excellent texts on Java and Unix:

- *Learning Unix for Mac OS X*, by Dave Taylor and Jerry Peek (O'Reilly)
- *Mac OS X for Unix Geeks*, by Brian Jepson and Ernest E. Rothman (O'Reilly)

Environment Variables

You may want to define some common environment variables for use in later sessions. Assuming you're sticking to the standard tsch shell, you can create a file called *.tcshrc* in your home directory. The contents of this file will be executed when you create a new tsch shell (for example, by opening a new Terminal window). Remember that files beginning with a period (.) will not appear in Finder windows or in ls views by default. Use the ls -a command to see all files, including those with periods.

One common convention is to set the JAVA_HOME environment variable, which on a Mac OS X machine is particularly relevant, considering that there is a single standard JVM directory. To set the JAVA_HOME environment variable, put the following contents in the *.tcshrc* file:

```
setenv JAVA_HOME /Library/Java/Home
```

 If you use a different shell, then the *.tcshrc* file won't execute. You can check your shell's documentation or use *.login*, which almost all shells execute on startup.

A common bugaboo is the CLASSPATH environment variable, a source of much Java heartache. Whenever possible, I recommend putting CLASSPATH environment variable settings into shell scripts specific to each application. Doing so will keep your single JDK installation healthier and more pristine. Debugging CLASSPATH problems is one of the most thankless tasks around, and is best avoided whenever possible.

Code Editors

More than a few code editors are available for Mac OS X, and no work on Java would be complete without at least mentioning these integrated development environments (IDEs). I've broken them up into several categories: those that are open source, those that are free, and those that are sold commercially. I'm a big fan of open source tools, but all the tools mentioned here get the job done, so pick your own poison.

Open Source Tools

Many available open source tools have been ported to or run under Mac OS X. These tools are all free (as are the tools in the next section), but also make their source code available.

NetBeans

NetBeans™ is a full-featured, commercial-grade IDE that was acquired and open-sourced by Sun Microsystems. Written in Java, it's easily configured to run on Mac OS X. You can download it for free from *http://www.netbeans. com/*.

To install and configure NetBeans, pull down a current version of the software. I'm currently using NetBeans 3.4.1. Go to the NetBeans web site, click on the download link, and agree to the NetBeans license. You can then download a release for Mac OS X in disk image format. On my system, the downloaded file was called *NetBeansIDE-release341-MacOSX.dmg*. Mac OS X will mount it, and you can then launch NetBeans from the disk image.

Before starting up NetBeans, though, you should copy the contents of the disk image into a folder on your hard drive, such as */Applications/netbeans*. I created this folder in the Finder and then copied the contents of the NetBeans disk image into the new folder. You can then drag the disk image to the trash to "eject" it.

NetBeans comes in a Mac OS X package called NetBeans Launcher. However, since we're all geeks here, let's look more closely inside this package. Control-click the launcher icon and select Show Package Contents. Navigate inside the revealed *Contents* directory. You'll see several files associated with Mac OS X packages (many of which are discussed in detail in Chapter 7), as well as *MacOS* and *Resources* folders. Open *Resources*, and then *netbeans*, and you'll find yourself in the actual NetBeans distribution. Figure 3-1 shows this directory structure.

Inside the distribution's *bin* directory, you will find several scripts and other files. Modify the contents for the *ide.cfg* file as follows:

```
-J-Xverify:none -J-Xdock:name=NetBeans -J-Xms64m -J-Xmx250m -J-Dcom.apple.
hwaccellist=ATIRage128_8388608 -jdkhome /Library/Java/Home
```

In this and other examples in this book, a single line has been broken into multiple lines due to the constraints of the printed page. Be sure to type commands like this all on a single line in your configuration file.

The -J option specifies that the following option should be passed to the underlying JVM. Note that I've extended the maximum amount of memory available by default to 250 MB by using the -Xmx switch. You can play around with similar options, depending on your system's configuration.

If you're working on a JDK 1.3, you'll want to change the -J-Dcom.apple.hwaccellist=ATIRage128_8388608 portion to match your video card and enable video acceleration (see "Hardware Acceleration" in Chapter 2). You can put in multiple strings separated by commas if you want.

Later versions of the Mac OS X JVM enable hardware acceleration by default.

You can actually run NetBeans with either the Apple look and feel (also known as Aqua) or with the Swing-standard Metal look and feel. There are advantages to both approaches. The Metal look and feel includes a user

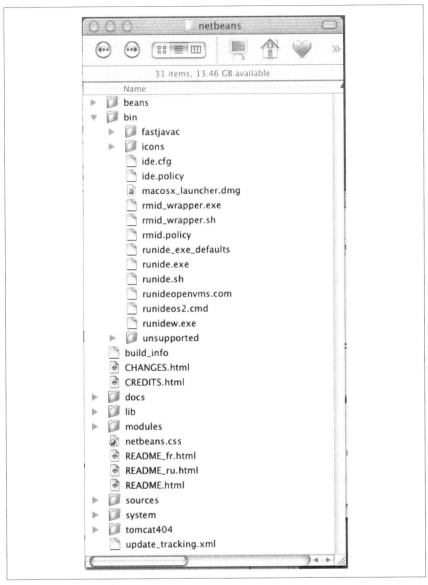

Figure 3-1. NetBeans directory structure

interface that is identical to the one you would see on other platforms, and also seems to be more stable than Aqua. The Aqua interface, though, is much more familiar to the Mac OS X user, and some native widgets seem to work better under Aqua than Metal (for example, the scrollbar). Note that

NetBeans relies heavily on the second mouse button, which can be emulated on Mac OS X using Control-click on a single mouse button system.

To actually launch the IDE, you should specify a look and feel and a user directory. The default look and feel is Metal. As of this writing, user directories are incompatible between Metal and Aqua. I created two files and two directories to test the various options; you can do the same. Figure 3-2 shows NetBeans running with the Metal look and feel.

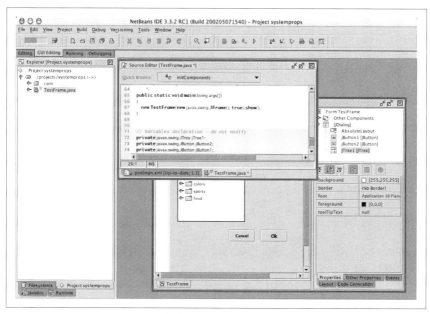

Figure 3-2. NetBeans running with the Metal look and feel

To launch NetBeans using the Metal look and feel, I first created an empty directory, /netbeans_userdir, on my system. Then I created a *launch_metal.sh* script with the contents shown in Example 3-2.

Example 3-2. Launching NetBeans with the Metal look and feel

```
./runide.sh -userdir /netbeans_userdir
```

To launch the Aqua look and feel, I created a *launch_aqua.sh* script with the options shown in Example 3-3. As with the Metal setup, you should create a directory for these settings. I used /netbeans_aqua.

Example 3-3. Launching NetBeans with the Aqua look and feel

```
./runide.sh -userdir /netbeans_aqua
        -ui com.apple.mrj.swing.MacLookAndFeel -fontsize 11
```

For Aqua fans, Figure 3-3 shows NetBeans running with that look and feel.

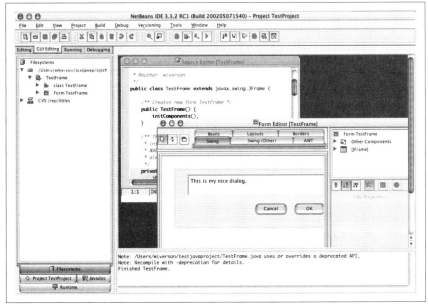

Figure 3-3. NetBeans running with the Aqua look and feel

 In this and other code examples, I inserted line breaks to increase the code's readability. However, you should *not* insert a line break in your own script, but should type the entire line continuously.

Try both versions and see which one you prefer. Note that the form designer will draw user interface widgets in the selected user interface as well.

To build applications that take advantage of Apple-specific options and to activate the NetBeans type-ahead feature in the text editor for the Apple extensions, add the following JAR file to the "Filesystems" tab:

```
/System/Library/Frameworks/JavaVM.framework/Versions/CurrentJDK/Classes/ui.jar
```

You can then right-click on the "JAR" entry and choose "Tools → Update Parser Database." This will bring up a dialog box, allowing you to name the parser database (for example, *apple_prefix*). The parser database may take a few moments to update, but you'll need to update this database only once. Then NetBeans will know about Apple's Java extensions. Figure 3-4 illustrates this process.

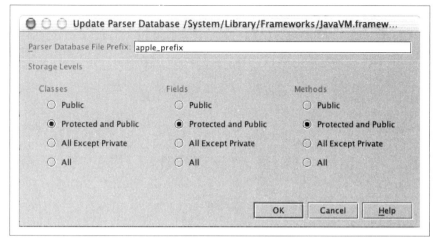

Figure 3-4. Adding Mac OS–specific type-ahead

NetBeans is probably one of my favorite IDEs. It's multiplatform, free, and the source is available. It's got a great API for writing extension modules. It supports CVS, and it's got a free, built-in auto-update mechanism. That said, it's also a bit of a Mac OS X newcomer, and rough edges pop up occasionally; still, a number of active NetBeans developers now use Mac OS X as their primary development environment. For more information on Net-Beans, check out *NetBeans: The Definitive Guide*, by Boudreau, Glick, Greene, Spurlin, and Woehr (O'Reilly).

Free Tools

Somewhere between open source and commercial tools lies freeware commercial software. You can't download the source code, but the price certainly can't be beat.

JBuilder Personal

Borland's JBuilder is another Java IDE that migrated over to Mac OS X. Borland officially supports Mac OS X as a release platform, meaning that if you purchase JBuilder, you can obtain support using it on a Mac. It has a wide, interesting feature set, and the Personal edition is free. You could purchase versions with additional features and commercial support, but you could also just play around with the Personal edition and get a feel for the editor and its overall responsiveness.

Figure 3-5 shows JBuilder in action. For more information on Borland's JBuilder or to download a copy, visit *http://www.jbuilder.com/*.

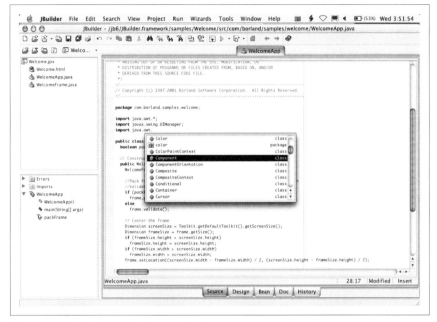

Figure 3-5. Borland JBuilder Personal edition

Project Builder

Project Builder is the latest incarnation of a set of GUI tools originally developed for the NeXT operating systems, now available for free to Mac OS X developers. It has interesting features and some curious omissions, but it also happens to be free, which gives it a certain appeal. Even if you don't use Project Builder for day-to-day development, you may want to use the default code generated by the assistants to give you a head start on application building.

If you've installed the Developer Tools CD,* you'll find Project Builder in the */Developer/Applications* directory. Start up Project Builder and select "File → New Project"; the resulting dialog box is shown in Figure 3-6.

When given a choice, choose "Pure Java → Java Swing Application." Then save the generated project in a new directory. You may wish to get in the

---

* The Developer Tools CD is included with any purchase of Mac OS X, and has a large suite of tools that aren't installed with the default operating system. This suite includes compilers, code editors, and other useful tools. If you don't have this CD, you may have to download the tools from *http://developer.apple.com/macosx*. Apple tends to update these tools fairly frequently, so you should check this site regularly.

Figure 3-6. Creating a new project with Project Builder

habit of saving files without spaces or unusual characters, as it tends to prevent problems later. In this example, I name my new project `TestSwingApp`.

Project Builder indexes and updates the parser database at project creation, and occasionally when you write code. You can more or less ignore this update. Although it takes time, it runs in the background, so you can still open Java source files while it's working. Once you've gotten past these steps, you'll see an editor window similar to that shown in Figure 3-7.

Be aware of the extent to which Project Builder focuses on Mac OS X development. For example, while browsing the source of the generated "Pure Java Swing Application", you'll see this line in your code:

```
import com.apple.mrj.*;
```

Several other Apple-specific classes are imported by default. Thus, using Project Builder's templates is a great way to get a feel for Apple extensions to the Java platform, but unless you pay attention, it can be a rude shock to see `com.apple.*` `ClassNotFoundExceptions` when you try to run your "Pure Java" application on another platform.

Figure 3-7. The Project Builder user interface

For now, select "Build → Build and Run..." to launch the application. You'll notice an "About TestSwingApp..." menu item under the TestSwingApp application menu, which opens a simple "About" dialog box when selected (as shown in Figure 3-8). This menu item and the related handler are Apple-specific extensions. Chapter 5 will look at these extensions more closely.

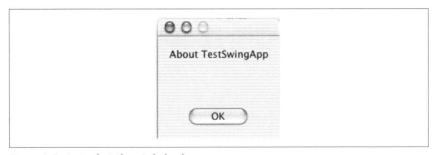

Figure 3-8. A simple "About" dialog box

Many other build options are also available. Go to the Project menu, select "Edit Active Target," and click on the "Application Settings" tab. Then click on the "Expert" button and change the "Java → Properties → com.apple. macos.useScreenMenuBar" value from true to false. Then click on the Java source file to return to the main display, and select "Build → Build and Run..." again. This time, the menu bar will appear in the window instead of in the Mac OS X menu bar, as shown in Figure 3-9.

Figure 3-9. Per-window menu bar

Project Builder is a sophisticated tool, but this text tries to be as IDE-neutral as possible, focusing on the underlying code rather than development tools. That said, you should explore Project Builder further, especially if you expect to develop several Mac OS X–specific applications, or if you use multiple programming languages.

JavaBrowser

In addition to Project Builder, Apple includes a tool called JavaBrowser (found in */Developer/Applications/*) for inspecting Java libraries, which are generally housed in JAR, ZIP, and class files. While this tool has only a few of these archives installed initially, you can easily add your own libraries to browse with this tool. Use the "File → Add Classes..." command to install any additional code you'd like to be able to browse. This installation lets you build your own library of Java classes to search and inspect, forming a nice Java API repository. Figure 3-10 shows an example of using Java-Browser when navigating through packages, classes, and even methods.

As shown in Figure 3-11, JavaBrowser can search for specific details very quickly, and results can be double-clicked to find additional information. This goes well beyond the class names, and even into the types of parameters and return values from methods.

I strongly recommend you use JavaBrowser, and always add the latest versions of your source files and classes to it; you'll have your own library of

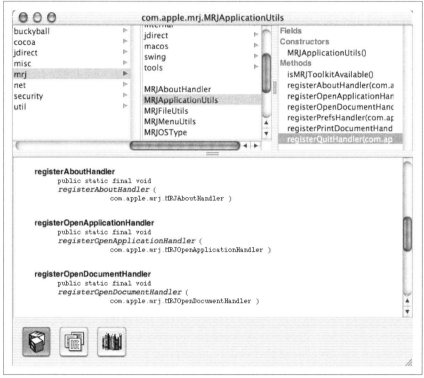

Figure 3-10. JavaBrowser navigation

code that you've written, which can really help when you've forgotten the signature of that odd method you wrote a few months ago.

Commercial Tools

Last but not least, plenty of not-free, not-open-source tools are out there. Don't let my description prejudice you, though; these tools can be very useful. First, paying for a tool generally means that you get some form of professional support. This support can be valuable at 2:00 A.M., when you can't get something seemingly trivial to work. Having someone a phone call away can save the day.

 Descriptions and screenshots in this section are intentionally sparse. I don't want to give you the impression that you must have these tools, or dissuade you twilight hackers from working through this book with nothing but Project Builder or a text editor.

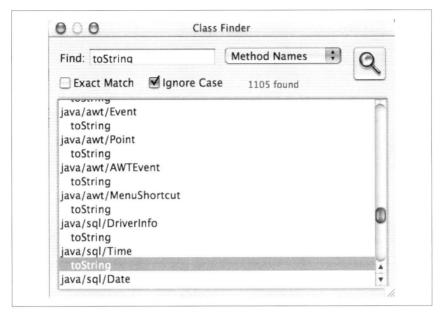

Figure 3-11. JavaBrowser Find capabilities

Metrowerks CodeWarrior

Metrowerks CodeWarrior is excellent native IDE for Mac OS X, and I strongly recommend it for Mac OS X development (especially if you will target multiple languages). Metrowerks earned tremendous respect back when Apple transitioned to the PowerPC chip for providing a compiler and IDE in the early through mid-1990s, and they have done an excellent job of tracking Apple technologies ever since.

For more information on Metrowerks CodeWarrior, visit *http://www.metrowerks.com/*.

Macromedia Dreamweaver MX

Macromedia Dreamweaver is principally a tool for building HTML-based user interfaces, but it includes support for building JSP-based web applications as well. It understands JavaBeans, JSP tags, JDBC, and web services, and it can build surprisingly sophisticated applications quickly. It also features integration with other tools such as Fireworks and Flash.

Chapter 12 describes how to install popular databases, and Chapter 13 connects to these databases by using JavaServer Pages (JSP). Macromedia Dreamweaver MX lets you do this visually by defining a connection and a query, as shown in Figure 3-12.

Figure 3-12. Setting up a Dreamweaver database connection

This connection, once defined, can create complex, interactive web pages visually, as shown in Figure 3-13.

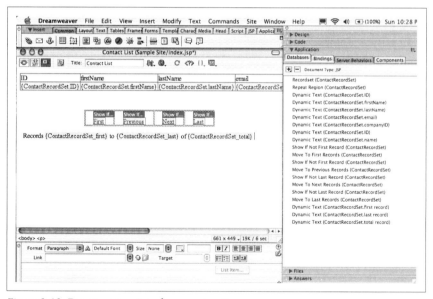

Figure 3-13. Dreamweaver interface construction

If you are using a web server locally, you can configure Dreamweaver MX to preview the application inside of the tool, as shown in Figure 3-14.

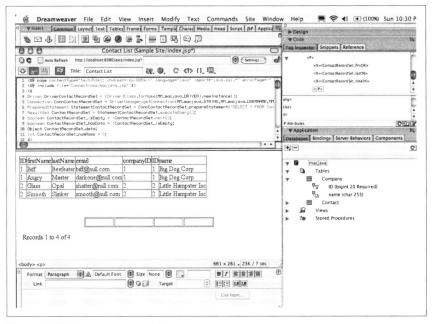

Figure 3-14. Dreamweaver preview

Dreamweaver MX is a highly productive tool used to create simple web applications very quickly. If most of your web application development consists of simple web user interface construction with lots of queries, you should probably evaluate Dreamweaver MX. For more information on the MX product line, visit *http://www.macromedia.com/*.

Jakarta Ant

As you work with Java, you'll often encounter references to Ant, an open source tool for managing build processes and other tasks. Ant is a great companion tool to IDEs and text editors, as it can manage complex build tasks, compilation, and even those nasty classpath issues discussed earlier. This section will describe Ant in some detail.

Ant is part of Apache's Jakarta project. Originally created to provide a cross-platform, portable replacement for the Unix make command, it has become a powerful development, deployment, and installation tool. To use Ant, run scripts from the command line, passing in an XML build file. Inside the build file, you can define variables and tasks to be performed at build time.

Installation and Setup

You can download Ant from *http://ant.apache.org/ant*. The latest version as of this writing is 1.5.1, and you can select a ZIP file or a gzipped version. I downloaded *jakarta-ant-1.5.1-bin.tar.gz*. Expand the file to *jakarta-ant-1.5.1* and copy the resultant directory somewhere easily accessible (I used *~/dev* for a user-specific installation). Then put the *bin* subdirectory in your path:

```
[Wills-Laptop:~] wiverson% setenv PATH ~/dev/jakarta-ant-1.5.1/bin:$PATH
```

To run Ant, use the *ant* script (*ant.bat* on Windows, and just plain *ant* on Unix-based systems such as Mac OS X):

```
[Wills-Laptop:~] wiverson% ant
Buildfile: build.xml does not exist!
Build failed
```

As the message here indicates, Ant expects a build file, generally called *build. xml*, to give it instructions.

Ant Basics

Let's look at writing a simple Ant project and building a file. Suppose you want to write a single Ant file that handles the drudgery of compiling an application, bundles the results into a JAR file, and then copies the resulting files into a new distribution directory.

First, create a new file and call it *build.xml*. As shown in Example 3-4, this file is perhaps one of the smallest possible useful build scripts.

Example 3-4. A simple build script

```
<project default="compile" basedir=".">
        <property name="src" location="src"/>
        <property name="build" location="build"/>

        <target name="compile">
                <javac srcdir="${src}" destdir="${build}"/>
        </target>
</project>
```

In this example, anything in the *src* directory is compiled, and the resulting class files are placed in the *build* directory. Both paths are based on the current working directory. This is a pretty complicated way to tell `javac` to compile a directory and place the results in another directory, but it's also very flexible. Let's look at some of the key syntax elements.

First, you'll notice that two `property` tags are supplied just inside the `project` tag. They are then referenced and expanded below by using the ${...} syntax. In addition to the properties you specify, you could also use ${basedir} to refer to the project base directory, as well as the different values available to the Ant JVM. These values would be available programmatically through System.getProperties() and related methods. For example, ${os.name} retrieves the operating system, and ${file.separator} retrieves the pesky file separator, which is platform-specific.

The next thing you'll notice is a target tag, which is named "compile". This is the default target (or task) that will be executed by the *build.xml* file. Target names are a way of breaking the Ant build file into different sections. Using these names can be useful for different stages in the development process, such as cleaning up, compiling, and deploying an application.

The javac task is a built-in task for Ant. You will find one or more tasks inside a target. A number of tasks are available from within Ant 1.5; popular tasks include creating JAR files and copying files to other locations.

Running the Build

Assuming that you've installed Ant as described above, an installation of Ant is available in your path. To give you an idea of how things work, assume the directory structure shown in Figure 3-15.

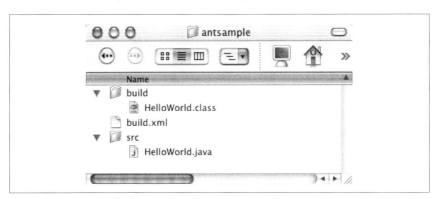

Figure 3-15. Ant sample directory

Given this structure, you can execute the following commands to build the single Java source file:

```
[Localhost:~] wiverson% cd antsample/
[Localhost:~/antsample] wiverson% ls
build     build.xml src
[Localhost:~/antsample] wiverson% /usr/local/ant/bin/ant
Buildfile: build.xml

compile:

BUILD SUCCESSFUL
```

```
Total time: 5 seconds
[Localhost:~/antsample] wiverson%
```

You'll notice the cd command at the beginning of this output. This command sets the current working directory, and Ant will automatically look for a file called *build.xml* to use as its instruction set.

If you have a more complex build script and would like to be able to call Ant scripts from within them without changing the current working directory, you can use the -buildfile option:

```
[Localhost:~] wiverson% ant -buildfile ~/antsample/build.xml
Buildfile: /Users/wiverson/antsample/build.xml

compile:

BUILD SUCCESSFUL
Total time: 4 seconds
[Localhost:~] wiverson%
```

Ant Documentation

For a complete reference on Ant, you should pick up *Ant: The Definitive Guide*, by Jesse Tilly and Eric Burke (O'Reilly). This book includes sections that explain how to expand Ant with your own custom tasks, as well as a wealth of information on Ant's built-in features.

Probably the most commonly requested item is a list of Ant tasks. For a complete list of these tasks, visit the Apache web site at *http://jakarta. apache.org/ant/manual/tasksoverview.html*. You'll also find a complete online manual at *http://jakartal.apache.org/ant/manual*. However, much of this information is available in printed form from O'Reilly.

Additional Tools

People get into bar fights over their choice of tools and IDEs. Here are some additional popular tools:

* IDEA IntelliJ (*http://www.intellij.com/idea/*), a commercial IDE that includes support for easily refactoring your application code.
* Eclipse (*http://www.eclipse.org/*), an open source IDE that also includes support for code refactoring.
* TogetherSoft Control Center (*http://www.togethersoft.com/*), a commercial development environment with support for Unified Modeling Language (UML).
* Bare Bones Software's BBEdit (*http://www.barebones.com/*), an excellent text editor.

## CHAPTER 4

GUI Applications

*Question: How many lines of code does it
take to display a window?
Answer: One, but you'll spend the rest of
your life rewriting it.*

OK, so it's not a particularly funny joke, but it does get to the heart of why so many people originally embraced the Java platform's promise of "write once, run anywhere." Here's a graphical user interface (GUI) development conundrum: each platform has a set of specific guidelines for what is considered the proper look and feel, yet users often want to access an application across multiple platforms. Just look at the variety of development tools described earlier; the installation for many IDEs, such as NetBeans, involves selecting which user interface you'd like to work with.

The long and the short of it is that there is no one right answer for GUI construction. From overt issues, such as the menu structure defaults (where is the placement of the Preferences menu item: the File, Edit, or Application menu?), to subtle ones, such as the default layout for dialog buttons, to paradigm decisions, such as requiring the use of the second mouse button—it's hard to imagine a single approach to GUI application programming that would satisfy all application development needs.

Instead of focusing on the theoretical debate, it is often more useful to consider two key factors: the intended audience and the available resources. If you know that you will develop a consumer application on a large budget, you may wish to build a multimedia-style interface, with an emphasis on graphics, single-click actions, and lots of mouse-rollover responses. If you're building a developer tool in your spare time, you'll probably want to rely on standard Java Metal user interface objects. If you're developing a general productivity application or an in-house application for a corporate environment, you may want to build and test for both Metal on Windows and Unix and Aqua on Mac OS X.

That said, it's often easiest for GUI programmers to begin with the Mac OS X Aqua interface rather than the standard Metal look and feel. Perhaps the best reason to start with Aqua is its sheer number of default components. Aqua has one of the largest sets of defaults for spacing and fonts of any platform. If you start with Aqua, you're less likely to have problems with other platforms (including both Motif and Windows) when you switch to Metal, because your defaults will all be set correctly. In addition, the graphics-intensive nature of the Aqua platform tends to push the limits of a graphics card; if your application responds well under Aqua, less sophisticated user interfaces should be at least as responsive, if not more so.

Swing and Aqua

Swing is the user interface toolkit of Java Foundation Classes (JFC). When Sun developed the original version of Java, it introduced the Abstract Windowing Toolkit (AWT), which drew user interfaces based on an abstract layer that sat on top of the native windowing toolkit. This caused many problems, as the abstraction tended to blur when faced with the peculiarities of many windowing platforms. To resolve these issues, JFC and Swing were introduced as a more sophisticated toolkit with much better cross-platform support. JFC and Swing are based on AWT, so the core AWT is still part of Java. You could even write a pure AWT application, although there's really no good reason to: if you're developing a rich user interface you'll want to stick to Swing APIs.

One of Swing's most interesting aspects is its notion of a "pluggable" look and feel. The entire Unix world has a high degree of customizability, at the cost of a staggering variety of different approaches to user interface design. At first, these custom behaviors and functionality seem ideal, but they soon become a headache for developers and users. To deal with this issue, Swing introduced a standard look and feel called "Metal" that provides a reasonably attractive user interface for all platforms. Metal looks the same, more or less pixel-for-pixel, on all supported platforms.

However, it is still possible to override Metal and use a custom look and feel instead. Windows users may choose to add a Windows-specific look and feel to their application instead of going with the standard Metal. On Mac OS X, the obvious choice is the native Aqua look and feel. Apple has done an excellent job with their implementation of the Java-based Aqua look and feel, with many graphical operations featuring native hardware acceleration.

Therefore, when developing applications in Java, it is useful to determine what your supported look and feel options are going to be. While it's possible to say that you intend to support Metal, Aqua, Motif, and Windows look and feel selections, you'll wind up having to test your application's appearance (including the length of localized strings—you were planning on making your application localizable, right?) on each supported look and feel. This is largely a matter of budget and resources, but in this section we will focus on comparisons between the standard Metal look and feel and the Mac OS X Aqua look and feel.

You may notice that, by default, Java applications on Mac OS X have the Aqua look and feel instead of Metal. This is a result of the default being set in a Mac OS X properties file (*/Library/Java/Home/lib/swing.properties*). If you wish, you could change the look and feel default to Metal, but in the interests of keeping your system as "virginal" as possible, it is probably best to change the settings on a per-application basis.

 You'll notice that this chapter does not detail the basics of Swing programming; instead, I've focused on the specifics of Swing as they relate to Aqua. If you're not comfortable in Swing land, you might want to pick up *Java Swing*, by Eckstein, Loy, and Wood (O'Reilly).

You can specify the default look and feel for a specific application in several different ways. Chapter 3 created scripts that specified two ways to launch the NetBeans IDE. Looking at the scripts, you can learn how to set the JDK and the default look and feel. While this may work for some applications, scripts like this are poor form and should be avoided for commercial (or even in-house) deployment. Instead, use global properties files (as Mac OS X does) or some other static method. It's a real pain to have to keep multiple versions of startup scripts, or to select a look and feel every time you start up an application.

A First Look at Aqua

The best way to get a sense of the Aqua look and feel is to examine the SwingSet2 demo application. On Mac OS X, you should find this application at */Developer/Examples/Java/JFC/SwingSet2/SwingSet2*.

If you view the application with the Terminal, you will notice that SwingSet2 actually appears as *SwingSet2.app*, which is in turn a directory. Chapter 10 will explore this topic more thoroughly. For now, double-click the SwingSet2 icon in the Finder.

The application may take some time to launch, but when it does, you should see the sample output shown in Figure 4-1.

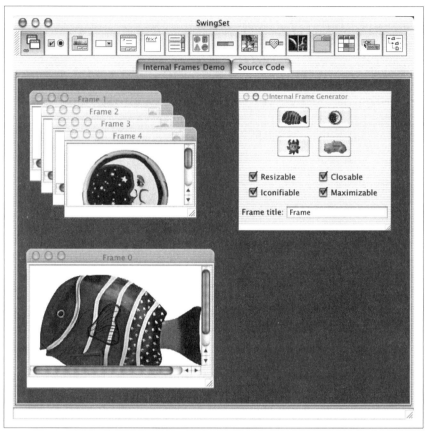

Figure 4-1. The SwingSet sample application

Playing around a bit with this application, you'll see that it is built on an instance of JDesktopPane. You should also notice that the application is a miniature version of a Mac OS X desktop, complete with a rather strange "mini-dock" at the top of the application interface. This is an odd arrangement, and it's a user interface concept you won't find referenced anywhere in Apple's documentation (aside from an admonishment in a *README* file against using it!). It's clearly provided for compatibility with multiple document interface (MDI) applications from other platforms, but is unlikely to be satisfactory for any real GUI programming task.

 If you're wondering how I knew that this application used a JDesktopPane, I simply clicked the "Source Code" tab on the application. There is also a *src* folder in the *SwingSet2* directory, which includes the source for the application.

Clicking on the second icon in the SwingSet2 button bar, we immediately confront the largest issue of the Aqua GUI: the radical difference in size required by common user-interface elements.

As you can see by comparing Figure 4-2 and Figure 4-3, the Aqua version of these buttons requires almost 50 percent more horizontal screen space than does the Metal version. This can reduce a nicely laid out Metal interface to a jumble of clipped text and ugly ellipses when converted to Aqua.

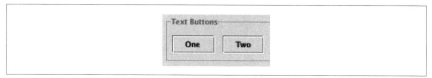

Figure 4-2. Metal buttons

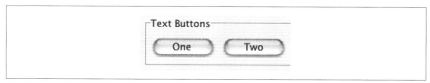

Figure 4-3. Aqua buttons

In Aqua, buttons by default have a gap of 12 pixels between them and are based on a 13-point font. This font can be a bit large when compared with other platform defaults. Rather than settling for a nasty-looking Metal interface based on these patterns, you may wish to standardize the "utility" UI patterns in Aqua for your Java applications. These smaller controls are closer to the control sizes of other platforms, and look good on Metal as well as Aqua. To support this smaller utility user interface, use controls based on an 11-point font and use a default control spacing of 8 pixels.

Another interesting contrast between Aqua and Metal can be found when comparing JList implementations (the seventh button from the left in the SwingSet2 mini-dock).

If you compare the user interface components in Figure 4-4 with those in Figure 4-5, you can see that while elements in the Aqua implementation are generally wider than those in Metal, they are often vertically shorter. So although Aqua interface widgets generally require more space than their Metal counterparts, this is not always the case.

The moral here is to be extremely careful when designing user interfaces for multiple look and feel motifs. The next section shows how you can minimize these problems.

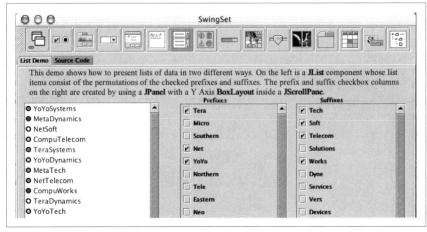

Figure 4-4. Metal JList component

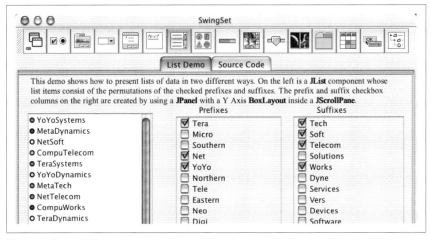

Figure 4-5. Aqua JList component

Look and Feel "Gotchas"

Unfortunately, many developers test their applications with the Metal look and feel, ignoring other platforms and look and feel packages. While that may be acceptable for Windows or Motif users, the Aqua look and feel implementation is excellent, and there is no reason not to test for and support it.

Sizing of elements

As pointed out so glaringly in the last section, the biggest issue you need to deal with is sizing elements. When you first run your application under Aqua, you may be taken aback by the number of places where element size will affect you—from buttons that are clipped short with an ellipse, to navigation tabs that are now centered and occupying two levels, to portions of the user interface that are now unusable or even completely hidden. All things are not created equal on Aqua and Metal.

If you are bringing an application over from another platform, this may be a good time to examine the interface. Often, an application that looks too busy on Aqua is actually too busy on all platforms; Aqua is just driving the point home, especially when compared to the quality of the user interface work put into other Mac OS X applications.

The bad news is that no mantra or special set of steps can convert a Metal-size application to an Aqua-size one. That means that you'll have to dig into your code by hand and space things out until they look good on Aqua. Be sure to use the "utility" UI patterns, which dictate 11-point fonts and 8-pixel spacings. The good news, though, is that you'll end up with a better-designed application, and reap the benefits of both look and feel motifs.

Background color

The default Aqua implementation of a JFrame is set to the textured background common to many Aqua applications. However, most developers prefer to use a plain white background, like one you'd see in a Finder folder or the various mail applications. To set the background to white (or some other color), you will need to use the following in your Swing code:

```
myJFrame.getContentPane( ).setBackground(java.awt.Color.white);
```

This explicit color setting ensures that defaults on different platforms don't change your application's background color without your knowing about it.

Dirty windows

Another difference between Mac OS X and other platforms is that Mac OS X applications consistently use a small dot to indicate when a window is "dirty," meaning that information has been changed and a save is in order. Figure 4-6 shows a "dirty" window icon, and Figure 4-7 shows the same icon once a save has been completed.

Figure 4-6. A "dirty" window

Figure 4-7. A window after saving

To set this "dirty" dot, use the following code:

```
myJFrame.getRootPane( ).putClientProperty("windowModified", Boolean.TRUE);
```

Use the following line to clear the dot after a save has occurred:

```
myJFrame.getRootPane( ).putClientProperty("windowModified", Boolean.FALSE);
```

Menu bars

The last major issue to think about is the location of actions on a menu bar. The standard Mac OS X menu bar is typically organized by the scope of the action. For example, consider the menu hierarchy detailed in Table 4-1, which indicates a menu bar's headings and the scope that each heading's actions should govern.

Table 4-1. Menu headings and their scope

Menu heading	Scope	Examples
Apple menu	Entire system (including global actions)	Restart, Sleep
Application	Entire application	Quit, Preferences, Hide, About
File	Entire document	New, Save, Print
Edit	Section of document	Find, Replace
Format	Changes appearance but not data	Font, Alignment
Window	Switches between documents	Tile, Cascade, Go To
Help	No effect on application, but easy to find	Help, Documentation

If you use these scopes as a standard set of rules for your own menu locations and choices, you'll find that users intuitively know where to look for items and will feel at home with your application quickly.

An Example Swing Application

This section introduces a fairly comprehensive Swing application and details its various components. This application is used throughout the rest of this book as the foundation application (so you can run each sample without having to create new windows, set up the menu bar, and perform other mundane tasks). For that reason, be sure to code and compile the application and have the source code handy before diving into future chapters.

 For those of you who don't like large code blocks, especially when it's mostly GUI setup code, understand that this section is a necessary evil; it's the basis for several future applications, all of which are made up of more interesting code fragments and concepts.

Source Code Listing

This application also demonstrates techniques that factor out and partition portions of your application to increase team development, as well as an introduction to concepts (such as dynamic class loading) used in later chapters. In this example, these modules are referred to as *plug-ins*. If you've used an application such as Adobe Photoshop or the NetBeans development environment, you've been exposed to applications that serve as a framework and then load other modules. Example 4-1 shows the entire class listing.

Example 4-1. The sample Swing application

```
package com.wiverson.macosbook;

import javax.swing.JMenuItem;
import javax.swing.JButton;
import javax.swing.JComponent;
import javax.swing.JMenu;
import java.awt.Cursor;
import java.awt.BorderLayout;
import java.util.Hashtable;
import java.awt.event.ActionEvent;
import java.awt.event.ActionListener;
import java.awt.event.KeyEvent;
import javax.swing.KeyStroke;

public class SimpleEdit extends javax.swing.JFrame
{
    // Used to set the number for new untitled windows
    private static int newWindows = -1;

    // Used to track all of the currently installed plugins
    private static Hashtable plugins = null;

    // The initial plugin configuration
    private static String[] argsconfig;

    /** Creates a new instance of SimpleEdit */
    public SimpleEdit()
    {
        init();
    }

/* -------------------- Application APIs ------------------------------- */

    /** Used by tools to get the text actual text area.
     * This wouldn't generally be recommended, but in this
     * case it's ok.
     *
     * In general, you'd want to use something to make the
     * interface more opaque (thereby freeing up options to
```

Example 4-1. The sample Swing application (continued)

```
 * switch to a different underlying toolkit), but in this
 * case it would cost readability (since everyone can look
 * up a JTextArea).
 */
public javax.swing.JTextArea getJTextArea( )
{
    return this.mainTextArea;
}


/** Used by tools to get the current text */
public String getDocumentText( )
{
    return this.mainTextArea.getText( );
}


/** Used by tools to set the current text */
public void setDocumentText(String in)
{
    mainTextArea.setText(in);
    mainTextArea.setCaretPosition(mainTextArea.getText().length( ));
    mainTextArea.requestFocus( );
}


/** Used by tools to add to the current text */
public void appendDocumentText(String in)
{
    setDocumentText(mainTextArea.getText( ) + in);
}


/** Used by tools to set the status text at the bottom
 * of a frame.
 */
public void setStatusText(String in)
{
    this.mainStatusText.setText(in);
}


/* -------------------- Initialization -------------------------------- */


// Sets up and creates a "pristine" window environment
private void init( )
{
    if(newWindows++ < 0)
        setTitle("Untitled");
    else
        setTitle("Untitled-" + newWindows);

    initPlugins( );
    initComponents( );
    initMenuBar( );
}
```

Example 4-1. The sample Swing application (continued)

```
/* -------------------- Initialization: Plugins  -------------------------- */

    // Installs all plugins as currently defined by the
    // private argsconfig.
    private void initPlugins()
    {
        if(plugins != null)
            return;
        if(argsconfig == null)
            return;
        if(argsconfig.length == 0)
            return;
        plugins = new Hashtable( );

        for(int i = 0; i < argsconfig.length; i++)
        {
            // This may very well fail, as we are going
            // to be loading classes by name, which is
            // prone to errors (e.g. typos, etc.)
            try
            {
                // This requests the classloader to find a
                // given class by name.  We are using this to
                // implement a plugin architecture, based on
                // expecting classes to implement a specific
                // interface (SimpleEditPlugin).  If the class
                // can be loaded and cast without failure,
                // we are good to go.
                Class myClass = Class.forName(argsconfig[i]);
                SimpleEditPlugin myPlugin =
                 (SimpleEditPlugin)myClass.getConstructor(null).newInstance(null);

                // Don't add the plugin if already installed. Allows for
                // eventual support for dynamically adding new plugins later.
                // Calls the Plugin init if this is the first time
                // it's being loaded.
                if(plugins.containsKey(myPlugin.getAction( )))
                {
                    return;
                } else
                {
                    myPlugin.init(this);
                }

                // If we made it this far, the plugin has been loaded
                // and initialized, so it's ok to add to the list of
                // valid plugins.
                plugins.put(myPlugin.getAction( ), myPlugin);
            }
            catch(Exception e)
```

Example 4-1. The sample Swing application (continued)

```
        {
            // This is not really adequate for a quality client
            // application, but it's acceptable for our purposes.
            System.out.println("Couldn't load Plugin: " + argsconfig[i]);
            System.out.println(e.getMessage( ));
            e.printStackTrace( );
        }
    }
}

/* -------------------- Initialization: GUI Components--------------------- */

    // The main visual components
    private javax.swing.JScrollPane mainScrollPane = new javax.swing.
JScrollPane( );
    private javax.swing.JTextArea mainTextArea = new javax.swing.JTextArea( );
    private javax.swing.JToolBar mainToolBar = new javax.swing.JToolBar( );
    private javax.swing.JTextField mainStatusText= new javax.swing.JTextField( );

    private void initComponents( )
    {
        this.getContentPane( ).setBackground(java.awt.Color.white);
        this.getContentPane( ).setLayout(new BorderLayout( ));
        this.getContentPane( ).add(mainScrollPane, BorderLayout.CENTER);
        this.getContentPane( ).add(mainToolBar, BorderLayout.NORTH);
        this.getContentPane( ).add(mainStatusText, BorderLayout.SOUTH);

        // This text field serves two purposes. It provides useful information
        // to the user, and also serves as a graceful "bump" for the Mac OS
        // grow box on the Mac OS platform.
        mainStatusText.setText("Ready.");

        mainStatusText.setCursor(
            Cursor.getPredefinedCursor(Cursor.DEFAULT_CURSOR));

        mainScrollPane.setViewportView(mainTextArea);

        mainTextArea.setEditable(true);
        mainTextArea.setCursor(Cursor.getPredefinedCursor(Cursor.TEXT_CURSOR));
        mainTextArea.setFont(
            new java.awt.Font("serif", java.awt.Font.PLAIN, 12)
            );

        // Perhaps a tool might be added later to control this dynamically?
        mainTextArea.setLineWrap(true);

        // Generally looks terrible on all platforms, and requires
        // a fair amount of work to get it to work right.
        mainToolBar.setFloatable(false);
        initToolBar(mainToolBar, this);
```

Example 4-1. The sample Swing application (continued)

```
        // Determine the offset value and stagger new windows
        // (with a reset every ten windows). A somewhat
        // unscientific mechanism, but it works well enough.
        int top_offset = 0;
        if((newWindows % 10) > 0)
        {
            top_offset =((this.newWindows) % 10) * 20 + 20;

            this.setLocation(
                new Double(getLocation().getX() + top_offset - 20).intValue( ),
                new Double(getLocation().getY() + top_offset).intValue( )
            );
        }
        int bottom_offset = 0;
        if (top_offset > 0)
            bottom_offset = top_offset - 20;

        // In a later chapter, we can use the JDirect and the
        // Carbon API GetAvailableWindowPositioningBounds( )
        // to properly position this.
        java.awt.Dimension screensize =
            java.awt.Toolkit.getDefaultToolkit().getScreenSize( );
        screensize =
            new java.awt.Dimension(640, screensize.height -128 - bottom_offset);
        this.setSize(screensize);
    }

    // Default items that always appear on the toolbar.
    // null items are treated as separators.
    String[] toolbarItems = {"New", "Open", null, "Timestamp"};

    private void initToolBar(javax.swing.JToolBar myToolBar, SimpleEdit myFrame)
    {
        JButton newButton;
        for(int i = 0; i < toolbarItems.length; i++)
        {
            if(toolbarItems[i] != null)
            {
                // It would be nice to provide icons
                // instead of just text labels.
                newButton = new JButton(toolbarItems[i]);

                // Used to track the targets more easily
                newButton.putClientProperty("window", myFrame);
                newButton.addActionListener(actionListenerHandler);
                myToolBar.add(newButton);
            } else
            {
                myToolBar.add(new javax.swing.JToolBar.Separator( ));
            }
        }
    }
```

Example 4-1. The sample Swing application (continued)

```
        // Load all plugins into the toolbar
        if(plugins != null)
            if(plugins.size( ) > 0)
            {
                java.util.Enumeration e = plugins.elements( );
                SimpleEditPlugin currentPlugin;
                while(e.hasMoreElements( ))
                {
                    currentPlugin = (SimpleEditPlugin)e.nextElement( );
                    newButton = new JButton(currentPlugin.getAction( ));
                    // We are using Swing client properties to
                    // track additional information without having
                    // to subclass - in effect, using the
                    // client properties mechanism as a form of
                    // delegation.
                    newButton.putClientProperty("window", myFrame);
                    newButton.putClientProperty("plugin", currentPlugin);
                    newButton.addActionListener(actionListenerHandler);
                    myToolBar.add(newButton);
                }
            }
    }


/* -------------------- Initialization: Menu Bar  --------------------------- */


    // The menu bar for the window
    private javax.swing.JMenuBar mainMenuBar = new javax.swing.JMenuBar( );

    // The menus attached to the menu bar
    private JMenu menuFile = new JMenu( );
    private JMenu menuEdit = new JMenu( );
    private JMenu menuTools = new JMenu( );

    // A Hashtable holding all of the default menu items, keyed by title
    protected static Hashtable menuItemsHashtable = new Hashtable( );

    /*
     * The items to be installed into the menus.
     * Each item consists of an identification string and
     * a corresponding virtual key.
     *
     * For a "real" application, the default item titles
     * and virtual keys would be loaded from resource bundles,
     * and ideally the user would be able to configure their
     * own toolbar and menu structure.
     *
     * For this demonstration, however, this is adequate.
     */
    private Object[][] fileItems =
    {
```

Example 4-1. The sample Swing application (continued)

```
        {"New", new Integer(KeyEvent.VK_N)},
        {"Open", new Integer(KeyEvent.VK_O)},
        {"Close", new Integer(KeyEvent.VK_W)},
        {null, null},
        {"Save", new Integer(KeyEvent.VK_S)},
        {"Revert to Saved", null},
        {null, null},
        {"Print...", new Integer(KeyEvent.VK_P)},
        {"Print Setup...", null}
    };
    private Object[][] editItems =
    {
        {"Undo", new Integer(KeyEvent.VK_Z)},
        {"Redo", new Integer(KeyEvent.VK_Y)},
        {null, null},
        {"Cut", new Integer(KeyEvent.VK_X)},
        {"Copy", new Integer(KeyEvent.VK_C)},
        {"Paste", new Integer(KeyEvent.VK_V)},
        {"Delete", null},
        {"Select All", new Integer(KeyEvent.VK_A)}
    };
    private Object[][] toolItems =
    {
        {"Timestamp", null}
    };

    private void dispatchEvent(ActionEvent evt, String tag)
    {
        SimpleEdit myFrame = null;
        SimpleEditPlugin myPlugin = null;
        if(evt.getSource() instanceof JComponent)
        {
            myFrame = (SimpleEdit)
              (((JComponent)evt.getSource()).getClientProperty("window"));
            myPlugin = (SimpleEditPlugin)
              (((JComponent)evt.getSource()).getClientProperty("plugin"));
        }

        // If it's a plugin, hand off to the plugin to handle
        if(myPlugin != null)
        {
            myPlugin.doAction(myFrame, evt);
            return;
        }

        // Handle minimal required functionality.
        // It could legitimately be argued that even this
        // functionality should be split off into an
        // overarching set of plugin functionality...
        // but this is adequate for now, and reinforces
        // the notion of certain "default" services.
```

Example 4-1. The sample Swing application (continued)

```
    if(tag.compareTo("New") == 0)
        doNew( );
    if(tag.compareTo("Close") == 0)
        doClose(myFrame);
    if(tag.compareTo("Timestamp") == 0)
        doTimestamp(myFrame);
}

/*
 * Default event processing.
 */
private void doNew( )
{
    (new SimpleEdit()).show( );
}

private void doTimestamp(SimpleEdit myFrame)
{
    if(myFrame != null)
        myFrame.mainTextArea.setText(myFrame.mainTextArea.getText( ) +
        System.getProperty("line.separator")  + new java.util.Date( ) + " : ");

        myFrame.mainTextArea.setCaretPosition(
        myFrame.mainTextArea.getText().length( ));
    myFrame.mainTextArea.requestFocus( );
}

// Used to track the number of open windows, and
// automatically quit when they are all closed.
private static int openWindows = 0;

// Overrides the default hide to see how many windows are currently
// showing. If none are visible, quit the app.
/** Hides the window. If no windows are visible, terminates quietly. */
public void hide( )
{
    super.hide( );
    openWindows--;
    if(openWindows == 0)
        System.exit(0);
}

public void show( )
{
    super.show( );
    openWindows++;
    // All ready to go, go ahead and get ready for input.
    this.appendDocumentText("");
}
```

Example 4-1. The sample Swing application (continued)

```
private void doClose(SimpleEdit myFrame)
{
    myFrame.hide( );
}

/* This variable is used to track the default accelerator
 * key for this platform.
 */
private int preferredMetaKey =
    Toolkit.getDefaultToolkit().getMenuShortcutKeyMask( );

private void setupMenu(JMenu myMenu, Object[][] menuconfig,
    SimpleEdit thisFrame)
{
    JMenuItem currentMenuItem;
    for(int i = 0; i < menuconfig.length; i++)
    {
        if(menuconfig[i][0] != null)
        {
            currentMenuItem = new JMenuItem( );
            currentMenuItem.setLabel((String)menuconfig[i][0]);

            if(menuconfig[i][1] != null)
            {
                int keyCode = ((Integer)menuconfig[i][1]).intValue( );
                KeyStroke key =
              KeyStroke.getKeyStroke(keyCode, preferredMetaKey);
                currentMenuItem.setAccelerator(key);
            }

            currentMenuItem.setEnabled(false);
            currentMenuItem.setActionCommand((String)menuconfig[i][0]);
            currentMenuItem.putClientProperty("window", thisFrame);

            currentMenuItem.addActionListener(actionListenerHandler);

            // Put the menu item into the menu hash to add handlers later
            menuItemsHashtable.put((String)menuconfig[i][0], currentMenuItem);
            myMenu.add(currentMenuItem);
        } else
        {
            javax.swing.JSeparator sep = new javax.swing.JSeparator( );
            myMenu.add(sep);
        }
    }
}

// A single default ActionListener that punts to dispatchEvent( ).
private ActionListener actionListenerHandler = new ActionListener( )
{
    public void actionPerformed(ActionEvent evt)
```

Example 4-1. The sample Swing application (continued)

```
    {
        Object src = evt.getSource( );
        if(src instanceof JMenuItem)
        {
            String input = ((JMenuItem)src).getLabel( );
            dispatchEvent(evt, input);
        }
        if(src instanceof JButton)
        {
            String input = ((JButton)src).getLabel( );
            dispatchEvent(evt, input);
        }
    }
};

private void initMenuBar( )
{
    mainMenuBar = new javax.swing.JMenuBar( );

    menuFile = new JMenu("File");
    setupMenu(menuFile, fileItems, this);
    mainMenuBar.add(menuFile);

    menuEdit = new JMenu("Edit");
    setupMenu(menuEdit, editItems, this);
    mainMenuBar.add(menuEdit);

    menuTools = new JMenu("Tools");
    setupMenu(menuTools, toolItems, this);
    mainMenuBar.add(menuTools);

    JMenuItem newMenuItem;
    if(plugins != null)
        if(plugins.size( ) > 0)
        {
            java.util.Enumeration e = plugins.elements( );
            SimpleEditPlugin currentPlugin;
            while(e.hasMoreElements( ))
            {
                currentPlugin = (SimpleEditPlugin)e.nextElement( );
                newMenuItem = new JMenuItem( );
                newMenuItem.setLabel(currentPlugin.getAction( ));
                newMenuItem.setEnabled(true);
                newMenuItem.setActionCommand(currentPlugin.getAction( ));
                newMenuItem.putClientProperty("window", this);
                newMenuItem.putClientProperty("plugin", currentPlugin);
                newMenuItem.addActionListener(actionListenerHandler);
                menuTools.add(newMenuItem);
            }
        }
```

Example 4-1. The sample Swing application (continued)

```
        ((JMenuItem)menuItemsHashtable.get("New")).setEnabled(true);
        ((JMenuItem)menuItemsHashtable.get("Timestamp")).setEnabled(true);
        ((JMenuItem)menuItemsHashtable.get("Close")).setEnabled(true);

        setJMenuBar(mainMenuBar);

    }
    /* ---------------- The Main Method: Menu Bar -------------------------
    */

    public static void main(String[] args)
    {
        argsconfig = args;
        (new SimpleEdit()).show();
    }
}
```

If you're new to Swing, you may wish to look up the reference material for imported classes. You'll also see several other classes named explicitly in the code (like javax.swing.JScrollPane) rather than imported, chiefly for self-documentation (and also because Swing occasionally has duplicate names in multiple packages). You'll also notice that the example class extends JFrame, a pretty standard technique in Swing, and calls an initialization routine in its constructor.

Using an init( ) method instead of working in the constructor allows you to recycle an object instead of allocating a new one:

```
// Create the object the first time
SimpleEdit editor = new SimpleEdit( );

// Do some work that changes the state of the editor object

// This takes more time and memory, depending on the JVM
editor = new SimpleEdit( );

// This approach is better and faster (instead of using new)
editor.init( );
```

Using an init( ) method is not actually required in this implementation, but it's a good pattern for instances in which you might reuse the object without creating a new one. For example, you could use the init( ) method to reset the window to a "pristine" state before loading a file from disk.

The Application API

After the constructor, you'll see several methods that aid in text manipulation (such as getDocumentText( ) or getJTextArea( )). While these examples could be considered utility methods, they form the backbone of this application's application programming interface (API). In other words, other applications could use this class as a module, with text editing capability, through these methods. The class provides a notebook-style framework that you could use in a code editor or journaling software, for instance. As a result, these utility methods become very important—applications using this class will depend on the methods for interaction with SimpleEdit.

Initialization

Moving back into the variable declaration section of the class, you'll see a private counter that keeps track of new and untitled document names:

```
// Used to set the number for new untitled windows
private static int newWindows = -1;
```

This counter determines the offset at which to place the document window, as well as the window identifier (to help the user keep multiple untitled windows distinct). It is also critical for the init( ) method:

```
// Sets up and creates a "pristine" window environment
private void init( )
{
    if(newWindows++ < 0)
        setTitle("Untitled");
    else
        setTitle("Untitled-" + newWindows);

    initPlugins( );
    initComponents( );
    initMenuBar( );
}
```

Loading plug-ins

What happens next is interesting: the init( ) method calls initPlugins( ), which then loads any plug-ins that the class is instructed to bring online (more on that in a minute). Of course, I just told you that this class has an API that other applications can use for accessing it. This means that the sample class suddenly has dual uses: as a framework to be used by other applications (basically a plug-in), and as an application in its own right, able to load its own plug-ins. This is a common concept in GUI programming: components are both containers and units that are contained. The API methods become more critical as applications external to the class use them to operate on the framework, and plug-ins internal to it might need to call back to them.

In the `initPlugins()` method, you'll see much of the heavy lifting performed as plug-ins are loaded. The plug-ins are specified by a set of command-line arguments that specify the class name of each desired plug-in. The JVM class loader then has to find the class by name.

Classes are loaded and then cached in a `Hashtable` (called, not surprisingly, `plugins`). This improves performance: the plug-ins are loaded only when the application is first launched. Traditionally, Mac OS users often expect delays when an application initially starts, but once they begin to work, lengthy delays are unacceptable.

You'll note that the plug-in classes are cast to the type `SimpleEditPlugin` (the next section deals with this interface, so don't get too impatient). Plug-ins are expected to implement this interface. Plug-in authors are given this interface and the application APIs, which are sufficient for writing additional modules that this framework can use.

GUI components

Next comes the `initComponents()` method, which creates the core interface of the application's main window. It's fairly straightforward. Check the Swing documentation for details on how the specific APIs are used.

This method then delegates additional GUI processing to `initToolbar()`, which does what it says it does: it deals with the application toolbar and its buttons. The application uses both the default application actions and the plug-in configuration options to create a user toolbar.

Menu bars

The menu bar configuration is handled via multiple-dimension arrays:

```
private Object[][] fileItems =
    {
        {"New", new Integer(KeyEvent.VK_N)},
        {"Open", new Integer(KeyEvent.VK_O)},
        {"Close", new Integer(KeyEvent.VK_W)},
        {null, null},
        {"Save", new Integer(KeyEvent.VK_S)},
        {"Revert to Saved", null},
        {null, null},
        {"Print...", new Integer(KeyEvent.VK_P)},
        {"Print Setup...", null}
    };
private Object[][] editItems =
    {
        {"Undo", new Integer(KeyEvent.VK_Z)},
        {"Redo", new Integer(KeyEvent.VK_Y)},
        {null, null},
```

```
    {"Cut", new Integer(KeyEvent.VK_X)},
    {"Copy", new Integer(KeyEvent.VK_C)},
    {"Paste", new Integer(KeyEvent.VK_V)},
    {"Delete", null},
    {"Select All", new Integer(KeyEvent.VK_A)}
};
private Object[][] toolItems =
{
    {"Timestamp", null}
};
```

This technique isn't very object-oriented, but it lays out the menu visually in the code, making it easy to see how the menu bar will look when rendered graphically.

Items defined as {null, null} are treated as separator bars. The action name is defined by the first element in each mini-array, and the second Integer element specifies the keyboard accelerator constant.

 You can look up these key constants in any good Swing reference.

A lot of code is associated with getting these menu bars to actually do something useful, beginning with the dispatchEvent( ) method. The event handling is performed mainly by a single handler, with Swing client property values used to store and handle event dispatching. Basically, the framework handles the most basic actions (calling upon the doNew( ), doTimeStamp( ), and doClose( ) methods), while everything else is handed off to the appropriate plug-in to handle on its own.

Once event handling is dealt with, add this trick to your toolkit:

```
/* This variable is used to track the default accelerator
 * key for this platform.
 */
private int preferredMetaKey =
    Toolkit.getDefaultToolkit().getMenuShortcutKeyMask( );
```

This little-known API is critical for proper cross-platform user interface application development. Mac OS X users expect to use the Meta key, officially referred to as the Command key (although I still tend to call it the "open apple" key). Windows applications, however, typically use the Control key. This application allows both options to map to the same UI action.

Many Java applications are hardcoded to use the control character as their default keyboard accelerator. Ironically, a user (or developer) used to Windows would consider this situation an ordinary feature: the same application running on two different platforms uses the same keyboard commands. However, it's terrible for any real Mac OS X user. Use this API when determining the default keyboard shortcuts and, if possible, include an interface that reassigns keyboard commands.

Finally, the menu can actually be created with the setupMenu( ) and initMenuBar( ) methods (the latter of which was called in the init( ) method). These methods use the arrays defined earlier to set up the menus, and the various event handlers to react to them. Some additional Swing client properties assist with event dispatching.

This menu bar is created and set for each window whenever a window is created. This serves an important purpose: on Windows and other windowing toolkits, each window is given a specific menu bar within the bounds of the window itself. On Mac OS X, a proper application has a single global menu bar shared by all windows. This application doesn't care which model is selected, and functions identically on all platforms.

Event processing

You learned about event processing and the dispatchEvent( ) method earlier, but now let's look at the doClose( ) method and its two helpers, hide( ) and show( ):

```
public void hide( )
{
    super.hide( );
    openWindows--;
    if(openWindows == 0)
        System.exit(0);
}

public void show( )
{
    super.show( );
    openWindows++;
    // All ready to go, go ahead and get ready for input.
    this.appendDocumentText("");
}

private void doClose(SimpleEdit myFrame)
{
    myFrame.hide( );
}
```

Note that the application terminates automatically when the final window is closed. This termination provides a relatively seamless user experience, minimizing the user's awareness of the application as a process that runs independently of any documents.

To get an idea of how this scenario affects your system, open Calculator, Address Book, and Internet Explorer. Now close out all your windows; note that while Calculator and Address Book are no longer running, Internet Explorer still waits for a "Quit" command. The example application behaves like Calculator and Address Book, assuming that when all windows are closed, the application should follow suit.

Last but not least, at the end of the code lies a simple main( ) method:

```
public static void main(String[] args)
{
    argsconfig = args;
    (new SimpleEdit()).show( );
}
```

With a solid set of methods already in hand, the main( ) method only has to configure the application and open a single window. It calls the constructor for the SimpleEdit class, which in turn calls the init( ) method, which then sets up the various plug-ins for the application.

The SimpleEditPlugin Interface

The SimpleEditPlugin interface allows the SimpleEdit application to deal with plug-ins at runtime, assuming that they implement this public interface. I've left the discussion of this interface for the end of this chapter so that you first learn how to use Swing with Mac OS X and don't get too hung up in inheritance and polymorphism.

This application demonstrates how to use dynamic class loading to let the same system add additional functionality without changing the core application. Chapter 5 uses a similar technique to isolate Mac OS X–specific code from the rest of the application. In a nutshell, the SimpleEditPlugin interface abstracts plug-in–specific (or platform-specific) details from SimpleEdit, and lets SimpleEdit handle all plug-ins generically.

The code shown in the initPlugins( ) method (see Example 4-1) relies on the fact that each plug-in implements a specific interface so it can easily call methods on a loaded class, as shown here:

```
Class myClass = Class.forName(argsconfig[i]);
    SimpleEditPlugin myPlugin =
        (SimpleEditPlugin)myClass.getConstructor(null).newInstance(null);
```

Example 4-2 shows the actual SimpleEditPlugin interface. As you can see, it is remarkably simple.

Example 4-2. The SimpleEditPlugin interface

```
package com.wiverson.macosbook;

public interface SimpleEditPlugin
{
    // Returns a list of actions which will be registered
    // The tool will then be notified if an action is
    // selected.
    public String getAction( );

    // Notification of an action which was registered by
    // this tool.
    public void doAction(SimpleEdit frame, java.awt.event.ActionEvent evt);

    // Called once when the plugin is first loaded
    public void init(SimpleEdit frame);

}
```

Code that implements this interface is loaded by SimpleEdit when it is launched with one or more command-line parameters with the fully qualified class name. As long as the interface is followed, SimpleEdit can interact with the plug-in.

Writing a plug-in

An example of a simple plug-in is one that simply beeps when the user invokes it from the menu bar or toolbar. Example 4-3 shows how easily you can code up such a plug-in.

Example 4-3. A beeping plug-in

```
package com.wiverson.macosbook.plugin;

import com.wiverson.macosbook.SimpleEdit;

public class BeepPlugin implements com.wiverson.macosbook.SimpleEditPlugin
{

    public BeepPlugin( )
    {
    }

    public void doAction(SimpleEdit frame, java.awt.event.ActionEvent evt)
    {
        java.awt.Toolkit.getDefaultToolkit().beep( );
        frame.setStatusText("Beep!");

    }
```

Example 4-3. A beeping plug-in (continued)

```
public String getAction( )
{
    return "Beep";
}

public void init(SimpleEdit frame)
{
    frame.setStatusText("Loaded BeepPlugin");
}

}
```

Assuming that this plug-in was compiled successfully, it is possible to launch SimpleEdit with this installed plug-in by executing the following command:

```
java com.wiverson.macosbook.SimpleEdit com.wiverson.macosbook.plugin.
BeepPlugin
```

Once the SimpleEdit application starts up and detects a command-line argument, it loads the named plug-in. The getAction( ) method tells SimpleEdit which text to display in the user interface, and when the user selects this option, the doAction( ) method is called. The arguments passed in allow the plug-in to affect the window and text area by working with the passed-in SimpleEdit object. In this manner, the plug-in is isolated from all user interface details of SimpleEdit.

In later chapters we will use this plug-in architecture to add everything from spellcheck capabilities to communication with web services. The next chapter uses this mechanism to add support for Apple-specific extensions to the Java platform.

## CHAPTER 5

Apple Extensions

Apple ships a nonstandard JVM with proprietary extensions. There—I've said it, and the cat is out of the bag. So why isn't Apple lumped into the same category as other vendors that ship proprietary JVMs? Why has Apple not been accused of trying to co-opt Java for sinister purposes? Put simply, Apple's JVM extensions are just that—extensions. They don't change what Java is, but add additional functionality on top of and around a normal Java environment. Apple ships a complete implementation of not just the Java Runtime Environment (JRE), but a full Java Development Kit (JDK). The extensions just include some icing on the standard Java cake.

Apple's Java implementation is fully compliant with any Java 2/JDK 1.3/4– based "pure" Java application. Certain vendors ship incomplete JVM implementations for strategically competitive reasons, in opposition to technologies such as RMI and CORBA. Apple's extensions to Java, however, principally address weaknesses in the Java platform. Careful application development lets you support these extensions while still maintaining excellent cross-platform compatibility. This chapter explores these extensions and shows how they can add to standard Java programs (like the editor from the last chapter).

 When comparing Apple's extensions to the efforts of other vendors (Microsoft in particular), keep the following in mind:

- Apple's extensions are (to the developer) just classes that allow you to more easily access Mac OS X functionality.
- The extensions do not add to the language model itself (e.g., additional keywords).
- The full Java 2 Standard Edition stack is included.
- Apple's JVM is compliant with all relevant Java specifications.

The Mac OS X Finder

Virtually every desktop client platform provides a standard that specifies application icons, associates documents with the application, and notifies the application of user requests generated by the desktop shell, be it the Finder, Explorer, or some X Windows–based system. However, the standard Java environment lacks mechanisms and APIs to deal with many of these conventions. Instead, you are given a main( ) method and the assumption that users can figure out what to do on their own. The result is a Java program that looks like Java, instead of a seamlessly integrated part of the user's desktop experience.

This section examines Apple's extensions that provide APIs for this desktop shell integration and describes how to support them while maintaining cross-platform compatibility.

 Apple provides new interfaces for these interactions under JDK 1.4.1 using a different set of packages (com.apple.eio and com.apple.eawt). However, the existing interfaces, described below, work under both JDK 1.3.1 and JDK 1.4.1. In addition, users are required to download JDK 1.4.1 separately, as it is not available for redistribution. Therefore, this section will focus on the JDK 1.3.1 extension mechanisms.

Finder Integration

When a Java application runs on Mac OS X, the system creates the default application menu shown in Figure 5-1. The default application name is the fully qualified class name of the launching main( ) class (which is really only acceptable during development, if at all).

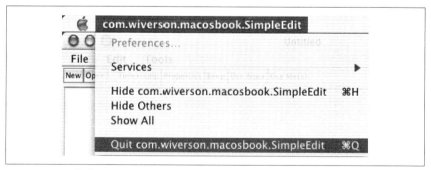

Figure 5-1. Default application menu

Each menu item needs to be accessible and integrated into the program so that code can respond to user actions. Apple provides hooks for integrating with these menu items via callbacks (or handlers). To implement these callbacks for the SimpleEdit application developed in Chapter 1, you will create a `SimpleEditPlugin` through the Java source file *FinderIntegrationPlugin.java*. This code, once compiled, will display the dialogs shown in Figure 5-2.

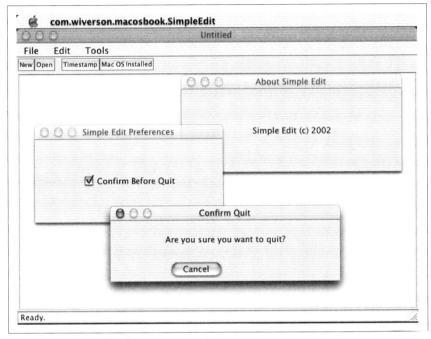

Figure 5-2. Menu callbacks trigger dialog boxes

While this process isn't overly complex, it does begin to add some polish to the application.

The Finder Plug-in

Launch this application from the Terminal. Use the `cd` command to navigate to the application's root directory (which should be in your classpath) and launch this application with the command shown here:

```
java -Dcom.apple.mrj.application.apple.menu.about.name=SimpleEdit com.
wiverson.macosbook.SimpleEdit com.wiverson.macosbook.plugin.
FinderIntegrationPlugin
```

As noted before, this is actually one long line of typing, broken up for readability. Do not use line breaks when typing the command into your Terminal window.

In addition to starting the program, this command sets and displays the name of the "About" menu item. You can do this for any OS X Swing application by using the com.apple.mrj.application.apple.menu.about.name property.

The plug-in shown in Example 5-1 interacts with the Mac OS X Finder, but it also introduces some important cross-platform considerations. Check out the source code, and soon you'll learn to handle non–Mac OS X platforms.

Example 5-1. The plug-in for Finder interaction

```
import com.wiverson.macosbook.SimpleEdit;

public class FinderIntegrationPlugin
    implements com.wiverson.macosbook.SimpleEditPlugin
{

    /** Creates a new instance of FinderIntegrationPlugin */
    public FinderIntegrationPlugin( )
    {
    }

    // Does nothing useful in this context.
    public void doAction(SimpleEdit frame, java.awt.event.ActionEvent evt)
    {
        return;
    }

    // Returns a status string only.
    public String getAction( )
    {
        if(isMacOS)
            return "Mac OS Installed";
        else
            return "Mac OS Not Available";
    }

    boolean isMacOS = false;

    /** Checks to see if Mac OS is available. If so,
     * goes ahead and loads the class by name that
     * actually performs the initialization. If not,
     * the class is never loaded. This helps prevent
     * classloader problems on non-Mac OS systems.
     */

    public void init(SimpleEdit frame)
    {
        if(System.getProperty("mrj.version") != null)
            isMacOS = true;

        if(isMacOS)
```

Example 5-1. The plug-in for Finder interaction (continued)

```
{
    try
    {
        // This requests the classloader to find a
        // given class by name. We are using this to
        // establish a firewall between the application
        // and Mac OS X dependencies. This helps isolate
        // the application logic for organizational purposes,
        // as well as ensure that we won't try to drag Mac OS
        // references into our crossplatform code.
        Class myClass =
            Class.forName("com.wiverson.macosbook.plugin.FinderIntegration");

        Object myObject = myClass.getConstructor(null).newInstance(null);
        myClass.getDeclaredMethod("execute", null).invoke(myObject,
null);;
    } catch (Exception e)
    {
        System.out.println("Unable to load FinderIntegration module.");
        e.printStackTrace( );
    }
}
}
}
```

This plug-in implements the SimpleEditPlugin interface from the last chapter, allowing it to integrate into SimpleEdit easily. Make sure you've got that interface compiled and on your classpath before compiling this class.

When reviewing the code for the plug-in shown in Example 5-1, you'll notice a lack of imports or references to Mac OS X–specific libraries; the code checks to see if it is running on a Mac OS system, and then loads the needed classes explicitly by name. This avoids ClassDefNotFound exceptions when running on platforms other than Mac OS X, as well as a miserable user experience.

Apple provides a stubs-only version of their MRJ classes that can be bundled with your application for distribution on non–Mac OS X platforms. However, using this version will make your application larger and require careful classpath management. You might find it easier to understand and maintain platform-specific code independently from your core application logic.

Once the plug-in is sure that it is running on an OS X platform, it begins to deal with Finder integration. Instead of handling this itself, though, it loads up another class, FinderIntegration, which does all the heavy lifting.

The FinderIntegration Support Class

To actually support the integration, the FinderIntegration class is filled with platform-specific code for handling Apple extensions. Example 5-2 shows the source code for this class.

Example 5-2. OS X–specific Finder functionality

```
/** In order for this plugin to function properly,
 * it must be loaded by the SimpleEdit application
 * and the proper system properties set before execution.
 *
 * For example, the following command, entered on a single line,
 * invokes the JVM and tells the system to display the About menu item
 * in the Mac OS X application menu.
 *
 * java -Dcom.apple.mrj.application.apple.menu.about.name=SimpleEdit
 * com.wiverson.macosbook.plugin.FinderIntegrationPlugin
 */
package com.wiverson.macosbook.plugin;

import javax.swing.JDialog;
import javax.swing.JLabel;
import java.awt.Dimension;
import java.awt.event.ItemEvent;
import java.awt.event.ItemListener;

import com.apple.mrj.MRJApplicationUtils;

import com.apple.mrj.MRJOpenApplicationHandler;
import com.apple.mrj.MRJPrefsHandler;
import com.apple.mrj.MRJQuitHandler;
import com.apple.mrj.MRJOpenDocumentHandler;
import com.apple.mrj.MRJAboutHandler;

public class FinderIntegration
    implements  MRJOpenApplicationHandler,
                MRJQuitHandler,
                MRJPrefsHandler,
                MRJOpenDocumentHandler,
                MRJAboutHandler
{

    /** Creates a new instance of FinderIntegration */
    public FinderIntegration()
    {
    }
```

Example 5-2. OS X–specific Finder functionality (continued)

```
    // Only want to install this once per application
    // to avoid getting multiple event notifications
    private static boolean installed = false;

    public void execute( )
    {
        if(!installed)
        {
            // Enables the menu item
            MRJApplicationUtils.registerPrefsHandler(this);

            // Overrides the default System.exit( ) behavior.
            MRJApplicationUtils.registerQuitHandler(this);

            // Requires com.apple.mrj.application.apple.menu.about.
name=Application
            // system property to be set to appear.
            MRJApplicationUtils.registerAboutHandler(this);

            // These require the application to be properly bundled for Mac OS X
            // for the events to be dispatched
            MRJApplicationUtils.registerOpenApplicationHandler(this);
            MRJApplicationUtils.registerOpenDocumentHandler(this);

            installed = true;
        }
    }

    // We only need one instance of the About dialog.
    static JDialog AboutDialog = null;

    public void handleAbout( )
    {
        new DoAbout().start( );
    }

    /** It may seem a bit strange to create a new Thread
     * just to display an about box.
     *
     * Unfortunately, due to the way the System interacts
     * between the native Carbon libraries and the JVM,
     * displaying a dialog will lock the user interface,
     * leaving kill to terminate the app.
     *
     * This simple thread just hangs on to a singleton
     * dialog, creating a new dialog if it's the first
     * time the dialog is displayed, hiding and reshowing
     * the dialog as needed.
     *
     * This isn't needed in the later Apple JVM's (including
     * JDK 1.4), but some earlier releases required this.
```

Example 5-2. OS X–specific Finder functionality (continued)

```
 *
 */
class DoAbout extends Thread
{
    public void run( )
    {
        if(AboutDialog == null)
        {
            AboutDialog = new JDialog( );
            AboutDialog.setResizable(false);
            AboutDialog.setTitle("About Simple Edit");
            AboutDialog.setSize(350, 150);
            Dimension screensize =
                java.awt.Toolkit.getDefaultToolkit().getScreenSize( );
            int width =
                new Double((screensize.getWidth() - 350) / 2).intValue( );
            int height =
                new Double((screensize.getHeight() / 2) - 150).intValue( );
            AboutDialog.move(width, height);
            JLabel myAppTitle = new JLabel( );
            myAppTitle.setHorizontalAlignment(myAppTitle.CENTER);
            myAppTitle.setText("Simple Edit (c) 2002");
            AboutDialog.getContentPane( ).add(myAppTitle);
        }
        AboutDialog.show( );
    }
}


/** Note that the application requires Mac OS X bundling
 * (as described in a later chapter) to be enabled.
 * The techniques for writing these handlers are similar
 * to the rest of the add-ons.
 *
 * Typically, you will want to use these handlers to call
 * your standard File -> Open... routines, simply bypassing
 * the standard file dialogs.
 * /
public void handleOpenApplication( )
{
    new DoOpenApplication().start( );
}

class DoOpenApplication extends Thread
{
    public void run( )
    {
        System.out.println("Open Application");
    }
}
```

Example 5-2. OS X–specific Finder functionality (continued)

```
public void handleOpenFile(java.io.File file)
{
    DoOpenFile myHandler = new DoOpenFile( );
    myHandler.setFile(file);
    myHandler.start( );
}


class DoOpenFile extends Thread
{
    private java.io.File theFile = null;
    public void setFile(java.io.File inFile)
    {
        theFile = inFile;
    }


    public void run( )
    {
        if(theFile == null)
            return;

        JDialog openedFileDialog = new JDialog( );
        openedFileDialog.setResizable(false);
        openedFileDialog.setTitle("File Open Request...");
        openedFileDialog.setSize(350, 150);
        Dimension screensize =
            java.awt.Toolkit.getDefaultToolkit().getScreenSize( );
        int width =
            new Double((screensize.getWidth() - 350) / 2).intValue( );
        int height =
            new Double((screensize.getHeight( ) / 2) - 150).intValue( );
        openedFileDialog.move(width, height);

        JLabel myFileName = new JLabel( );
        myFileName.setHorizontalAlignment(JLabel.CENTER);
        myFileName.setText("File name: " + theFile.getName( ));
        openedFileDialog.getContentPane( ).add(myFileName);

        JLabel myFilePath = new JLabel( );
        myFilePath.setHorizontalAlignment(JLabel.CENTER);
        myFilePath.setText("File path: " + theFile.getPath( ));
        openedFileDialog.getContentPane( ).add(myFilePath);

        openedFileDialog.show( );
    }
}

 public void handlePrefs( ) throws java.lang.IllegalStateException
{
    new com.wiverson.macosbook.plugin.FinderIntegration.DoPrefs().start( );
}
```

Example 5-2. OS X–specific Finder functionality (continued)

```
// This is the one preference we are tracking, which
// only relates to Mac OS X specific behavior anyways.
// Note that we aren't persisting the user's preferences.
public static boolean pref_askToClose = true;

static JDialog PrefsDialog = null;
class DoPrefs extends Thread
{
    public void run( )
    {
        if(PrefsDialog == null)
        {
            PrefsDialog = new JDialog( );
            PrefsDialog.setResizable(false);
            PrefsDialog.setTitle("Simple Edit Preferences");
            PrefsDialog.setSize(300, 150);
            Dimension screensize =
                java.awt.Toolkit.getDefaultToolkit().getScreenSize( );
            int width =
                new Double((screensize.getWidth()  - 300) / 2).intValue( );
            int height =
                new Double((screensize.getHeight() / 2) - 150).intValue( );
            PrefsDialog.move(width, height);

            javax.swing.JCheckBox myQuitPrefButton =
                new javax.swing.JCheckBox("Confirm Before Quit");
            myQuitPrefButton.setHorizontalAlignment(
                javax.swing.SwingConstants.CENTER);
            myQuitPrefButton.setSelected(true);
            myQuitPrefButton.addItemListener(new ItemListener( )
            {
                public void itemStateChanged(ItemEvent evt)
                {
                    pref_askToClose =
                        (evt.getStateChange( ) == ItemEvent.SELECTED);
                }
            });
            PrefsDialog.getContentPane( ).add(myQuitPrefButton);
        }

        PrefsDialog.show( );
    }
}

/* Note that the Quit thread is slightly more complex
 * than the other threads.
 *
 * There is a bug which manifests as of Mac OS X 10.1, JDK 1.3.1
 * Update 1 which causes it to generate multiple events
 * for a single selection of the Quit menu item on the native
 * application menu.
```

Example 5-2. OS X–specific Finder functionality (continued)

```
 *
 * If you know you'll only be running on JDK 1.4 or later, this
 * isn't necessary.
 *
 * Therefore, to avoid a deadlock, a new thread is created,
 * tracked, and communicated with.  It's arguably overkill for
 * what is supposed to be a modal quit confirmation dialog...
 * but it works.
 */
com.wiverson.macosbook.plugin.FinderIntegration.DoQuit quitThread = null;

public void handleQuit( ) throws java.lang.IllegalStateException
{
    if(pref_askToClose)
    {
        if(quitThread == null)
        {
            quitThread = new DoQuit( );
            // Make sure the application doesn't hang around
            // waiting for this thread.
            quitThread.setDaemon(true);
            quitThread.start( );
        }
        else
            quitThread.show( );
    } else
    {
        // If the user set a preference not to be
        // prompted, go ahead and bail out.
        System.exit(0);
    }
}

class DoQuit extends Thread
{
    private  QuitConfirmJDialog myQuitDialog = null;
    // Operations on ints are inherently atomic,
    // and we aren't doing anything too fancy
    // requires fancier semaphores & locking.
    int showDialog = 0;
    public void show( )
    {
        showDialog = 1;
    }

    public void run( )
    {
        if(myQuitDialog == null)
            myQuitDialog =
                new QuitConfirmJDialog(new javax.swing.JFrame( ), true);
```

Example 5-2. OS X–specific Finder functionality (continued)

```
        showDialog = 1;
        // Now that the Quit dialog is ready, go ahead and sit
        // around waiting for a semaphore notification to redisplay.
        while(true)
        {
            if(showDialog == 1)
            {
                myQuitDialog.show( );
                showDialog = 0;
            }
        };
    }
  }
}
```

You'll notice several Apple-specific imports. Each imported handler describes specific methods that must be implemented and ensures that the class can be cast properly. Additionally, Apple provides a lot of "out-of-the-box" functionality for working with GUIs, so it makes no sense to reinvent these pieces of code when you can simply implement some standard interfaces.

Registering handlers

The class uses the Apple-supplied MRJApplicationUtils class to register this class as an implementation of the various handlers:

```
// Enables the menu item
MRJApplicationUtils.registerPrefsHandler(this);

// Overrides the default System.exit( ) behavior.
MRJApplicationUtils.registerQuitHandler(this);

// Requires com.apple.mrj.application.apple.menu.about.name=Application
// system property to be set to appear.
MRJApplicationUtils.registerAboutHandler(this);

// These require the application to be properly bundled for Mac OS X
// for the events to be dispatched
MRJApplicationUtils.registerOpenApplicationHandler(this);
MRJApplicationUtils.registerOpenDocumentHandler(this);
```

This class lets any other application using standard Apple controls know that the application can work seamlessly with this class (and the plug-in that uses it).

The "About" dialog box

Like other menu items that have event handlers associated with them, you can use a simple callback method to deal with the "About" dialog box. One of its unusual features, though, is the creation of a new thread that displays the dialog box:

```
public void handleAbout( )
{
    new DoAbout().start( );
}

class DoAbout extends Thread
{
    public void run( )
    {
        if(AboutDialog == null)
        {
            AboutDialog = new JDialog( );
            AboutDialog.setResizable(false);
            AboutDialog.setTitle("About Simple Edit");
            AboutDialog.setSize(350, 150);
            Dimension screensize =
                java.awt.Toolkit.getDefaultToolkit().getScreenSize( );
            int width =
                new Double((screensize.getWidth() - 350) / 2).intValue( );
            int height =
                new Double((screensize.getHeight( ) / 2) - 150).intValue( );
            AboutDialog.move(width, height);
            JLabel myAppTitle = new JLabel( );
            myAppTitle.setHorizontalAlignment(myAppTitle.CENTER);
            myAppTitle.setText("Simple Edit (c) 2002");
            AboutDialog.getContentPane( ).add(myAppTitle);
        }
        AboutDialog.show( );
    }
}
```

This use of threading is a result of interactions with Mac OS X's native libraries. Threading is not necessary when using Apple's JDK 1.4 implementation, but the limitation does exist on JDK 1.3, and the required overhead is relatively trivial. If your "About" box does perform more sophisticated work across threads, however, you might need to pay attention to synchronization and other threading issues. Of course, getting your system upgraded to JDK 1.4 takes care of this problem, so these threading concerns will only be a legacy issue for most Mac OS X developers.

The "Open" and "Preferences" handlers

Once you've gotten the "About" box handled, you can move on to more standard handlers such as the "Open" and "Preferences" menu items. In each, the same basic threading principles are applied: the handler starts a thread, and then the thread handles the actual actions associated with the requested action.

To enable the handlers registered for the "Open" item, you'll need to launch the application using Apple's packaging format as described in Chapter 7. While launching is an inconvenience now (you'll have to get a little further in the book to use these features), it results in much better application code.

The preferences dialog created by the DoPrefs thread is very basic and doesn't actually do much. In fact, the settings it allows are not persisted, so they would have to be reset each time the application is restarted. Several strategies are available for persisting user preferences, from the Preferences API included in JDK 1.4 to Java serialization and JDBC. The actual selected mechanism depends on the overall use of the application. Regardless of the mechanism, options available from this dialog should be global to the application, not specific to the current running instance.

The "Quit" handler

The "Quit" handler shown in Example 5-2 is perhaps the most complex example of a "Quit" dialog you'll see, but it's necessary in applications that are backward-compatible with Apple's JDK 1.3 implementation.

This text often discusses how to make code work on JDK 1.3. While you probably keep up with the latest versions and system upgrades and have JDK 1.4 installed, you shouldn't expect your user base to do the same. Building in support for JDK 1.3 is generally simple and well worth a little extra effort. The end result is code that works on nearly all Mac OS X systems, not just on systems that are completely up to date.

Consider this unusual bit of code:

```
if(pref_askToClose)
{
    if(quitThread == null)
    {
        quitThread = new DoQuit( );
        // Make sure the application doesn't hang around
        // waiting for this thread.
        quitThread.setDaemon(true);
        quitThread.start( );
    }
    else
        quitThread.show( );
} else
{
```

```
        // If the user set a preference not to be
        // prompted, go ahead and bail out.
        System.exit(0);
    }
```

A bug in Mac OS X 10.1 and JDK 1.3.1 (including Update 1) requires a lot of extra work. On those platforms and JDKs, multiple events are fired off for a single selection of the "Quit" menu item. Consequently, multiple threads can be created and deadlocked, resulting in an apparently frozen application. This turns out to be a lot of work for such a simple task, but if anything annoys a user, it is the thought that his or her application has locked up (even if the user was just trying to quit).

 If your application doesn't provide a "Quit" handler, the "Quit" menu item is still available to the user. When the user selects it, System.exit(0) is automatically called (which can have undesirable effects if you haven't saved your work).

To make things easier, a dialog pops up to ensure that the user wants to quit:

```
if(myQuitDialog == null)
    myQuitDialog = new QuitConfirmJDialog(new javax.swing.JFrame( ), true);
```

Example 5-3 is the code for the "Quit" confirmation dialog.

Example 5-3. The "Quit" confirmation dialog box

```
package com.wiverson.macosbook.plugin;

import javax.swing.JDialog;
import javax.swing.JFrame;
import java.awt.Frame;

public class QuitConfirmJDialog extends JDialog
{

    /** Creates new form QuitConfirmJDialog */
    public QuitConfirmJDialog(Frame parent, boolean modal)
    {
        super(parent, modal);
        initComponents( );
    }

    private void initComponents( )
    {
        buttonPanel = new javax.swing.JPanel( );
        cancelButton = new javax.swing.JButton( );
        okButton = new javax.swing.JButton( );
        jLabel1 = new javax.swing.JLabel( );
```

Example 5-3. The "Quit" confirmation dialog box (continued)

```java
setTitle("Confirm Quit");
setModal(true);
setResizable(false);
addFocusListener(new java.awt.event.FocusAdapter( )
{
    public void focusGained(java.awt.event.FocusEvent evt)
    {
        formFocusHandler(evt);
    }
});

addWindowListener(new java.awt.event.WindowAdapter( )
{
    public void windowClosing(java.awt.event.WindowEvent evt)
    {
        closeDialog(evt);
    }
});

cancelButton.setText("Cancel");
cancelButton.addActionListener(new java.awt.event.ActionListener( )
{
    public void actionPerformed(java.awt.event.ActionEvent evt)
    {
        cancelButtonHandler(evt);
    }
});

buttonPanel.add(cancelButton);

okButton.setText("OK");
this.getRootPane( ).setDefaultButton(okButton);
okButton.addActionListener(new java.awt.event.ActionListener( )
{
    public void actionPerformed(java.awt.event.ActionEvent evt)
    {
        okButtonHandler(evt);
    }
});

buttonPanel.add(okButton);

getContentPane( ).add(buttonPanel, java.awt.BorderLayout.SOUTH);

jLabel1.setText("Are you sure you want to quit?");
jLabel1.setHorizontalAlignment(javax.swing.SwingConstants.CENTER);
jLabel1.setHorizontalTextPosition(javax.swing.SwingConstants.CENTER);
getContentPane( ).add(jLabel1, java.awt.BorderLayout.CENTER);

pack( );
java.awt.Dimension screenSize =
```

Example 5-3. The "Quit" confirmation dialog box (continued)

```
        java.awt.Toolkit.getDefaultToolkit().getScreenSize( );
        setSize(new java.awt.Dimension(366, 116));
        setLocation((screenSize.width-366)/2,(screenSize.height-116)/2);
    }

    private void formFocusHandler(java.awt.event.FocusEvent evt)
    {
        okButton.requestFocus( );
    }

    private void cancelButtonHandler(java.awt.event.ActionEvent evt)
    {
        okButton.requestFocus( );
        this.hide( );
    }

    private void okButtonHandler(java.awt.event.ActionEvent evt)
    {
        System.exit(0);
    }

    private void closeDialog(java.awt.event.WindowEvent evt)
    {
        this.hide( );
    }

    public static void main(String args[])
    {
        new QuitConfirmJDialog(new JFrame(), false).show( );
    }

    private javax.swing.JPanel buttonPanel;
    private javax.swing.JButton okButton;
    private javax.swing.JButton cancelButton;
    private javax.swing.JLabel jLabel1;

}
```

It should be fairly easy to adapt these classes to your own application, providing Mac OS X–specific features while maintaining seamless cross-platform compatibility. As long as you use the FinderIntegrationPlugin or something similar, you can check for the existence of a Mac OS X platform and respond to it quickly and efficiently.

Native Access

The preferred mechanism for accessing native functionality on Mac OS X is the standard Java Native Interface (JNI). This section builds a simple JNI library using Apple's Project Builder tool, found in */Developer/Applications/*.

In the past, Apple supplied a technology known as JDirect, a set of bindings between native code and Java that is much simpler than JNI. Specifically, JDirect allows access to native libraries without the cumbersome header generation of JNI. Apple has deprecated JDirect, however, and strongly encourages the use of JNI. In fact, the latest versions of the JDK (1.4+) remove JDirect altogether.

To begin, launch Project Builder and select "File → New Project." Select the "Java → Java JNI Application" option, as shown in Figure 5-3. On the next panel, name your project and give it a location (here, we'll name it "JNIExample"). Then save it in ~/JNIExample/.

Figure 5-3. JNI's new project

The assistant will generate several files for you automatically, as shown in Figure 5-4. Before looking at the files, however, consider the build process and the targets, as shown in Figure 5-5. When building applications with JNI, you should usually first write Java application code, and then flag methods that will have a native implementation using the native keyword:

```
native boolean loginAsRoot(String username, String password);
```

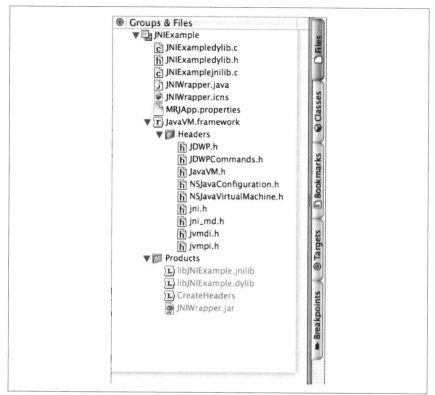

Figure 5-4. JNI files

This Java source file is then read by the javah tool (a standard JDK command-line tool), and an appropriate C header file is generated. You then write a native implementation in C, build a library appropriate for the target platform, and ship both the original Java source file and the native library.

For occasional use of native functionality, or when it's easy to segment the Java and native portions of an application, this model works fairly well. In particular, it allows shipment of identical Java code on multiple platforms as long as an appropriately built native library is present and accessible by the JVM. Unfortunately, no existing tool easily handles the other, rather common scenario: quickly and easily building Java bindings for existing C- and C++-based native libraries. For those situations, either contact the vendor of the native library or build JNI wrappers yourself—and consider sharing them.

The project generated by Project Builder includes all these steps as targets in its build process. The JNIWrapper target compiles the *JNIWrapper.java*

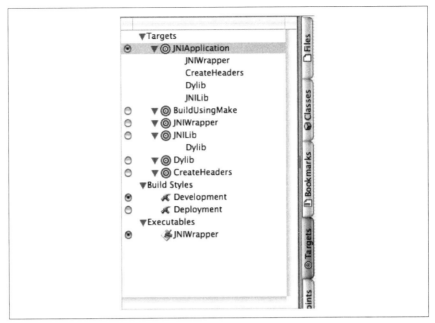

Figure 5-5. JNI targets

source file and archives it into a JAR. The CreateHeaders target calls javah on that JAR file. This scenario is shown in Figure 5-6, accessible by clicking on the "Targets" tab, and then clicking on CreateHeaders.

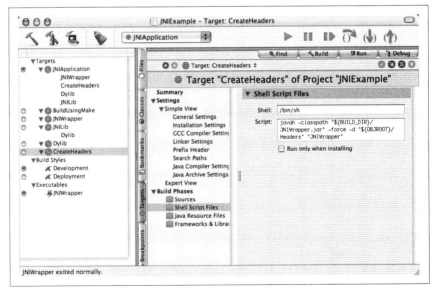

Figure 5-6. JNI CreateHeaders target

The final stage is building a JNI library and creating a sample *dylib* library. The JNI library conforms to library conventions as required by JNI, whereas a *dylib* is the preferred format for Mac OS X native libraries (similar to a DLL on Windows). Mac OS X native libraries are typically shipped as *dylib* libraries, and it's important to know how to call from a JNI library to a *dylib* library so you can access most Mac OS X native functionality. To facilitate this process, Project Builder provides the JNILib target, which builds the JNI library, and the Dylib target, which builds a sample *dylib* library.

JNI and Dependencies

A common problem for JNI developers coming from other platforms is an assumption that JNI dynamic libraries can be built with interdependencies. For example, *libA.jnilib* contains a function foo( ). *libB.jnilib* needs to link against *libA.jnilib* in order to use foo( ). This linkage will *not* work on Mac OS X because JNI libraries are bundles, and all symbols are private to a bundle. This effectively makes the foo( ) method private and inaccessible by libB.

One way to solve this dependency problem is to put the common functions into separate *dynamic* libraries (*libC.dylib*, for example) rather than JNI libraries, and link both *libA.jnilib* and *libB.jnilib* to *libC.dylib*. In other words, JNI native libraries can link only to external native functions in dynamic libraries, not to other JNI library functions.

The rest of this section adds a new native method to access a system function to the JNIExample application. First, create a new method called test_method( ) in a *JNIWrapper.java* source file, as shown in Example 5-4. Be sure and do this in your new JNI Application project in Project Builder to avoid having to perform the JNI setup steps manually.

Example 5-4. The JNIWrapper source file

```
import java.util.*;

public class JNIWrapper {

    static {
        // Ensure native JNI library is loaded
        System.loadLibrary("JNIExample");
    }

    public JNIWrapper( ) {
        System.out.println("JNIWrapper instance created");
    }
```

Example 5-4. The JNIWrapper source file (continued)

```
native int native_method(String arg);
native String test_method(String arg, int arg2);

public static void main (String args[]) {
    // insert code here...
    System.out.println("Started JNIWrapper");
    JNIWrapper newjni = new JNIWrapper( );
    int result = newjni.native_method("Hello World !");

    System.out.println(newjni.test_method("Test", 1));

    System.out.println("Finished JNIWrapper. Answer is " + result);
    }

}
```

Build the application in Project Builder by selecting "Build → Build." The application will rebuild, but its execution will result in a java.lang. UnsatisfiedLinkError. To get the application to build properly, add the native implementation for the native_method( ) and test_method( ) methods.

When you build the project, Project Builder generates a *JNIWrapper.h* file, which can be found in *~/JNIExample/build/Headers/*. After opening this file, you'll see the declarations shown here:

```
/* DO NOT EDIT THIS FILE - it is machine generated */
#include <jni.h>
/* Header for class JNIWrapper */

#ifndef _Included_JNIWrapper
#define _Included_JNIWrapper
#ifdef __cplusplus
extern "C" {
#endif
/*
 * Class:     JNIWrapper
 * Method:    native_method
 * Signature: (Ljava/lang/String;)I
 */
JNIEXPORT jint JNICALL Java_JNIWrapper_native_1method
  (JNIEnv *, jobject, jstring);

/*
 * Class:     JNIWrapper
 * Method:    test_method
 * Signature: (Ljava/lang/String;I)Ljava/lang/String;
 */
JNIEXPORT jstring JNICALL Java_JNIWrapper_test_1method
  (JNIEnv *, jobject, jstring, jint);
```

```
#ifdef __cplusplus
}
#endif
#endif
```

Of particular interest is the declaration for test_method. Copy and paste this declaration into the *JNIExamplejnilib.c* file, and add arguments and an implementation to the method, as shown in Example 5-5.

Example 5-5. Adding native code

```
/*
 *  JNIExamplejnilib.c
 *  JNIExample
 *
 *  Created by Will Iverson on Mon Dec 16 2002.
 *  Copyright (c) 2002 __MyCompanyName__. All rights reserved.
 *
 */

#include "JNIWrapper.h"
#include "JNIExampledylib.h"

JNIEXPORT jint JNICALL Java_JNIWrapper_native_1method(JNIEnv *env, jobject this,
                                                      jstring arg) {
  /* Convert to UTF8 */
  const char *argutf  = (*env)->GetStringUTFChars(env, arg, JNI_FALSE);

  /* Call into external dylib function */
  jint rc = shared_function(argutf);

  /* Release created UTF8 string */
  (*env)->ReleaseStringUTFChars(env, arg, argutf);

  return rc;
}

JNIEXPORT jstring JNICALL Java_JNIWrapper_test_1method
  (JNIEnv * env, jobject argObject, jstring argString, jint argInt)
{
  return (*env)->NewStringUTF(env, "Greetings from the native library.");
}
```

 You'll notice that the implementation for the other method (Java_JNIWrapper_native_1method, which translates to native_method( ) in Java) uses GetStringUTFChars( ) and ReleaseStringUTFChars( ). The implementation of the new method also uses a NewStringUTF( ) method to convert the native code string to a regular Java String. Using these UTF methods ensures that you don't get unexpected results when converting between programming languages.

With these methods defined, you can now compile and run the application. Select "Build → Build and Run…" and you will see the output shown here:

```
Started JNIWrapper
JNIWrapper instance created
Greetings from the native library.
Finished JNIWrapper. Answer is 42
shared_function called with Hello World !

JNIWrapper has exited with status 0.
```

When working with native application code, you need to pay attention to the rest of the native environment you're working in. As shown in Figure 5-7, the Mac OS X JDK 1.3 user interface implementation relies on Carbon. Carbon is Apple's legacy interface provided for compatibility with Mac OS Classic applications that are recompiled (but not rewritten) for Mac OS X.

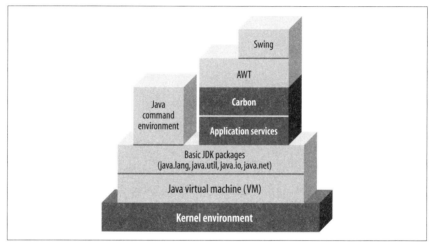

Figure 5-7. JDK 1.3 JVM implementation

 If your JDK 1.3 application uses the Carbon layer, you may need to perform locking (as described in Apple's tech note at *http://developer.apple.com/technotes/tn/tn1153.html*).

Apple's JDK 1.4 implementation replaces the Carbon layer with an implementation based on Cocoa. For information on Cocoa and Mac OS X Unix interfaces, visit Apple's web site at *http://developer.apple.com/*, or check out *Learning Cocoa with Objective-C*, by James Duncan Davidson and Apple Computer, Inc.

## CHAPTER 6

Cross-Platform Programming

In the last chapter, you learned how to provide users with Mac OS X features "on the fly," depending on what platform an application runs on. While that chapter focused on menuing options, you can apply the same techniques to any of the other Mac OS X features (such as QuickTime or Spelling, both discussed in future chapters). However, you need to consider a lot of other issues when writing a cross-platform application. While some techniques require code to determine what platform is used, others are simply good programming practices that make any application run better, on any platform.

This chapter, then, is a mixed bag of suggestions and tricks. It's organized by problem area: each section deals with one particular aspect of cross-platform programming. Generally, these are areas of concern where things can go wrong if you aren't careful. Occasionally, you may see some general programming tips mixed in with them, as good development practices often take care of many of these issues implicitly.

GUI Construction

Chapter 4 covered this topic in detail, but it's worth reviewing. Generically, for maximum cross-platform compatibility, stick with the Metal look and feel, and perform sanity checking to ensure that the user interface operates correctly on both platforms. For the best performance (and user experience) on Mac OS X, however, be sure to let users run the application with the Aqua look and feel. Doing so involves using appropriate fonts and spacing so that Metal and Aqua interfaces look good on every platform.

While Apple's Aqua GUI is excellent and the implementation allows first-class application appearances, the same cannot be said for the standard Windows look and feel. Determining whether you want to support one or more native look and feel targets is largely a matter of budget and resources (mostly consumed by the testing personnel). Whatever you decide, though, you need to test your GUI applications on every platform they will run on. This might mean buying some extra hardware (or better yet, salvaging those old 486 and Pentium II machines), installing Windows and Linux, and actually seeing what your application looks like on each platform. Despite the best advice from this book, things can go wrong when running an application on a platform it wasn't designed for or developed on. Your own eyes are always the best verification.

New Line

In the old days, developers built applications for terminal and simple daisy-wheel feed printers. They had agreed on the ASCII standard for 7-bit text encoding, with the eighth bit reserved for system specific uses (such as character-based graphics). These developers neglected, however, to specify the precise encoding for generating a new line. Some systems used a carriage return (CR) to return the printer head to the start of a new line, and then a line feed (LF) to tell the printer to roll up the paper a line.

However, many developers decided that using two characters for a line feed was wasteful and redundant. This led to the use of *either* a CR or LF code (but not both) to indicate the end of a line. For these developers, the single character was sufficient to tell the printer or terminal character generator that a new line should be generated. Of course, fragmentation occurred and applications didn't always use the same line feed character, or didn't correctly interpret documents and applications that used a different character than they were programmed to interpret.

Since then, we've moved to a world of WYSIWYG and GUI, where users typically associate the return key with a new paragraph break, not a new line. Today, the Windows environment is standardized on the CR/LF value (the original double-character line feed), the Classic Mac OS is standardized on the CR value, and the Unix world on LF. As you can see, this is the worst possible scenario—three major platforms with three different line feed standards. Therefore, a Java developer doesn't know which of these bits actually renders the proper logical result. Since Java is intended to be a multiplatform language, this situation can be quite a problem.

Fortunately, Java developers have a standard mechanism that queries the system's properties for the current system's correct value:

```
System.getProperty("line.separator",".");
```

However, this mechanism doesn't help text-file users copy one system to another. Many of today's popular text editors take a "best guess" by scanning through the document until they find a CR, LF, or CR/LF sequence, and then assuming that what they find is the proper new line sequence for the file. This can lead to problems, however, if the user opens the file with one line feed syntax and then pastes in data from an application that uses a different line feed syntax.

For general text processing, the best solution is to keep track of the original line break preference of the text document, normalize the line breaks in memory to the platform standard, and then convert the output back to the original when the document is saved. You may wish to expose new line preferences to the user as well. This means that you have to work harder at opening and saving documents. Opening now involves an initial scan to get the line feed syntax, a possible conversion, and then any normal opening steps; saving involves the same process in reverse. However, your users will never notice your work (which may seem frustrating) and never have problems with your applications (which is definitely good).

You will also encounter this issue in the source files of the code you write. A variety of tools is available for dealing with this, including several programming text editors for Mac OS X and other platforms that can deal with these issues seamlessly. If you're aware of the problem, though, it's much easier to avoid.

File Encoding

This surprisingly critical issue gets slighted in most application development texts. Normally, it comes up in discussions of multiple-language support, but even if you target only English-speaking users, you'll run into encoding when multiple platforms are taken into account.

In its simplest form, ASCII text is a slightly more elaborate version of the simple "secret decoder" that kids play with. The decoder rings would let you map a letter to a number, and you would need the right decoder rings to convert a string of text to numbers (and back to text). ASCII defines a standard set of characters that convert to numbers, with uppercase and lowercase letters, numbers, spaces, and a few extra symbols thrown into the mix.

That said, only seven bits of a number are defined. The eighth bit, often called the *high bit*, is unspecified. Some systems, such as the Apple II series or the Commodore PET line, use these so-called high-bit characters to generate graphics onscreen. For example, the high-bit letter "r" might draw a smiley face character. There are many high-bit encodings with systems sold to non-English-speaking users who need extra characters for certain languages. Other non-English systems throw out ASCII entirely and use their own character encodings.

When the original Macintosh was released, graphics could be drawn in multiple fonts simultaneously. The smiley face character (and all of its friends) was moved to the Dingbats fonts. Normal user fonts, such as Times, now used the high-bit characters for accents and non-English punctuation. Apple could sell a Macintosh in France with a different keyboard that would generate the proper high-bit characters, and French users could now enter text and share that text with English users without any additional software. Users of Chinese, Japanese, and other pictographic-based systems ended up using *double-byte* systems, as the 256 slots available to a single 8-bit value could not adequately represent their character sets.

These encodings made multiple-language management a huge undertaking. Developers wound up having to support multiple custom encoding import and export tables, with no standard for normalizing the data.

Enter Unicode

At this point, Unicode entered the scene in an attempt to clear up this large and confusing mess. Unicode defines a single "decoder ring" set of values for pretty much any language you're likely to support (and a great deal beyond, including several dead languages). Thus, a Unicode-aware system maps the A to the number 35, the Japanese character for rice to 11263, and so on. You can be sure that this system will be consistent across character sets, in any language.

However, the Unicode character set is not a standard means of writing (or encoding) these values to disk, or even specifying a method for storing the values in memory. The most popular method for saving and reading Unicode text for persistence (e.g., writing to disk or sending text to another system on the network) is a format called UTF-8. UTF-8 is a *multi-byte* format, which means that the amount of storage required to save a specific character varies depending on the location of the character in the Unicode number chart. The lower, English values map to the old 7-bit ASCII values. Higher values are "escaped" and represented by two, three, or four characters.

The big problem with UTF-8 is that it is impossible to access linearly; that is, if you load a UTF-8 character stream into memory, you don't know if the 8-bit character at offset 48 is actually character 12, 24, 48, or something else. Java takes care of this by converting all character data internally into UTF-16, a double-byte format. This is what the Java marketing folk mean by Unicode-enabled Java. A Java developer can specify an encoding format, open a text file, and the JVM will convert the text internally from whatever the original text was to UTF-16.

Java, Unicode, and UTF

It's possible to use the standard Java APIs with a character set that is specified programmatically:

```
java.io.OutputStreamWriter.OutputStreamWriter(
  OutputStream out, String charsetName
)
```

For information on all of the available character sets and their names, check Sun's online documentation at *http://java.sun.com/j2se/1.4.1/docs/guide/intl/ encoding.doc.html*.

Unfortunately, there is no consistent way for a developer to auto-detect the encoding format of a text file, which means that you'll have to either guess or require that your users know their encoding format. To see how unlikely this latter prospect is, ask your Windows users if they are aware that "Cp1252" is the standard Windows text file encoding format. That said, you can usually assume that a file uses the system's default encoding, which is obtained through the following system property:

```
System.getProperty("file.encoding")
```

 You can also set the character set for the entire JVM by specifying the system property `file.encoding`.

Windows and Mac OS X systems have different defaults for this property, which explains why the topic comes up in a discussion of cross-platform compatibility. You can assume that any high-bit characters a user specifies will cause problems, and with tools like Word and AppleWorks automatically converting straight quotes to curly quotes even for English users, there will probably be high-bit characters sneaking into your text files for any but the most basic applications.

If you expect users to share text files between different platforms, you'll need to decide how you want to manage these encoding issues. If users move files across platforms (or different language operating systems), they will at least have a rudimentary familiarity with language encodings. Consider Figure 6-1, an example of what is presented to a user when he or she saves a text file. In this case, the default encoding is UTF-8, which is probably a safe bet for most operations (especially for exported files and your application's default document saving functionality). UTF-8 shares the same text encoding for the first 127 characters as for normal ASCII; this fact in addition to UTF-8's flexibility and growing popularity make it an ideal choice for your application's default. For sophisticated applications, you should probably add the ability to specify file encodings on a per-file basis as well.

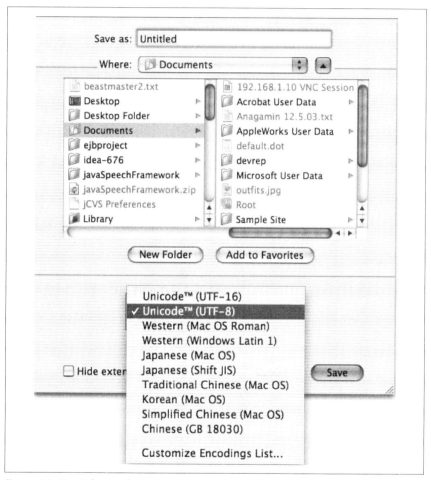

Figure 6-1. TextEdit encodings

Threading

It's beyond the scope of this book to fully cover threads and the difficulties surrounding their use. However, the threading models that underlie different JVMs (even on the same OS) can exhibit different behavior. If your application is not properly designed, previously unexposed issues might appear due to thread scheduler differences resulting from a move to another platform (or a different JVM).

For more information on problems (and solutions) to threading issues, read *Java Threads* by Scott Oaks and Henry Wong (O'Reilly) and *Concurrent Programming in Java* by Doug Lea (Addison-Wesley). The threading issues that appear result from (incorrect) assumptions—that the threading model is based on the underlying JVM implementation, or regarding the use of deprecated threading APIs, such as `Thread.stop( )`, `Thread.resume( )`, and `Thread.suspend( )`.

File Separator

You should also learn to use characters in different operating systems to represent a directory path in a file hierarchy. The file separator is always a problem when dealing with multiple platforms.

Consider the following paths, all valid for their respective operating systems:

* Windows: *C:\myfolder\mydocument.txt*
* Unix: */usr/myuser/mydocument.txt*
* Classic Mac OS: *Hard Drive:My Folder:My Document*

Each path describes a typical location for a user document, located in a nested folder. Each OS uses a different character to represent a directory: \, /, or :. Make sure your application does not make assumptions about which of these characters to use, but rather relies on the value returned by the system specific to that platform:

```
System.getProperty("file.separator");
System.getProperty("path.separator");
```

The `file.separator` is the system property containing the character (or characters) that delimits file and directory names. This character is usually / or \. The `path.separator` is the character used to separate path entries on a single line (such as multiple entries in the system's classpath).

Generally, either you will have a base directory and need to construct paths relative to this directory, or you will work with user-specified files and use standard file dialogs.

Class Loader Issues

When writing Java applications, it's common to write code that contains a reference to a platform-specific class and then dynamically load that class. Consider the following pseudo-code snippet:

```
if(ismacos)
{
    com.apple.system.Utility myAppleClass= new Utility( );
    myAppleClass.beep( );
} else
{
    doSomething;
}
```

In the case above, even if the code is run on Windows (and therefore the ismacos variable never evaluates to true), the com.apple.system.Utility class will still be loaded by reference by the class loader, which in turn will throw a ClassDefNotFound or similar exception. At compile time, this action will create errors and can be caught and dealt with. However, developing on a system where the dynamically loaded class is present can be worse—in this case, compilation succeeds, and it isn't until the application is run on a different platform that errors occur. The result, unsurprisingly, is often an unhappy user.

One way to solve this problem is to place platform-specific code into another set of classes and then load them dynamically. There are a couple of strategies for dealing with this, depending on the range and scope of the classes to be loaded dynamically.

One strategy is simply to load a single class by name, construct method references, and then call that class as needed. Consider the following code snippet:

```
Class myClass = null;
try
{
    myClass = Class.forName("java.lang.String");
    java.lang.reflect.Method myMethod = myClass.getMethod("length", null);
    Object myString = myClass.getConstructor(null).newInstance(null);
    Object myResult = myMethod.invoke(myString, null);
    System.out.println(myResult);
} catch (Exception e)
{
    e.printStackTrace( );
}
if(myClass == null)
    System.out.println("java.lang.String unavailable!");
```

Since there is no explicit reference to the class java.lang.String, if java.lang.String were unavailable, the application would merely report the exception and continue. Obviously, building the references to the various methods manually (not to mention the laboriousness of building the parameter lists) can become oppressive with this method. Therefore, you may wish to cast dynamically loaded objects to a specific, required interface, as the following code snippet (taken from Chapter 4) shows:

```
Class myClass = Class.forName(argsconfig[i]);
SimpleEditPlugin myPlugin =
    (SimpleEditPlugin)myClass.getConstructor(null).newInstance(null);
...
// Call methods from the SimpleEditPlugin interface on myPlugin as you wish.
```

Testing Cross-Platform Compatibility

The most reliable way to ensure that your application runs on another platform is to test it out—run your code on as many platforms as possible *before*
releasing it or considering the development complete. Testing compatibility
will reveal some of your most obvious problems, such as GUI elements that
don't display correctly. That said, some specific areas of your application
should be tested rigorously.

File I/O

Make sure your application can read and write files correctly. If the platform supports path or file names with spaces (such as on Mac OS X), see if
your application handles this task correctly. Also, find out how the application handles high-bit characters (for example, ™, ä, ê, and ó).

Preference and Resource Files

You'd be surprised how often you'll see a hardcoded reference to a path in a
Java application. Try opening the preferences dialog, changing and saving
preferences, and quitting and reopening the application. If you use JDK 1.4's
Preferences API, be aware that preferences are not guaranteed to migrate
across platforms (or even different systems running the same platform). If
migration is a requirement, you might want to consider a different preferences mechanism. If you're using ordinary Java property files, remember that
they are saved to disk as 7-bit text files, and users who try to edit them manually might encounter difficulties with high-bit characters.

Instead, rely on JAR files to contain resources and values returned from
standard file dialogs. For more information on packaging applications with
relative links and storing resources in JAR files, consult Chapters 7 and 8.

Native Code

When building cross-platform applications, anything that interacts with
native or platform-specific code is obviously at risk. If you've written native
code, you're probably breaking portability, but if your application should
still function on a pure Java environment, make sure it does. Add checks to

your code to verify that classes that rely on native code can actually be loaded (fortunately, you can use the same dynamic class loading techniques described above).

If at all possible, try to build a version of your application that still runs (perhaps with limited functionality) in a so-called "pure" Java environment. To test this application, remove the native library from the JVM search path and try to launch the application. Depending on the application, you may wish to display a dialog to the user indicating that some functionality is not available on this platform, or simply note the reduced functionality in a log. You might also want to include a mechanism for users to report their desired platform so you can get a sense of the demand for your application on that environment.

Native GUI Elements

Besides the guidelines and suggestions described in Chapters 4 and 5, test the various "Minimize" and "Maximize" controls and other native user interface elements. On Mac OS X, this will require testing the application's behavior for the red, yellow, and green buttons in various combinations. You'll also want to test the application's response to messages sent from the Dock and various system events (for example, if a user tries to shut down). You should duplicate these tests on other supported platforms as well.

Threading

If your application uses threads extensively, stress-test it on different platforms to see if you can force deadlocks or other issues to appear. For example, if your application is a multithreaded GUI FTP client, try to initiate as many downloads as possible. If it's a web application, use a web testing tool such as Apache Jakarta's JMeter (*http://jakarta.apache.org/jmeter*).

If your application allows user-controlled thread generation, you may wish to provide more graceful handling of thread generation control than merely allowing the user to continue creating threads until the JVM fails. For example, you may wish to limit the number of simultaneous downloads in your FTP client to a maximum of ten. Unfortunately, it's almost impossible to determine in advance the specific number of threads that will result in failure. Some applications, such as web servers, let users control the maximum number of threads that may be created via a preference (defaulting to a fairly conservative value), and if your system administrator intends to make your application highly tunable, you may wish to offer a similar option.

For More Information

Cross-platform application development is a rich and interesting field, and generally, your application will be more robust if you test it on several different platforms. This chapter discussed the possibility of targeting multiple platforms, but you might work on a team that also develops on multiple platforms; in this case, you'll probably want to verify that your version-control systems and development tools are configured properly. The issues involved are generally similar to those described above—in particular, you might need to consider file encodings. To better understand this topic, consider reading *Crossing Platforms: A Macintosh/Windows Phrasebook (A Dictionary for Strangers in a Strange Land)*, by Adam Engst and David Pogue (O'Reilly).

CHAPTER 7
Standalone Applications

Even if you manage to nail all aspects of cross-platform programming and write a great application, you can still create a horrendous user experience through poor application packaging. The delivery of an application, its installation, and even the way it is launched affect what a user thinks about an application. You'll want to spend as much time packaging up your application as you do tweaking control and font sizes, editing line separators, and monitoring threads in your code.

When actually packaging and delivering an application experience to an end user, several different options are available to developers on the Java platform. However, when boiled down to their basic states, there are really just two categories of application delivery:

Standalone applications
> These applications are installed and run completely on the end user's physical machine. The user buys a CD, runs an installation program, and buys new software to perform an upgrade. Typical examples are word processors, spreadsheets, music players, and anything else you might buy in a box at your local computer store.

Web-delivered applications
> Web-delivered applications may run on a user's machine, but are installed from an online web site. They are often more volatile in nature, releasing upgrades (also installed from a web site) every few months, if not every few weeks. All the updates installed via the Mac OS X System Preferences control panel are web delivered.

This chapter looks at the first of these two categories and details Mac OS X support for standalone applications. The next chapter explores web-delivered applications. You'll understand how both are options on a Mac OS X platform, as well as how to package and deliver each.

Packaging

The first issue you must consider when dealing with a standalone application is its packaging. End users are used to loading a CD, installing a program, and then clicking an icon that launches the application. These users of desktop software typically don't want to deal with lots of configuration files and subdirectories, or with components of an application scattered all over a hard drive. Developers, however, need to be able to create applications with some degree of sophistication, which often means including a large number of files in a single distribution of an application. Trying to balance these conflicting desires is the first goal in application packaging.

Packaging on Windows

The latest versions of Java support a more or less cross-platform approach through the Java JAR mechanism, whereby JAR files are launched by an application distributed as part of the JDK. On Windows, this application is called javaw, and is also used to launch Java applications for which one does not want a DOS terminal to appear.

The "double-clickable JAR" approach lacks sophistication, however. For example, it has no support for defining an icon, for binding the application to specific documents, or other application packaging details. These deficiencies lead to a less than stellar user experience.

Packaging on Mac OS X

Native Mac OS X applications, on the other hand, use a specific application packaging format for delivering desktop applications. At the core of this format, the base desktop navigation user interface (the Finder) maintains the illusion that directories with specific names or settings should be treated as applications. There are no fancy resource forks to be dealt with, and generally, application directory packages can be copied across foreign filesystems without damage.

This chapter looks at how to build double-clickable applications and how to create Mac OS X directory packages.

JAR Files

Virtually all delivery mechanisms for Java applications depend on packaging the .class files created from your .java source files into one or more Java Archive (JAR) files. Think of a JAR file as a special sort of ZIP archive, with a very specific set of expected characteristics and layout. You can use the jar tool included with the JDK, an Ant task, or the specific capabilities of your preferred Java development environment to create a JAR file.

The standard way to create a JAR file, of course, is to use the command-line jar command included with Mac OS X's JDK. Open the Terminal, type jar, and a list of options will appear:

```
Usage: jar {ctxu}[vfmOM] [jar-file] [manifest-file] [-C dir] files ...
Options:
    -c  create new archive
    -t  list table of contents for archive
    -x  extract named (or all) files from archive
    -u  update existing archive
    -v  generate verbose output on standard output
    -f  specify archive file name
    -m  include manifest information from specified manifest file
    -O  store only; use no ZIP compression
    -M  do not create a manifest file for the entries
    -i  generate index information for the specified jar files
    -C  change to the specified directory and include the following file
If any file is a directory then it is processed recursively.
The manifest file name and the archive file name needs to be specified
in the same order the 'm' and 'f' flags are specified.

Example 1: to archive two class files into an archive called classes.jar:
       jar cvf classes.jar Foo.class Bar.class
Example 2: use an existing manifest file 'mymanifest' and archive all the
       files in the foo/ directory into 'classes.jar':
       jar cvfm classes.jar mymanifest -C foo/ .
```

Creating a JAR File

If you work with the source for the SimpleEdit application presented in Chapter 4, you should have it organized as shown in Figure 7-1.

Let's package the core SimpleEdit files into a single JAR, which you will make double-clickable (and therefore executable by an end user). Suppose that you have compiled the source files already, either using javac, Ant, or an IDE.

To make the JAR double-clickable, you'll need a manifest file to specify the main class in the JAR. Create a text file called *manifest.mf* with contents as shown in Example 7-1. Save this file inside the *src* directory of your application folder. Note that this *manifest.mf* file is *very* particular about the carriage return sequence used (see Chapter 6 for more information about carriage returns). You may wish to use the Terminal's more command to display your *manifest.mf* file—if you see any ^M characters in it using that command or when viewing the file with *vi* or *emacs*, you've got a problem.

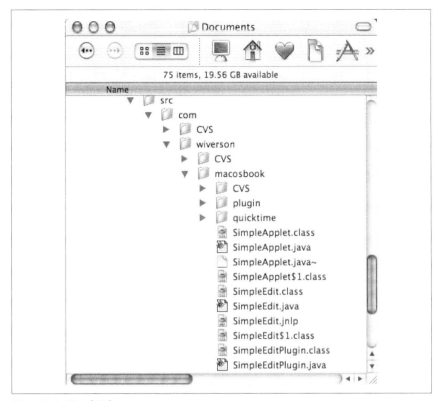

Figure 7-1. SimpleEdit source tree

Example 7-1. A simple manifest file

```
Main-Class:com/wiverson/macosbook/SimpleEdit
```

This scenario is pretty self-explanatory: the manifest file will instruct Java on the class to launch when the JAR it is included within is double-clicked. You can specify any Java class as the main class, but make sure that it's a class that actually has a main( ) method, or you'll encounter errors when distributing your application.

Open the Terminal and use the cd and pwd commands to navigate to the *src* directory. In this directory, type the JAR command as shown:

```
jar cvfm SimpleEdit.jar manifest.mf ./com/wiverson/macosbook/*.class
    ./com/wiverson/macosbook/plugin/*.class
```

After entering this command and pressing return, you should see something similar to the following output:

```
added manifest
adding: com/wiverson/macosbook/SimpleApplet$1.class(in = 770) (out=
425)(deflated 44%)
```

```
adding: com/wiverson/macosbook/SimpleApplet.class(in = 909) (out=
527)(deflated 42%)
adding: com/wiverson/macosbook/SimpleEdit$1.class(in = 1187) (out=
625)(deflated 47%)
adding: com/wiverson/macosbook/SimpleEdit.class(in = 11062) (out=
5521)(deflated 50%)
adding: com/wiverson/macosbook/SimpleEditPlugin.class(in = 323) (out=
206)(dcflatcd 36%)

... omitted for space...

adding: com/wiverson/macosbook/plugin/QuitConfirmJDialog.class(in = 4367)
(out= 1917)(deflated 56%)
adding: com/wiverson/macosbook/plugin/SystemPropsPlugin.class(in = 1827)
(out= 892)(deflated 51%)
```

Launching the JAR File

If all goes well, double-clicking on the generated JAR file will automatically launch the SimpleEdit application. This JAR file can be moved to other platforms, and users of JDK 1.2 or later should be able to move it as well.

Even if you distribute the JAR file by using another mechanism (for example, as part of an application bundle, delivered as a web applet, or as a Web Start application), it's often useful to deliver the JAR file with a Main-Class specified in a manifest file for development and testing purposes.

Applications launched as double-clickable JARs will use the most recent Mac OS X JDK installed (either JDK 1.3.1 or JDK 1.4.1). If you distribute your application in this manner, you should therefore test it on both JVMs. If you wish to force JDK 1.3.1 or require JDK 1.4.1, you should use an application bundle, as described in the next section.

Application Bundles

Native Mac OS X applications are delivered in packages known as *application bundles*. These packages contain the application's executable code, images, sounds, icons, localizable strings, and other resources. An application, as shown in the Finder, is actually just a specific directory structure with a few additional attributes.

These application bundles are displayed in the Finder with a simple name (for example, TextEdit). Users can double-click on these application names, complete with colorful icons, and the system automatically launches the application. Alternatively, users can drop documents on the application, and the launched application will attempt to open the selected document.

For a developer, however, an application bundle is a directory with an *.app* suffix and a specific internal file structure. You can explore these bundles on your system from the Finder by Control-clicking on an application and selecting "Show Package Contents," as shown in Figure 7-2.

Figure 7-2. Opening an application package

Layout of an Application Bundle

Once you peel back the layers of an application bundle, you'll find quite a few directories, each with several files. Figure 7-3 shows the structure of a typical application bundle for a Java application (in this case, the open source Java application PCGen; for more information on PCGen, visit *http://sourceforge.net/projects/pcgen/*).

 If you installed NetBeans according to the instructions in Chapter 2, you saw another example of an application bundle.

The *Info.plist* file in the *Contents* folder is probably the most significant element of any Mac OS X application. For Java applications, this file is used to specify information for the JVM execution of the application.

Icons for the Mac OS X Finder are placed in the *Resources* folder. The preferred format is the proprietary Mac OS X file type designated by the *.icns* suffix, as this file type includes support for different bit depths and icon sizes in a single file. Use the Icon Composer application installed in */Developer/Applications* to create icon files, or investigate online for freeware and shareware tools that accomplish the same task.

Your Java code, in either JAR or class files, is put into *Resources/Java*. A native executable file in the *MacOS* folder launches the appropriate classes.

Figure 7-3. Sample application bundle

This native stub library, referenced by the *Info.plist* file, is the component that actually launches the application.

While understanding all of these steps is useful (especially in an automated build environment), a couple of different tools allow you to set up and work with application bundles without having to work through these details manually. One tool, MRJAppBuilder, is included with Apple's tool set. This chapter covers this tool in more detail later.

Property List Attributes for Java Applications

Before digging into specific tools, though, you need to understand the *Info. plist* file that keeps coming up. In fact, by browsing through applications and various configuration directories on Mac OS X, you'll notice the frequent use of XML files with a *.plist* extension. These files are called property lists, and can be edited easily with the bundled Mac OS X Property List Editor (as shown in Figure 7-4).

The *Info.plist* file in a Mac OS X application's *Contents* folder is no different from these other property lists. While you can use tools to generate these

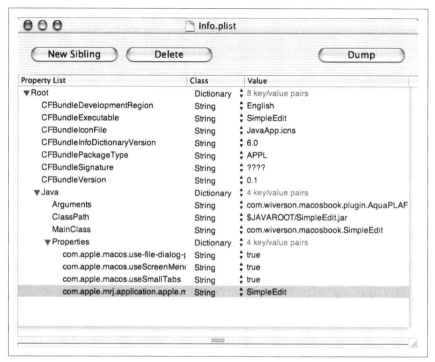

Figure 7-4. Mac OS X Property List Editor

files, try to understand what was created for you and how to modify the auto-generated files.

> Since the various *.plist* files are in XML, you can modify them with any text editor. The Property List Editor is generally a better option, though, as it ensures that you maintain well-formed XML.

Example 7-2 shows an example property list for the SimpleEdit application created in Chapter 4.

Example 7-2. Info.plist for SimpleEdit

```
<?xml version="1.0" encoding="UTF-8"?>
<!DOCTYPE plist PUBLIC "-//Apple Computer//DTD PLIST 1.0//EN"
                "http://www.apple.com/DTDs/PropertyList-1.0.dtd">
<plist version="1.0">
<dict>
    <key>CFBundleDevelopmentRegion</key>
    <string>English</string>
    <key>CFBundleDocumentTypes</key>
    <array>
```

Example 7-2. Info.plist for SimpleEdit (continued)

```
<dict>
    <key>CFBundleTypeExtensions</key>
    <array>
        <string>text</string>
        <string>txt</string>
        <string>*</string>
    </array>
    <key>CFBundleTypeMIMETypes</key>
    <array>
        <string>text/plain</string>
    </array>
    <key>CFBundleTypeName</key>
    <string>Text File</string>
    <key>CFBundleTypeOSTypes</key>
    <array>
        <string>****</string>
    </array>
    <key>CFBundleTypeRole</key>
    <string>Editor</string>
</dict>
</array>
<key>CFBundleExecutable</key>
<string>SimpleEdit</string>
<key>CFBundleIconFile</key>
<string>JavaApp.icns</string>
<key>CFBundleInfoDictionaryVersion</key>
<string>6.0</string>
<key>CFBundlePackageType</key>
<string>APPL</string>
<key>CFBundleSignature</key>
<string>????</string>
<key>CFBundleVersion</key>
<string>0.1</string>
<key>Java</key>
<dict>
    <key>Arguments</key>
    <string>com.wiverson.macosbook.plugin.AquaPLAFPlugin
com.wiverson.plugin.BeepPlugin
com.wiverson.macosbook.plugin.FinderIntegrationPlugin
com.wiverson.macosbook.plugin.SystemPropsPlugin</string>
    <key>ClassPath</key>
    <string>$JAVAROOT/SimpleEdit.jar</string>
    <key>MainClass</key>
    <string>com.wiverson.macosbook.SimpleEdit</string>
    <key>Properties</key>
    <dict>
        <key>com.apple.macos.use-file-dialog-packages</key>
        <string>true</string>
        <key>com.apple.macos.useScreenMenuBar</key>
        <string>true</string>
        <key>com.apple.macos.useSmallTabs</key>
```

Example 7-2. Info.plist for SimpleEdit (continued)

```
        <string>true</string>

    <key>com.apple.mrj.application.apple.menu.about.name</key>
        <string>SimpleEdit</string>
        </dict>
    </dict>
</dict>
</plist>
```

About dictionaries

This property list is divided into hierarchical *dictionaries*. The top-level dictionary contains the information that the operating system needs to launch the application. The keys in this section are prefixed by CFBundle and are more or less self-explanatory. One exception is CFBundleDocumentTypes, which tells the system that this particular application will open any file as a text document by default. Identifying files in this manner lets users drag and drop files on your application's icon, either in the Finder or the Dock. You'll want to create a new file type and extension if you want to handle custom data file types. Finally, you should set the proper options for the Java dictionary.

CFBundle dictionary keys

Per Apple's documentation (installed at */Developer/Documentation/ Essentials/SystemOverview/PropertyListKeys/Bundle_Keys.html*), the keys in Table 7-1 are used to build Java applications. The comments shown below are based on Apple's documentation. Keys not used by Java applications have been omitted.

Table 7-1. CFBundle dictionary keys

Key	Type	Required	Summary
CFBundleDevelopment- Region	String	No	The native region for the bundle. Usually corresponds to the author's native language.
CFBundleDisplayName	String	No	The bundle's localized display name.
CFBundleDocumentTypes	Array	No	An array of dictionaries describing the document types supported by the bundle. For more information, see the next section.
CFBundleExecutable	String	Yes	Name of the bundle's executable file.
CFBundleGetInfoHTML	String	No	A string for displaying richer (HTML) content in the Finder's "Get Info" panel.
CFBundleGetInfoString	String	No	A string for display in the Finder's "Get Info" panel.

Table 7-1. CFBundle dictionary keys (continued)

Key	Type	Required	Summary
CFBundleIconFile	String	Yes	The filename for an icon image file.
CFBundleIdentifier	String	Yes	A unique identifier string for the bundle. This string should be in the form of a Java package name, such as *com.apple.myapp*.
CFBundleInfoDictionary Version	String	Yes	Version information for the *Info.plist* format.
CFBundleName	String	Yes	The short display name of the bundle. Should be less than 16 characters.
CFBundlePackageType	String	Yes	The four-letter code identifying the bundle type. For applications (including Java applications) you should set this value to "AAPL".
CFBundleShortVersion-String	String	Yes	The marketing-style version string for the bundle
CFBundleSignature	String	Yes	The four-letter code identifying the bundle creator.
CFBundleVersion	String	Yes	The executable's build number.

CFBundleDocumentTypes dictionary keys

Per Apple's documentation (installed at */Developer/Documentation/ Essentials/SystemOverview/PropertyListKeys/Bundle_Keys.html*), the keys in Table 7-2 describe the kinds of documents that your application supports.

Table 7-2. CFBundleDocumentTypes dictionary keys

Key	Type	Description
CFBundleTypeExtensions	Array	This key contains an array of filename extensions that map to this type. To open documents with any extension, specify an extension with a single asterisk (*). This key is required.
CFBundleTypeIconFile	String	This key specifies the name of the icon file to be used when displaying documents of this type. The icon filename can have an extension or be without one. If it is without an extension, the system appends an extension appropriate to the platform (for example, *.icns* in Mac OS 9).
CFBundleTypeName	String	This key contains the abstract name for the document type and is used to refer to the type. This key is required and can be localized by including it in the corresponding *InfoPlist.strings* files. This value is the main way to refer to a type, and it is recommended that you use a Java-style package identifier to ensure its uniqueness. If the type is a common Clipboard type supported by the system, you can use one of the standard types listed in the NSPasteboard class description.

Table 7-2. CFBundleDocumentTypes dictionary keys (continued)

Key	Type	Description
CFBundleTypeOSTypes	Array	This key contains an array of four-letter type codes that map to this type. To open documents of any type, specify the four-letter type code '****'. This key is required.
CFBundleTypeRole	String	This key specifies the application's role with respect to the type. The value can be Editor, Viewer, Printer, Shell, or None. This key is required.

Generally, most Mac OS X Java applications work with document types based on file extension (as opposed to the four-letter creator codes), as file extensions survive cross-platform exchange. Therefore, to support a launch of your application types, register the file extensions that your application supports (for example, *.txt, .gif, .jpg,* and *.jpeg*). It's usually best to err on the side of supporting a larger variety of document file extensions and file types for the purposes of receiving Finder notifications (relying on the wildcard options above). Then you should perform error checking on the data files from within your application.

 For more information on how your Java application is notified of opening files, see Chapter 5.

Java dictionary keys

At the end of the CFBundle keys, a Java key designates the beginning of the Java dictionary. Two top-level keys in the Java dictionary are required in the property list of a Java application bundle:

MainClass

This key value should be set to the fully qualified class name of the application's main entry method. The value of this key can be retrieved at runtime by querying the com.apple.mrj.application.main system property.

ClassPath

This key lets you set the classpath for your application. The string value for this key should specify the fully qualified path to the directories where your class files are, or to your JAR files. You'll note the use of the $JAVAROOT variable to point to the *Resources/Java* directory. If your application bundles third-party JAR files, you'll want to include them here and reference them with the $JAVAROOT variable. You can discover this value by querying the com.apple.mrj.application.classpath system property.

In addition to these required keys, you may wish to specify additional keys in the Java dictionary:

Arguments
: This value is tokenized into a String array, and passed into the application's main( ) method. This can be a convenient way to package applications that expect specific command-line arguments. This value can be introspected through the com.apple.mrj.application.parameters system property.

WorkingDirectory
: When an application is launched, this key sets the working directory. By default, the current working directory is set to the application bundle's parent directory. You can use the $APP_PACKAGE variable to refer to the root of the application bundle. The value of this key is available via introspection through the com.apple.mrj.application.workingdirectory system property.

 You may prefer to use the standard Java APIs for determining the user's home and working directory. This has the added flexibility of adapting to changes the user makes to the working directory while the application is running.

VMOptions
: The space-delimited value of the VMOptions key can set the JVM options normally referred to by the -X and -XX options. The typical use of this key is to set the minimum and maximum heap size for the JVM launching the application. Your application can read this value by looking at the com.apple.mrj.application.vm.options system property.

JVMVersion
: This can be used to specify either a specific version of the JVM to use (e.g., "1.3.1" or "1.4.1") or the latest version in a series (e.g., "1.3+" or "1.4+"). Note that even if the user has installed JDK 1.4.1, your application will default to the latest JDK 1.3 JVM.

 This means that if you are building an application that requires JDK 1.4.1 or later, be sure to include the JVM-Version key!

The Properties dictionary

The keys in the Properties dictionary include both Mac OS X–specific options and general Java options. Mac OS X–specific keys and values that you may add to this dictionary of the property list include:

`com.apple.hwaccel`

This property defaults to `true`. It turns on hardware graphics accelera-tion for the video cards not commented out of the */Library/Java/Home/ lib/hwexclude.properties* file. If it is set to `false`, hardware acccleration is turned off. You can use it in conjunction with the `com.apple. hwaccelexclude` property.

`com.apple.hwexclude`

This property defaults to `none`. When specific video card designation strings are passed in with this property, hardware graphics acceleration is *not* turned on for the specified video cards. When this property is set, */Library/Java/Home/lib/hwexclude.properties* is ignored.

 This property is useful when you know that specific video cards (hopefully just one or two) cause problems with your application when hardware acceleration is turned on. You are testing for this, right?

`com.apple.macos.use-file-dialog-packages`

This property defaults to `false`. When set to `true`, it causes `java.awt. FileDialog` to show application packages (with both *.app* and *.pkg* extensions) as if they were files, prohibiting the user from selecting spe-cific files inside the application bundle. This option is not available for use on JDK 1.4.1.

`com.apple.macos.useScreenMenuBar`

This property defaults to `false`. Setting it to `true` causes Swing menus that use the Aqua look and feel to appear in the global application menu bar at the top of the screen (instead of inside the window). This is the proper behavior for Mac OS X applications, but may require some test-ing before your application supports it properly. Note that `JMenuBars` in `JDialogs` are *not* moved to the Mac OS X menu bar. Under JDK 1.4.1, use `apple.laf.useScreenMenuBar` instead. Note that you can include both properties with no ill effects.

`com.apple.macos.smallTabs`

This property is not defined by default. If defined and set to `true`, tab controls in Swing applications more closely resemble the Metal look and feel (which can be very helpful if your application expects smaller tabs). If the property is set to `false`, the tabs assume a larger size that is simi-lar to the default Aqua controls. This option is not available for use on JDK 1.4.1.

`com.apple.macosx.AntiAliasedTextOn`

This property defaults to `true`. When rendering text, it tells the application to use anti-aliasing. Occasionally you might want to switch this value to `false`. If your application draws text to the same location twice, it can look blurry, as each application of the text to the screen is incrementally darker. Conversely, if your application expects to erase text by drawing the background color over previously rendered text, anti-aliasing artifacts can be left over. Under JDK 1.4.1, use `apple.awt.textantialiasing` instead (as described in the next section). Note that you can include both properties with no ill effects.

`com.apple.macosx.AntiAliasedGraphicsOn`

This property also defaults to `true`. Like the potential issues around anti-aliased text, the default Mac OS X rendering of graphics can lead to blurry graphics. You may see a small performance increase by setting this property to `false`.

`com.apple.mrj.application.apple.menu.about.name`

If defined, this property adds an "About" command to the top of the application menu. Your application can be notified when the user selects this menu item by registering a `com.apple.mrj.AboutHandler`, as described in Chapter 5.

`com.apple.mrj.application.growbox.intrudes`

This property defaults to `true` and causes a growbox (a resizing control) to intrude into AWT frames. For certain applications, this growbox can obscure other important GUI features, such as scrollbars. If turned off (by setting the value to `false`), the bottom of the window is pushed down 15 pixels. Setting this value to `false` is appropriate only as an intermediate stopgap—you are strongly encouraged to rework your application's user interface so the growbox control looks natural and doesn't block other important controls. Under JDK 1.4.1, use `apple.awt.showGrowBox` instead. Note that you can include both properties with no ill effects.

`com.apple.mrj.application.live-resize`

This property defaults to `false`, but setting it to `true` enables live resizing of windows. You should test this property on a variety of machines (and perhaps make it a user-configurable preference), as the performance of live window resizing for your application can vary dramatically between different systems and JVMs. This option is not available for use on JDK 1.4.1.

`apple.awt.brushMetalLook`

Allows you to specify that your main application window should use the brushed Metal appearance, similar to that used by Apple applications such as iTunes and Safari. This is set to false by default. It is available only on JDK 1.4.1.

JDK 1.4.1 rendering

JDK 1.4.1 introduces more sophisticated control over rendering via Java 2D. For more information on Java 2D, examine the standard Java documentation on java.awt.Graphics2D. In the section below, references are made to various rendering hints via settings such as KEY_ANTIALIASING and KEY_TEXT_ANTIALIASING—these are references to the Java 2D APIs.

The following properties are available only when using JDK 1.4.1 or a later JVM.

apple.awt.antialiasing
Specifies that standard graphic primitives (such as line, arc, rectangle, etc.) are drawn anti-aliased. By default, text will also take this setting, but you can override that using apple.awt.textantialiasing. You can override this setting via the KEY_ANTIALIASING rendering hint for specific objects. By default this is set to false for Metal applications, and to true for Aqua applications. Even if it is set to false, standard Aqua user interface components will still be drawn anti-aliased.

apple.awt.textantialiasing
Sets the default Java 2D rendering hint for KEY_TEXT_ANTIALIASING. Although this inherits the same setting as apple.awt.antialiasing, you can override that setting explicitly. The default value is false unless you are using the Aqua look and feel.

apple.awt.rendering
Determines whether Graphics 2D objects prioritize speed or quality. It sets the Java 2D hint KEY_RENDERING so that it accepts either VALUE_RENDER_SPEED or VALUE_RENDER_QUALITY as an argument.

apple.awt.interpolation
Allows you to set the Java 2D KEY_INTERPOLATION rendering hint to determine which algorithm is used in image transformations. Options include VALUE_INTERPOLATION_NEAREST_NEIGHBOR, VALUE_INTERPOLATION_BILINEAR, and VALUE_NTERPOLATION_BICUBIC.

apple.awt.fractionalmetrics
Allows you to specify that the Java 2D KEY_FRACTIONALMETRICS hint should use floating-point font metrics instead of the default integer metrics. Options include VALUE_FRACTIONALMETRICS_ON and VALUE_FRACTIONALMETRICS_OFF.

JDK 1.4 full screen display

JDK 1.4 introduces the ability to run your application in "full screen" mode, where the application takes over the entire screen, hiding default user interface elements such as the menu bar. This can be particularly useful for such applications as kiosk displays and games.

apple.awt.fakefullscreen
This flag causes full screen applications to be displayed in a window. You may wish to make this a user preference, or use it to assist with debugging. The default value is false.

apple.awt.fullscreencaptureal ldisplays
When you have multiple displays, entering full screen mode darkens any secondary screens that might be attached to the system. Setting this to false overrides this default behavior so that secondary screens are not darkened (allowing you to still see the content displayed, such as debugging output or logs). The default value is true.

apple.awt.fullscreenhidecursor
Hides the mouse cursor when in full screen mode. Many entertainment applications, such as games, may wish to hide the mouse. The default value is true.

apple.awt.fullscreenusefade
Mac OS X automatically provides a "fade" effect when changing screen resolutions. You may find it more aesthetically pleasing to see this fade effect whenever you switch to full screen mode, even if you don't initiate a resolution change. To do this, set this property to true instead of the default value of false.

JDK 1.4 window positioning

In the JDK 1.4 release, Apple provides additional functionality to assist with window positioning. This is particularly useful for when you store the current window position, and the user changes the screen to a smaller resolution—the window may no longer appear on screen! This functionality is controlled via the following properties:

apple.awt.window.position.forceSafeCreation
New windows are always created on screen, not outside the desktop where users would not be able to access them. The default value is false.

apple.awt.window.position.forceSafeUserPositioning
This option disallows users from moving windows into a position where they would no longer be able to access them. The default value is false.

You can test any of these options from the command line by using the -D option to the java command. For example, if you want to run an application with standard Aqua menu styles and the name "SimpleEdit", you could pass in two keys, com.apple.macos.usescreenmenubar and com.apple.mrj.application.apple.menu.about.name, as shown here:

```
java -Dcom.apple.macos.useScreenMenuBar=true
    -Dcom.apple.mrj.application.apple.menu.about.name=SimpleEdit
    com.wiverson.macosbook.SimpleEdit
```

If you get the results that you expect, you can then add these two properties into your Properties dictionary in the *Info.plist* file. Using the -D option allows you to test options quickly before editing your property lists.

Why Use Application Bundles?

Using double-clickable JAR files is easy, so why bother with application bundles? Bundles require a lot of properties to be set, and it takes time to get used to property lists. However, you can benefit from packaging your application as a Mac OS X application bundle:

- The application launches on a double-click (as a JAR file would).
- The application becomes a single, self-contained structure that is portable across different filesystems.
- You can optionally specify a custom icon to appear in the Dock and the Finder.
- You can set specific system properties to more closely emulate the behavior of a native application.
- You can bind specific document types to the application. The Finder keeps track of which applications can open which documents and document types, which lets users double-click on a document in the Finder to open your application, drag and drop a document on your application, or use the "Open With" command in the Finder.

 To take full advantage of document type bindings, implement the document event handlers in your application as described in Chapter 5.

- You can set specific configuration and runtime details that would otherwise require the user to enter a complex command-line command (such as memory configuration or default file encoding).

Building an Application from Scratch

This section builds a Mac OS X application from scratch. It will start with the base SimpleEdit JAR file that was built in Chapters 4 and 5, and then add the necessary elements to convert it to a full Mac OS X application bundle. It will build out the directory structure shown in Figure 7-5; you might want to refer to this figure as you walk through this example.

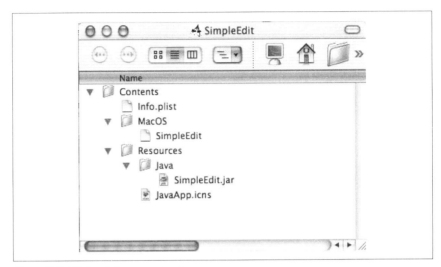

Figure 7-5. Minimal directory structure

Directory Layout

Create a new folder called *SimpleEdit* in your home directory (~) by using the Finder. Add a folder inside this new directory called *Contents*. This is where you'll add the *Info.plist* file. Next, create a *MacOS* folder (no space) inside the *Contents* directory. Here, add a "stub" file that acts as a native launcher stub for the application.

Create a *Resources* folder inside *Contents*. This is where you will add an *icns* file, an icon that will be displayed in the Finder and standard file dialogs. Finally, add a *Java* directory to the *Resources* folder. This is where you'll put the required Java libraries (JAR files).

Property List

Directly inside the *Contents* folder, add an *Info.plist* file with the contents shown back in Example 7-2.

Several of the properties are already set, including the main class and some arguments passed in to load SimpleEdit plug-ins (specifically, the SimpleEdit plug-ins developed in Chapter 9). Understanding this point will help you understand how plug-ins affect your property lists. If you don't want to jump to Chapter 9, you can always comment out these portions of the file.

Once you have a base *Info.plist* file, use the Property List Editor to make any necessary additions or changes.

Launcher Stub

To launch your application, you'll need a small native stub file. Copy the file *JavaApplicationStub* from the directory */System/Library/Frameworks/JavaVM.framework/Versions/A/Resources/MacOS*. You can rename this stub whatever you want, as long as the stub file matches the entry for CFBundleExecutable in *Info.plist*. A new stub is included with each JVM release from Apple, and you'll generally want to use the latest available stub.

Application Icon

In the *Resources* folder inside *Contents*, add an *icns* file (a Mac OS X icon file). For development purposes, you can borrow an icon file from another application to test, but you should eventually use the IconComposer tool (shown in Figure 7-6) to create attractive icons. You can find IconComposer in */Developer/Applications/*.

It's also worth pointing out that the photorealistic icons used by Mac OS X are sometimes best created in a commercial application and then imported into IconComposer. Specifically, Adobe Photoshop does an excellent job of creating an application icon, including generating transparency masks, and IconComposer will import Photoshop's PSD files.

Java Libraries

Obviously, you need to add your Java application code to the package. Copy the *SimpleEdit.jar* file into the *Java* directory inside the *Resources* folder. If you were building an application that relied on several other Java libraries, you'd want to place those libraries here as well, and update the *Info.plist* classpath entry (using the $JAVAROOT/ directive to indicate this relative, dynamic path).

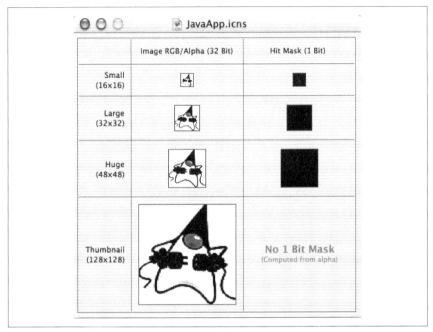

Figure 7-6. IconComposer

Finder Recognition

Finally, rename the base directory from *SimpleEdit* as *SimpleEdit.app*. The Finder will automatically recognize the new folder name and display the folder as an application (hiding the *.app* extension, even if the Finder preferences are set to always show file extensions).

You can now use the Finder to drag and drop files on the application's icon. Assuming you've added the Finder "Open" file handlers (as described in Chapter 5), you'll also be able to open files by using standard features such as the Finder's "Open With" command (as shown in Figure 7-7). The default handler in Chapter 5 displays a dialog showing the path of the file shown in Figure 7-8. Depending on your application, you'll probably want to use the passed-in path to open the file and read the data by using standard Java file I/O APIs.

Congratulations! You've now built a complete Mac OS X application.

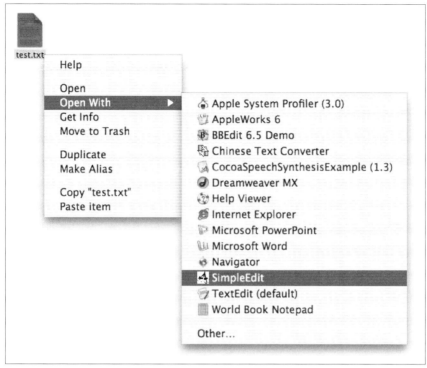

Figure 7-7. Open With command

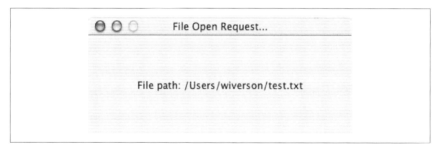

Figure 7-8. SimpleEdit "Open File" notification

MRJAppBuilder

MRJAppBuilder is a utility that packages already-compiled Java applications to run as Mac OS X applications. When you first convert your application to Mac OS X, it may be useful to create a skeleton application with MRJApp-Builder rather than creating one from scratch, as described in the last section. However, MRJAppBuilder has a serious limitation—once you've used the utility to generate your application wrapper and quit MRJAppBuilder, you'll have to make changes by hand or re-enter everything.

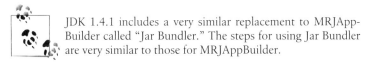 JDK 1.4.1 includes a very similar replacement to MRJApp-Builder called "Jar Bundler." The steps for using Jar Bundler are very similar to those for MRJAppBuilder.

MRJAppBuilder can be found in your */Developer/Applications* directory. When you launch the application, you'll see the interface shown in Figure 7-9.

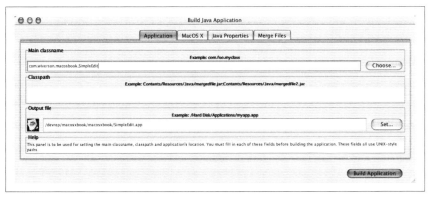

Figure 7-9. MRJAppBuilder main properties

Technically, the information in the "Application" pane is all you need to make a Mac OS X application. All three fields are required. The "Main class-name" field lets you specify the fully qualified class that contains the main( ) method you want executed on application startup. This field represents the value of the property com.apple.mrj.application.main (in effect, it sets the MainClass key). Whatever JAR file you select when you follow the dialog is added to the "Classpath" field automatically.

If you want to use JAR or class files that will not be included in the resulting application bundle, add the following classpath entry:

```
$APP_PACKAGE/../SimpleEdit.jar
```

$APP_PACKAGE is a special path string that represents the application bundle directory.

The last required field is the "Output file" field. This specifies the directory where the resulting application bundle will be built. You can also set the application icon in this pane, which is optional (but recommended). Click the icon in the "Output file" section to bring up a file chooser dialog for selecting an *.icns* file.

Settings in the "Mac OS X," "Java Properties," and "Merge Files" panes are all optional. The "Mac OS X" pane, shown in Figure 7-10, lets you set values specific to the Mac OS X application bundle format. If you do not specify `CFBundleExecutable` or `CFBundleName`, they are set based on the name of the output file you choose.

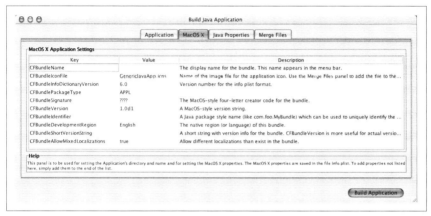

Figure 7-10. MRJAppBuilder application properties

The "Java Properties" pane, shown in Figure 7-11, lets you set specific runtime properties as described earlier in this chapter.

Figure 7-11. MRJAppBuilder Java properties

The "Merge Files" pane provides a way to add files, such as ZIP or JAR files, to the application bundle. Each item added to the merge list is copied into the application's *Contents/Resources/Java* directory. Each item you add to the merge list is automatically added to the classpath. Since *.class* files aren't supported here, you'll need to package your class files as a ZIP or JAR for inclusion.

When you finish making your selections, click "Build Application." MRJApp-Builder does not provide an import mechanism or other ability to save your choices; once you build your application and quit, you'll need to make all your selections in MRJAppBuilder again, or modify the *Info.plist* and *MRJApp.properties* files by hand.

Next Steps

Applications built in this manner are static, standalone desktop applications. When the user installs the application, either by copying it from a CD-ROM or downloading a compressed archive, the application no longer has contact with the publisher (unless it is added by custom application development).

For small utilities or very large monolithic applications, this technique works well. For many classes of software, however, you might want to deploy your applications via the Web, as discussed in the next chapter.

## CHAPTER 8

Web-Delivered Applications

In the last chapter, you learned how to package and distribute standalone applications, where most bytecode was delivered to and ran on an end user's desktop machine. This chapter examines the other delivery option—web-delivered applications. This type of application, which is housed on remote servers rather than on a CD in a box (in a store), avoids some problems associated with standalone applications. The primary disadvantage of a standalone application is that it is typically "cut off" from further updates (without extensive additional work and/or a commercial update system). Users have to buy new versions of software to get new features, bug fixes, and updated documentation. This difference is one of the core strengths of a web-delivered application, which allows web updates (and it even auto-updates itself).

When Java was first introduced, small applications were often delivered via the Web; these mini-applications were called *applets*. The idea was for a web browser to automatically load and execute Java applets in a secure *sandbox*, where the applets would run inside a web page. Unfortunately, many issues—some technical, some political—led to the untimely death of applets for most Java developers.

Sun has since introduced a new model, under the name Web Start, that delivers Java applications via the Web. Web Start eliminates many problems associated with desktop applications (developing an auto-updatable application is fairly straightforward) while cutting the browser out of the equation, vastly improving cross-platform compatibility.

This section looks at how the applet and Web Start models distribute a web-based application and compares the advantages and disadvantages of each approach.

Applets

An applet is a restricted Java application invoked by and running inside of an ordinary web browser. It has a specific base class (java.applet.Applet) with some lifecycle APIs added to interact with the browser. Most of the complexity associated with developing applets (as opposed to ordinary Java applications) derives from the interface and interactions between the JVM and the HTML-based web browser. The basic delivery model for an applet is illustrated in Figure 8-1.

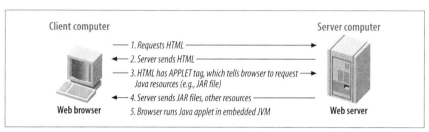

Figure 8-1. Applet delivery

Note that the browser controls resource loading and the manner in which the JVM is embedded. There is no support for running an application if the user is not connected to the Web.

Mac OS X Web Browsers

Several different browsers are available for Mac OS X, each with a different level of support for applets. All rely on the underlying JDK installed with Mac OS X.

For applets, the JVM version used is completely under the control of the browser, with no way to specify older or newer JVMs. As of March 2003, all of the popular Mac OS X browsers support at least JDK 1.3.1. However, if you have Safari and JDK 1.4.1 installed, your applets will only run using JDK 1.4.1—there is no way to tell Safari that your applet requires JDK 1.3.1 instead.

Mac OS X provides a robust environment for applet development through the use of Sun's Java Plug-in (although some browsers rely on the Java Embedding Framework). This means that applets use the same VM used by Java applications. Unfortunately, the default Java installation included with other operating systems (notably, most releases of Windows) is woefully out of date, and typically based on JDK 1.1.7 or 1.1.8 releases. You'll need to pay careful attention to the APIs used if you wish to maintain compatibility with these ancient releases. You may consider requiring that your users upgrade to JDK 1.3 or 1.4, in which case you might consider migration to Java Web Start, discussed later in this chapter.

If you do decide to use applets, you should expect behavior similar to that of applets running on other platforms that use Sun's Java Plug-in. To properly manage the execution of your applet, you'll need to understand how web browsers interpret your HTML code to launch the applet.

Creating an Applet

Example 8-1 shows the source code for a simple applet. It defines an applet and adds a button that, when pressed, launches the SimpleEdit application developed in Chapter 4.

Example 8-1. A simple applet

```
package com.wiverson.macosbook;
public class SimpleApplet extends javax.swing.JApplet
{
    private javax.swing.JButton launchButton;

    public SimpleApplet( )
    {
        launchButton = new javax.swing.JButton( );
        launchButton.setText("Launch SimpleEdit");
        launchButton.addActionListener(new java.awt.event.ActionListener( )
        {
            public void actionPerformed(java.awt.event.ActionEvent evt)
            {
                com.wiverson.macosbook.SimpleEdit.main(null);
            }
        });

        getContentPane( ).add(launchButton, java.awt.BorderLayout.CENTER);
    }
}
```

To launch the applet, you will use a set of tags within an HTML page. You'll structure the HTML as shown in Example 8-2. You should then place this file, saved as *SimpleEditLauncher.html*, in a *~/Sites* directory.

Example 8-2. HTML for launching an applet

```
<HTML>
<HEAD>
   <TITLE>Applet HTML Page</TITLE>
</HEAD>
<BODY>
```

Example 8-2. HTML for launching an applet (continued)

```
<H3><HR WIDTH="100%">SimpleEdit<HR WIDTH="100%"></H3>
<P>
<APPLET archive="SimpleEdit.jar"
        code="com/wiverson/macosbook/SimpleApplet"
        width="160" height="35">
</APPLET>
</P>
</BODY>
</HTML>
```

Deploying an Applet

To deploy the application, place the *SimpleEdit.jar* file created in Chapter 7 and the launcher HTML file into your *~/Sites* directory, and turn on Personal Web Sharing via "System Preferences → Sharing → Services" (as shown in Figure 8-2).

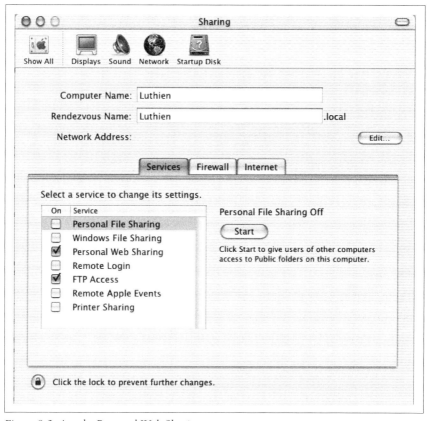

Figure 8-2. Apache Personal Web Sharing

If you want to place content in the "root" of your system, not in a specific user's directory, use */Library/WebServer/Documents/* instead.

Assuming you have placed the files in the *~/Sites* directory, you should be able to view the applet by going to *http://127.0.0.1/~username/SimpleEditApplet.html*. This 127.0.0.1 (or loopback) IP address won't work for deployment, but it is useful when developing and testing an application.

When the applet is run, clicking on the button will launch a new window from inside the browser. This is shown in Figure 8-3 on Internet Explorer (the default web browser that ships with Mac OS X), and in Figure 8-4 on Camino (a Mozilla/Gecko-based browser).

Camino, available at *http://www.mozilla.org/projects/camino/*, is an excellent Cocoa-based web browser that uses the Gecko HTML rendering engine from the Mozilla open source project.

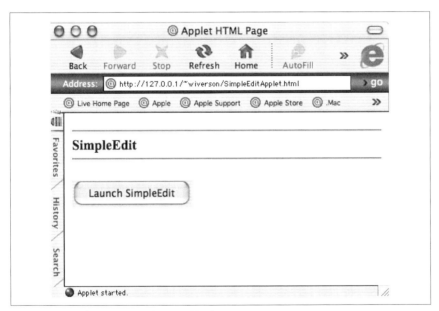

Figure 8-3. Applet running in Internet Explorer

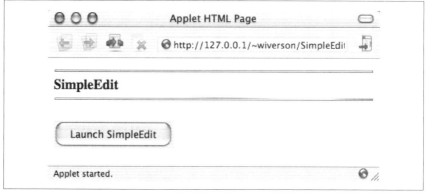

Figure 8-4. Applet running in Camino

Accessing Mac OS X–Specific Properties from Applets

Mac OS X includes specific system properties that you might want to use in your applets, as described in Chapter 7. Except for the com.apple.macos. useScreenMenuBar and mrj.version properties, unsigned applets cannot access these Mac OS X–specific properties (and useScreenMenuBar is ignored by most current browsers). If you want to use any of the properties discussed in Chapter 7, you must grant permission to access them by adding a line to your systemwide *java.policy* file located at */Library/Java/Home/lib/ security/*. The line should be in the following form:

```
java.util.PropertyPermission systemPropertyName, read ;
```

The Java Applet Plug-in

Some web browsers use the Java Embedding Framework (based on Sun's reference appletviewer class) to embed Java applets in web pages, and other browsers rely on the Java Plug-in. The Java Plug-in is considered a superior solution, but unfortunately you usually have little control over the installation and configuration of this plug-in in user desktop browsers. When examining interactions between the applet and the browser, this is another variable to keep in mind.

The default tag for an applet, for both the Java Plug-in and the Java Embedding Framework, is the well-known <APPLET>. However, this tag does not always work as well as the <OBJECT> or <EMBED> tags in different situations.

Figure 8-5 shows the effect of the <APPLET> tag compared to the <OBJECT> and <EMBED> tags. You can see that the <APPLET> tag maps to the Java Plug-in only for users of Mozilla, Netscape, or Camino browsers. This means that you may get different results on an Internet Explorer browser than on a Mozilla or Camino browser (a very bad thing!).

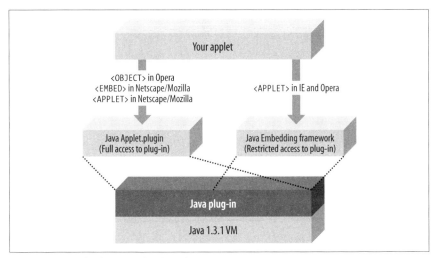

Figure 8-5. Applet functionality based on tag usage

To work around the different interpretations of the <APPLET> tag, you have a few options. If you know that your application is targeted for a specific web browser, you can use the appropriate tag, as listed in Table 8-1. This assumes that one specific browser is targeted, though, and that is an extremely rare situation. A better approach is to use a tool that creates HTML that works in any browser. This tool, called the HTML Converter, is provided by Sun and is available online at *http://java.sun.com/products/plugin/1.3/docs/htmlconv.html*. This converter processes an HTML file and generates HTML and JavaScript that should work across any platform. Using this tool will ensure that the Java Plug-in is activated, regardless of the browser used.

 Sun's HTML Converter is reliable, but you should still perform extensive testing on multiple browsers to make sure you get the results you expect.

Table 8-1. Applet HTML tags for common browsers

Browser	<APPLET>	<OBJECT>	<EMBED>
Microsoft Internet Explorer 5.2.x	Targets the Java Embedding Framework	Functions normally	Functions normally
Netscape / Mozilla / Camino	Treated as <EMBED> tag, which maps to *application/x-java-applet* mime type	Functions normally	Targets the Java Plug-in

Table 8-1. Applet HTML tags for common browsers (continued)

Browser	<APPLET>	<OBJECT>	<EMBED>
OmniWeb	Functions normally		Targets the Java Plug-in
Opera	Functions normally	Targets the Java Plug-in	Functions normally

Generally, applets that run with the Java Plug-in have more functionality than those that run within the Java Embedding Framework. The following sections deal with the specific affected areas. Because of these features, you'll want to target the Java Plug-in whenever possible.

JAR caching

The Java Plug-in is smart enough to cache JAR files for repeated use. This cache is stored in the user's home folder in *Library/Caches/Java*. To take advantage of JAR file caching, you may need to modify your HTML with the tag shown here:

```
<!-- Turns on JAR caching -->
<PARAM NAME ="cache_option" VALUE="plugin">

<!-- Optional tag, identifies specific JAR files to cache
<PARAM NAME ="cache_archive" VALUE="SimpleEdit.jar">
```

JAR cache versioning

You can also use the Java Plug-in to cache certain versions of JAR files, and download new files only if needed. The following HTML shows an optional tag used to specify the version number of the JAR files an applet uses:

```
<!-- Turns on JAR caching -->
<PARAM NAME ="cache_option" VALUE="plugin">

<!-- Optional tag, identifies specific JAR files to cache
<PARAM NAME ="cache_archive" VALUE="SimpleEdit.jar">

<PARAM NAME ="cache_version" VALUE="1.0">
```

The version number is designated with the cache_archive attribute. Each value corresponds to the respective JAR files designated with cache_archive. If the version value is higher than the value of the cached JAR file, the JAR is downloaded again. Thus, if a new version of the *SimpleEdit.jar* file were published, you would increment the cache_version to 1.0.0.1 or some other appropriate value. If this tag is omitted, the plug-in always checks the server to see if a newer version is available and then caches that version.

The default JAR-caching implementation for Mac OS 10.2 conforms to the Java 1.3.1_03 standard, not Java 1.4 (unless the browser vendor has updated to support the 1.4 release). When developing for this target, therefore, you should remember that:

- JAR files specified with the ARCHIVE tag are not cached.
- The cache_version_ex parameter is not supported.
- There is no JAR file indexing support.

For better forward compatibility, you should use the cache_ archive and cache_version parameters instead of these other, now unsupported, options.

The Java Plug-in settings application

The Java Plug-in settings application is a useful utility found in /Applications/Utilities/Java/. Installed on every Mac OS X system by default, it allows users to configure options related to applet behavior. However, users may have different settings than those you have on your development system, and you need to test for those settings as well as your own. You may even want to create multiple users on your own system and give each user different preferences. Each user's settings are stored in ~/Library/Preferences/com.apple.java.plugin.properties131. Figure 8-6 shows the settings application in action.

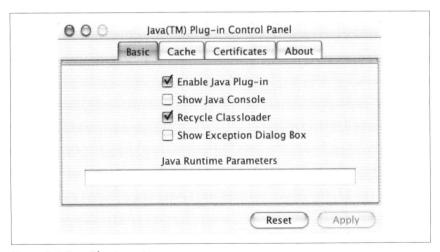

Figure 8-6. Java Plug-in settings

Turning on the option "Show Java Console" is particularly relevant. This console views any text output your applet generates (including the System.out and System.err streams). It can also be used to view thread information interactively and force garbage collection. To enable viewing the console, select "Show Java Console" in the Java Plug-in settings application.

Java Web Start

Java Web Start is a new standard for distributing Java applications, based on a blend between applet advantages (delivered and automatically updated via the Web) and standalone applications (without any dependencies on a web browser). The documentation, several demonstrations, and implementations for Windows and Solaris users are available for download from *http://java.sun.com/products/javawebstart/*. Fortunately for Mac OS X users, an implementation of Java Web Start is included in every distribution of Mac OS X (specifically, Java Network Launching Protocol & API (JNLP) Specification, v1.0.1). There's nothing to configure and nothing to set up—it's just there, waiting for you to take advantage of it!

As shown in Figure 8-7, users will typically first encounter a Web Start application while browsing the Web. Clicking on a link to a Web Start JNLP file causes the browser to launch a helper application, which in turn downloads the resources for the Java application and then launches it. From that point on, users can launch a Web Start application without launching a web browser. In addition, if the application is properly designed and makes sense, Web Start applications can be launched independently of a network connection.

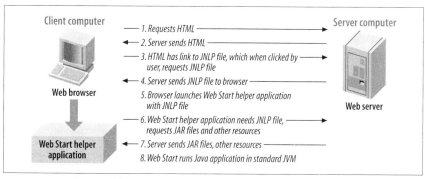

Figure 8-7. Web Start delivery

Consider, for example, a Tic-Tac-Toe game in which the user plays against the computer or a remote opponent. A user surfing the Web with a laptop clicks a link to a JNLP file to launch the game. The browser downloads the JNLP file, which is then launched by Web Start. Web Start downloads the game resources, saves them in a cache, and then launches the application.

The user can play the game against remote opponents and the computer, quitting the browser if desired. Later, the user disconnects the laptop from the network and gets on a plane. The user can still launch the game by using the Java Web Start utility (located in */Applications/Utilities/Java/*), even without a network connection. The user can only play against the computer, however, as no network connection is available.

At the heart of Web Start is the JNLP file (essentially, an XML configuration file that describes the application and application resources). This section will turn the previously developed SimpleEdit application into a Web Start–packaged application.

Before starting, it's worth spending some time looking at the Web Start management application stored in */Applications/Utilities/Java* (shown in Figure 8-8). This is the only real user interface to Web Start beyond whatever interface you present as part of your application.

Figure 8-8. The WebStart user interface

By default, users who launch a Java Web Start application more than twice are prompted to save the application as a standard Mac OS X application, as shown in Figure 8-9. This is a standard Web Start behavior, designed to encourage use of Web Start applications outside the confines of the browser. The application is still a Java Web Start application, but now users can work with the application like other Mac OS X applications (for example, by adding its icon to the Dock).

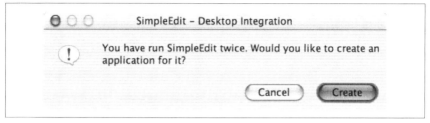

Figure 8-9. Java Web Start desktop integration

Note that even though users won't have to launch a web browser every time a Web Start application is launched, Web Start checks the network connection and attempts to download any updates. If an update is available, Web Start automatically downloads and installs the latest version of the application before launching.

 Java Web Start caches its data in the user's */Library/Caches/ Java Web Start* directory, which can be managed directly via the Web Start GUI; you shouldn't need to work with this directory manually.

Web Start Runtime Environment

When building JNLP-based applications, consider the restrictions on the environment and the packaging. From Sun's Web Start documentation (at *http://java.sun.com/products/javawebstart/1.2/docs/developersguide.html#dev*), the following list details the required attributes of JNLP-delivered applications:

- An application must be delivered as a set of JAR files.
- All application resources, such as files and images, must be stored in JAR files, and they must be referred to by using the getResource( ) mechanism in the Java 2 platform (see the "JAR Resources" section below).
- An application is allowed to use the System.exit( ) call.
- An application that needs unrestricted access to the system must be delivered in a set of signed JAR files. All entries in each JAR file must be signed.

If an application is written to run in a secure sandbox, it must follow these additional restrictions:

- No access to local disk is available.
- All JAR files must be downloaded from the same host.

- Network connections are enabled only to the host from which the JAR files are downloaded.
- No security manager can be installed.
- No native libraries can be installed or utilized.
- Limited access is provided to system properties. The application has read/write access to all system properties defined in the JNLP file, as well as read-only access to the same set of properties that an applet has access to.

Mac OS X Web Start Differences

You need to be aware of only a few differences between the Mac OS X implementation of Java Web Start and that of the Windows and Solaris versions. First, Mac OS X does not support dynamic downloading of additional Java Runtime Environments (JREs). Mac OS X includes J2SE 1.4 (and 1.3.1 is easily available), so if your application specifically requires JRE 1.2 or prior, it will not work. Users who need the latest JVM should use their standard Mac OS X Software Update functionality (available in System Preferences) to download Apple JDK releases. Specifications for version numbers that can expand to include 1.4 will work, though (for example, 1.2+ or 1.3+). It also isn't necessary to set up proxy information explicitly in the Web Start application on Mac OS X—this is automatically configured via the Network control panel proxy settings.

JAR Resources

Java Web Start maintains strict control over the class loading configuration. It transfers JAR files from the web server to the client machine, and chooses where to store the JAR files; an application cannot use disk-relative references to resources such as images and configuration files.

Therefore, application resources should be retrieved from the JAR files specified in the resources section of the JNLP file, or retrieved explicitly by an HTTP request to the web server. It's easiest to store resources directly in the JAR files, since they will be cached on the local machine by Java Web Start (preventing a potentially expensive or even unreachable network connection).

The code example shown in Example 8-3 shows how to retrieve images from a JAR file. The example assumes that the entries *images/save.gif* and *images/ cut.gif* exist in the application's JAR files.

Example 8-3. Accessing resources in a JAR

```
// Get current classloader
ClassLoader cl = this.getClass().getClassLoader( );
// Create icons
Icon saveIcon  = new ImageIcon(cl.getResource("images/save.gif"));
Icon cutIcon   = new ImageIcon(cl.getResource("images/cut.gif"));
```

Developers sign code for use with Java Web Start much like they do for Java applets: by using the standard jarsigner tool from the Java 2 SDK. The documentation for the jarsigner tool shows how to sign code, create test certificates, and other signing-related issues. For more on jarsigner, visit *http://java.sun.com/j2se/1.3/docs/tooldocs/win32/jarsigner.html*.

Delivering a Web Start Application

In this case, you'll use the built-in Mac OS X implementation of Apache to serve JNLP files. To do this, you need to add the line shown below to your *mime.types* file, located in */etc/httpd/*.

```
application/x-java-jnlp-file jnlp
```

Using this implementation will ensure that Web Start applications are associated with JNLP and the proper programs on your Mac OS X machine. The easiest way to ensure this is to use a one-time execution of a command-line text editor from within Terminal:

```
cd /etc/httpd/
sudo pico mime.types
```

You'll need to enter your password, and you'll see the text editor shown in Figure 8-10. Make the needed changes and quit out of Pico.

 To save the file, type Control-X and press return.

You'll then want to restart Apache in the "System Preferences → Sharing" control panel (as shown back in Figure 8-2).

Creating a JNLP File

Before building a Web Start–based application, you'll need a JAR file. In this case, use the JAR file built in Chapter 7. You've been getting some mileage out of this application, as it was already deployed earlier in this chapter as an applet.

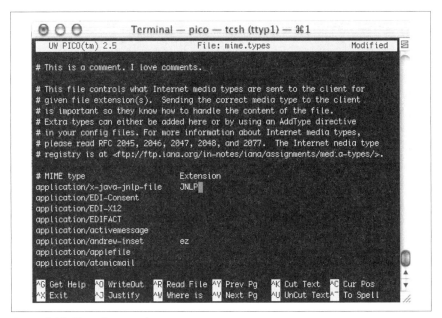

Figure 8-10. Using Pico to edit mime.types

Then create a JNLP configuration text file, as shown in Example 8-4. Save this file as *SimpleEdit.jnlp* in your *~/Sites* directory.

Example 8-4. JNLP configuration file

```
<?xml version="1.0" encoding="utf-8"?>
<!-- JNLP File for SimpleEdit -->
<jnlp
  spec="1.0+"
  codebase="http://127.0.0.1/~wiverson/"
  href="SimpleEdit.jnlp">
  <information>
    <title>SimpleEdit</title>
    <vendor>Will Iverson</vendor>
    <homepage href="http://127.0.0.1"/>
    <description>An extremely minimal text editor</description>
    <description kind="short">An extremely minimal (but extensible) text editor.
</description>
    <icon href="images/notset.jpg"/>
    <icon kind="splash" href="images/notset.gif"/>
    <offline-allowed/>
  </information>
  <resources>
    <j2se version="1.3"/>
    <jar href="SimpleEdit.jar"/>
  </resources>
  <application-desc main-class="com.wiverson.macosbook.SimpleEdit"/>
</jnlp>
```

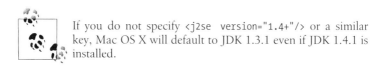
If you do not specify <j2se version="1.4+"/> or a similar key, Mac OS X will default to JDK 1.3.1 even if JDK 1.4.1 is installed.

Next, create a simple HTML file to link to this JNLP file (so users have something to click on in their web browser). Save the contents of Example 8-5 as *SimpleEditWebStart.html* in the *~/Sites* directory.

Example 8-5. HTML to launch a JNLP application

```
<HTML>
<HEAD>
<TITLE>SimpleEdit WebStart</TITLE>
</HEAD>
<BODY>
<A HREF="SimpleEdit.jnlp">Launch SimpleEdit</A>
</BODY>
</HTML>
```

You should now be able to view the HTML page in your web browser by viewing *http://127.0.0.1/~username/SimpleEditWebStart.html*. Clicking on the "Launch SimpleEdit" link will, depending on your web browser, prompt the user to save the JNLP file to disk or automatically launch Web Start. If the file is saved to disk, the user can then launch Web Start (and the Simple-Edit application) by double-clicking on the JNLP file.

JNLP in Detail

As you can see from the example, a JNLP file is a standard XML file. Most of the information contained in the file is fairly self-explanatory, but you'll need to modify some items to deploy your application on a "real-world" server. These items are listed here:

jnlp *element,* codebase *attribute*
 The base URL for all relative HREF URLs in the rest of the JNLP file. If your test system is *http://127.0.0.1/~wiverson* but your production system is *http://www.mycompany.com/games/*, you can change just this attribute's value.

jnlp *element,* href *attribute*
 This attribute's value should be set to the name of the JNLP file.

jnlp/information/title
 This element should indicate the application's human-readable name. This becomes the default name for the application, and should be kept short.

jnlp/information/homepage
: This URL appears automatically in the Java Web Start management application as a clickable link.

jnlp/information/icon
: This graphic is automatically converted to a local system icon if users save an application to their system. The graphic should be square, 64 × 64 pixels (Java Web Start will automatically resize this graphic as needed).

: If an icon with the splash attribute is provided, this icon will be used when Java Web Start downloads or updates the application.

jnlp/information/offline-allowed
: This tag must be present if the application is to be launched when not connected to the network. There are no configurable options; for more sophisticated control, you will probably want to include this option and then perform network availability checks within your application.

jnlp/resources/jar
: You should include one or more of these entries to refer to the various JAR files required by your application.

jnlp/application-desc
: This entry is used to specify the main class for your application. Sub-entries can be provided to pass arguments to the application via argument tags. For example, if you wanted to load a SimpleEdit plug-in, you might pass in an argument as shown below:

```
<application-desc main-class="com.wiverson.macosbook.SimpleEdit">
    <argument>
        com.wiverson.macosbook.webservices.XmlRpcAsynchClientPlugin
    </argument>
</application-desc>
```

GUI Application Delivery Comparison

Several options are available for delivering your Java-based, client-side GUI application on Mac OS X. Table 8-2 provides a chart comparing these various delivery mechanisms.

Table 8-2. Packaging options for GUI applications

	Double-clickable JAR	Mac OS X bundled application	Applet	Web Start
Packaging requirements	Entry in JAR manifest	Specific directory and packaging requirements	HTML file	HTML file and JNLP file

Table 8-2. Packaging options for GUI applications (continued)

	Double-clickable JAR	Mac OS X bundled application	Applet	Web Start
Development complexity	Minimal (standard Java development)	Additional Mac OS X configuration	Use Applet Runner	Significant relaunching within Web Start
Portability	Closest to "pure" Java	Doesn't force incompatibility; unfamiliar to non-Mac OS X users	Extensive browser testing required	Closest to "pure" Java with network connectivity
Functionality	Full	Full	Limited by Sandbox, browser JVM	Limited by digital signature
Sandbox	None	None	Browser	Web Start
Mac OS X user experience	Varies per testing on Mac OS X	Preferred	Varies per testing on Mac OS X	Generally preferred over applets for network-delivered applications

Next Steps

These solutions offer the richest possible user experience, but at a cost—both development and use are complicated. Many applications can be delivered more simply, to a greater range of users and platforms, by using standard HTML and a web browser.

These delivery mechanisms all assume that you've written your application properly. Although this book has covered the basics of Java on Mac OS X, it has yet to delve into the system's real bells and whistles. The next several chapters do this by looking at Mac OS X's support for speech, QuickTime, and spelling. It then continues its exploration of Java on the Mac by examining platform enterprise applications.

## CHAPTER 9

The Mac OS X Speech Framework

Your Macintosh wants to talk to you…and it's even willing to listen to what you have to say. Mac OS computers have been able to speak for a long time—ever since the introduction of PlainTalk and Speech Recognition in the pre-Mac OS 8 days (the early 1990s).

Speech is a very interesting concept, but it's one that has been sadly under-supported by most Mac OS applications. One of Classic Mac OS's most interesting features was its support for a feature called "talking dialogs." You could specify a few basic options, and the alerts that appeared would be spoken automatically. No application support was needed, as the appropriate text string was detected automatically by the alert/dialog API. This feature wasn't reimplemented for Mac OS X until the release of Jaguar (Mac OS 10.2). In addition to this basic functionality, Mac OS X features a number of other speech capabilities.

First, Mac OS X can perform speech recognition. Broadly speaking, there are two classes of speech recognition: systems that can understand specific words or phrases (such as the engine in Mac OS X) and systems that are capable of full dictation services. Some packages available from third parties provide full dictation for Mac OS X, but they require an independent commercial license and are beyond the scope of this book. This chapter focuses on the ability of an OS X system to recognize words and on how your Java programs can use that functionality.

Additionally, Mac OS X still supports text-to-speech conversion. This conversion allows plain text, such as that typed into TextPad or a Microsoft Word document, to be converted into a binary audio format and read back to the user. This conversion is a bit of a niche feature, but is pretty cool and worth knowing about.

Apple has made Java-based frameworks for both text-to-speech and voice recognition available as freely downloadable packages from the Apple

Developer Connection (ADC). The native support is already included in Mac OS X, but the downloadable frameworks include the required Java bindings and documentation to make them useful programmatically. You'll need to register with the ADC to download the toolkit; free registration is available at *http://www.apple.com/developer/*.

 Currently, the Speech Framework relies on Apple's JDirect implementation (as described in Chapter 5). Since JDirect isn't included in the Mac OS X JDK 1.4 implementation, it may be some time before an implementation of the Speech Framework is made available for JDK 1.4–based applications. Visit *http://developer.apple.com/java/* for the latest information. In the meantime, you'll have to consider speech a JDK 1.3–only feature.

Before diving into the code, consider this advice before using speech in your applications:

- You can't require speech input for your application unless you are willing to constrain the use of your application. I wrote most of this chapter in a coffee shop. Text-to-speech worked well with my headphones, but I wasn't bold enough to talk to my iBook in public. If I'm hesitant, your users might be, too.

- It's easier and (arguably) more useful to add text-to-speech to your application than to add speech recognition. Also, just because you add one, it doesn't mean that you must add both. I'd suggest adding text-to-speech capabilities first and speech recognition second.

- When using text-to-speech, include an easy way for the user to stop the system from speaking. If you use a talking alert dialog, turn off the sound if the user clicks the mouse anywhere, not just on a button. Include an option that turns speech off and on easily and globally in your application. If you're working on a game, pause the speech engine when you pause the rest of the game.

- Don't forget that the hardware and environment can affect the utility of both technologies. Also, non-native English speakers can sometimes find speaking systems difficult to use or understand.

The Speech API

Two main sections in the Speech API are used to create spoken words from text strings and to listen to words spoken by the user. This section covers a few basic classes you should be familiar with when working with the Speech API.

The Synthesizer Class

When you simply want Mac OS X to speak text, you'll work primarily with the com.apple.speech.synthesis package. Synthesizer is the most important class for converting text to spoken words. This class has a few basic methods to work with, such as speakText(String) and stopSpeech( ). In addition, several methods allow control over other speech options, including:

- Notification of specific events while speaking text, including when individual words or individual phonemes are spoken, or when speech is started, finished, or paused.
- The ability to embed special commands via delimiters (*http://developer. apple.com/techpubs/mac/Sound/Sound-200.html#HEADING200-0*).
- Changing of pitch, pitch modulation, rate, voice, and volume.
- Pausing of the current speech synthesis immediately, or at the end of the current sentence or word.

All methods for these classes are detailed in the included Javadoc documentation for the Speech Framework. Rather than deal with each individually, the rest of this chapter will put the framework into action, giving you practical experience in working with OS X, Java, and speech.

Setting Speech Defaults

Although programmatic options control the speech playback as described above, the "System Preferences → Speech" control panel sets default speech configuration, as shown in Figure 9-1.

Speech Recognition

Recognizing speech from a user is a bit trickier than generating speech from text, and is handled by the com.apple.speech.recognition package. The package's core class is Recognizer, which lets you specify which words and phrases are known by the recognition package. You also need to specify the language style to be used, through the LanguageModel class. This class allows you to specify the type of speech so the recognition engine can try to make intelligent decisions about combinations of words it "hears." You'll then add phrases to the model and add that model to the Recognizer (Recognizer. setLanguageModel( )).

Once you've registered all the words and phrases, you then need to add event handlers to the Recognizer. This class lets you deal with recognized and unrecognized events. You can launch programs, continue listening,

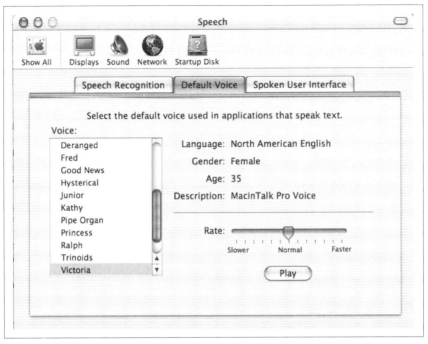

Figure 9-1. Speech preferences

show (or speak) error messages if a phrase isn't understood, and do anything else that Java programming supports.

Putting Speech to Work

Once you've decided that you want to play around with the speech API, it's actually pretty simple to put it into action. This section will discuss how to put speech into basic dialog boxes, as well as more useful applications of text-to-speech and speech recognition.

Getting Set Up

As mentioned earlier, these steps assume that you are a member of the Apple Developer Connection (ADC), for which you can sign up for free. Visit *https://connect.apple.com* and log in to the developer connection. You'll be given several menus and submenus on the left. Select "Download Software" and then "Java." Then download the Speech Framework as a Mac binary file (in *.dmg* format). Once you have mounted the disk image, start the included installer.

The installer will place several items of interest on your disk. First, it will place a JAR file, *JavaSpeechFramework.jar*, in the standard extensions directory of your *JavaVM.framework* folder, at */System/Library/Frameworks/JavaVM.framework/Versions/CurrentJDK/Home/lib/ext/* (see Chapter 2 for more information on the Mac OS X JVM directory layout). It will place documentation in the directory */Developer/Research/JavaSpeechFramework/Documentation/*, and sample code in the directory */Developer/Research/JavaSpeechFramework/Examples/*.

The *JavaSpeechFramework.jar* file, therefore, is of great interest. You'll need to make sure this library is on the classpath for your compiler and application before you use the framework.

You can put this JAR file in the *ext* directory and not worry about classpath issues.

The TalkingJDialog Class

The class `TalkingJDialog`, shown in Example 9-1, is a simple extension to the standard Swing `JDialog`. This class extends the basic `JDialog` dialog box with additional information to provide for spoken text.

This class is *not* cross-platform and will fail on non–Mac OS X systems. Chapters 5 and 6 show how to provide support for Apple-specific extensions while retaining cross-platform compatibility.

Check for both the Speech Framework and the Mac OS X platform to ensure that users who don't have the update won't be confused by error messages.

Example 9-1. Extending JDialog for speech

```
package com.wiverson.macosbook.speech;

/* This single class does the vast bulk of the
   heavy lifting of actually making Mac OS X talk.

   Don't blink or you'll miss it.
 */
import com.apple.speech.synthesis.Synthesizer;

/* This class describes a very generic version of
   JDialog with a few methods added for speech recognition
   and related user interface. It's extraordinarily
   straightforward.
 */
```

Example 9-1. Extending JDialog for speech (continued)

```java
public class TalkingJDialog extends javax.swing.JDialog
    implements java.awt.event.MouseListener
{

    public TalkingJDialog()
    {
        this.setResizable(false);
        this.addMouseListener(this);
    }

    /* This method is used to allow the user to click
     anywhere and immediately cancel out of the
     speech playback - even if the dialog isn't
     dismissed
     */
    public void mousePressed(java.awt.event.MouseEvent mouseEvent)
    {
        if(mySynthesizer != null)
            mySynthesizer.stopSpeech();
    }

    // Needed to complete the MouseListener interface
    public void mouseReleased(java.awt.event.MouseEvent mouseEvent)
    {}
    public void mouseExited(java.awt.event.MouseEvent mouseEvent)
    {}
    public void mouseEntered(java.awt.event.MouseEvent mouseEvent)
    {}
    public void mouseClicked(java.awt.event.MouseEvent mouseEvent)
    {}

    public void dispose()
    {
        super.dispose();
    }

    public void hide()
    {
        super.hide();
        // If the dialog goes away, be sure to stop talking.
        mySynthesizer.stopSpeech();
    }

    private Synthesizer mySynthesizer = null;

    public void show()
    {
        super.show();
        // Get a synthesizer for this dialog
        // if one isn't already available
        if(mySynthesizer == null)
```

Example 9-1. Extending JDialog for speech (continued)

```
            mySynthesizer = new Synthesizer( );
    // Start talking!
    mySynthesizer.speakText(getNotificationText( ));
}

    // Storage & accessors for the text to be spoken
    private String spokenText;
    public void setNotificationText(String inString)
    {
        spokenText = inString;
    }
    public String getNotificationText( )
    {
        return spokenText;
    }
}
```

A Talking Dialog Box

On its own, this class is pretty useless, as is JDialog without an additional
extension. To use it, extend TalkingJDialog with your own dialog box and
listen to Mac OS X read your messages. Example 9-2 provides a simple,
user-friendly standalone example of a talking dialog.

Example 9-2. A simple talking alert box

```
package com.wiverson.macosbook.speech;

public class TalkingAlertJDialog
    extends com.wiverson.macosbook.speech.TalkingJDialog
{

    /** Creates new form TalkingAlertJDialog */
    public TalkingAlertJDialog(String alert)
    {
        setNotificationText(alert);
        initComponents( );
        this.getRootPane( ).setDefaultButton(okButton);
        pack( );
        java.awt.Dimension screenSize =
            java.awt.Toolkit.getDefaultToolkit().getScreenSize( );
        setSize(new java.awt.Dimension(374, 128));
        setLocation((screenSize.width-374)/2,(screenSize.height-128)/4);
    }

    private void initComponents( )
    {
        alertText = new javax.swing.JLabel( );
        stylePanel = new javax.swing.JPanel( );
        okButton = new javax.swing.JButton( );
```

Example 9-2. A simple talking alert box (continued)

```
        setTitle("Alert");
        setResizable(false);
        alertText.setText(getNotificationText());
        alertText.setHorizontalAlignment(javax.swing.SwingConstants.CENTER);
        getContentPane().add(alertText, java.awt.BorderLayout.CENTER);

        okButton.setText("OK");
        okButton.addActionListener(new java.awt.event.ActionListener()
        {
            public void actionPerformed(java.awt.event.ActionEvent evt)
            {
                okButtonActionPerformed(evt);
            }
        });

        stylePanel.add(okButton);

        getContentPane().add(stylePanel, java.awt.BorderLayout.SOUTH);

    }

    private void okButtonActionPerformed(java.awt.event.ActionEvent evt)
    {
        setVisible(false);
    }

    public static void main(String args[])
    {
        new TalkingAlertJDialog("Help! I've fallen and I can't get up!").show();
    }

    private javax.swing.JLabel alertText;
    private javax.swing.JPanel stylePanel;
    private javax.swing.JButton okButton;
}
```

While a picture may be worth a thousand words, you'll have to try this one out on your own to really appreciate Mac OS X's speech features. Still, Figure 9-2 shows `TalkingAlertJDialog` in action.

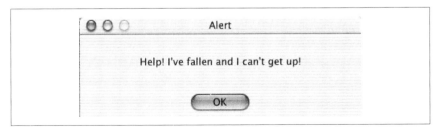

Figure 9-2. A talking alert box

Ask Mac OS X

Next, write a small utility application that sits in the background and answers common questions. This section shows you how to set up the voice recognizer, teach it a few phrases, and make it answer common questions. This lesson should familiarize you with other useful applications of the Speech Framework. Example 9-3 includes the source listing for this utility.

Example 9-3. Speech utility listener

```
package com.wiverson.macosbook.speech;

import javax.swing.JLabel;
import javax.swing.JComboBox;
import java.awt.BorderLayout;

public class SpeechListener
    extends javax.swing.JDialog
    implements java.awt.event.ActionListener,
               com.apple.speech.recognition.UnrecognizedEventListener,
               com.apple.speech.recognition.DetectedEventListener,
               com.apple.speech.recognition.DoneEventListener
{

    // Set up the speech recognition engine
    static com.apple.speech.recognition.Recognizer mySpeechRecognizer = null;
    static com.apple.speech.recognition.LanguageModel myLanguageModel = null;

    // Set up the text-to-speech engine
    static com.apple.speech.synthesis.Synthesizer mySynthesizer = null;


    public SpeechListener()
    {
        this.getContentPane().setLayout(new BorderLayout());
        statusLabel = new JLabel("Ready.");
        statusLabel.setHorizontalTextPosition(statusLabel.LEFT);
        this.getContentPane().add(statusLabel, BorderLayout.CENTER);

        manualCommandMenu = new JComboBox();
        manualCommandMenu.setModel(new javax.swing.DefaultComboBoxModel(tasks));
        manualCommandMenu.addActionListener(this);

        this.getContentPane().add(manualCommandMenu, BorderLayout.EAST);

        this.pack();
        this.setSize(300, 50);
        this.setTitle("Address me as " + computerName);

        // Set up to talk have the computer talk back.
        if(mySynthesizer == null)
            mySynthesizer = new com.apple.speech.synthesis.Synthesizer();
```

Example 9-3. Speech utility listener (continued)

```
    try
    {
        // Hack for workaround of bug which
        // prevents Java apps from receiving
        // AppleEvents in Mac OS X 10.0
        com.apple.ae.AppleEventFunctions.initAE( );

        // Create the SpeechRecoginizer.
        // Speech is activated lazily upon startup.
        mySpeechRecognizer = new com.apple.speech.recognition.Recognizer( );

        // Create & setup the LanguageModel which we will add our phrases to.
        myLanguageModel = new com.apple.speech.recognition.LanguageModel( );
        mySpeechRecognizer.setLanguageModel(myLanguageModel);

        // Add the phrases we are looking for.
        // Note that we need to add the computer's address first.
        // Still, easier than using the more complex API
        String[] full_tasks = new String[tasks.length];
        for(int i = 0; i < tasks.length; i++)
            full_tasks[i] = computerName + tasks[i];

        myLanguageModel.setPhrases(full_tasks);

        // Start the recoginizer
        mySpeechRecognizer.start( );

        // Listen for speech events
        mySpeechRecognizer.addDoneEventListener(this);
        mySpeechRecognizer.addUnrecognizedEventListener(this);
        mySpeechRecognizer.addDetectedEventListener(this);
    }
    catch(Exception e)
    {
        e.printStackTrace( );
    }
}

private JLabel statusLabel;
private JComboBox manualCommandMenu;
private String computerName = "Computer ";

static final private int DAY = 0;
static final private int SONG = 1;
static final private int QUIT = 2;
static final private int BEEP = 3;

private String[] tasks =
{
    "what day is it",
    "sing a song",
```

Example 9-3. Speech utility listener (continued)

```
        "quit",
        "beep"
    };

    static void main(String[] args)
    {
        (new SpeechListener()).show( );
    }

    public void doCommand(String input)
    {
        statusLabel.setText("I heard " + input);

        if(input.compareTo(tasks[DAY]) == 0)
        {
            mySynthesizer.speakText(new java.util.Date().toString( ));
        }

        if(input.compareTo(tasks[SONG]) == 0)
        {
            mySynthesizer.speakText("Sorry, I'm shy");
        }

        if(input.compareTo(tasks[QUIT]) == 0)
        {
            System.exit(0);
        }

        if(input.compareTo(tasks[BEEP]) == 0)
        {
            java.awt.Toolkit.getDefaultToolkit().beep( );
        }
    }

    public void handleDoneEvent(com.apple.speech.recognition.DoneEvent doneEvent)
    {
        String command = doneEvent.getPhraseRecognized( );
        if(command != null)
        {
            command = command.substring(computerName.length(), command.length( )
);
            doCommand(command);
        } else
        {
            statusLabel.setText("Can't understand...?");
        }
    }

    public void actionPerformed(java.awt.event.ActionEvent actionEvent)
    {
        if(actionEvent.getSource( ) instanceof JComboBox)
```

Example 9-3. Speech utility listener (continued)

```
        {
        doCommand
            (
                (
                (JComboBox)actionEvent.getSource( )
                ).getSelectedItem().toString( )
            );
            }
        }

    public void handleDetectedEvent(
        com.apple.speech.recognition.DetectedEvent detectedEvent)
    {
        statusLabel.setText("Listening...");
    }

    public void handleUnrecognizedEvent(
        com.apple.speech.recognition.UnrecognizedEvent unrecognizedEvent)
    {
        statusLabel.setText("Unrecognized...");
    }
}
```

Fire up this application:

```
java com.wiverson.macosbook.speech.SpeechListener
```

 Make sure you've got the Mac OS X speech packages in your classpath before using this program, or you won't be able to compile or execute it.

Once started, the program sits quietly in the background, waiting for the user to speak a phrase such as "Computer, what day is it?" The computer will then respond, using the voice synthesizer to answer the question.

 To add additional tasks to the example above, you'll need to add additional phrases to the tasks array, branching logic to the doCommand( ) method and the relevant implementation.

If you're adding support for voice recognition, you'll probably want to integrate the voice commands into your application's existing event dispatching system. Ideally, you should provide a customizable interface for users to specify the specific phrases they'd like to use to trigger events.

Custom Language Models

Besides adding tasks, you can install your own "grammar" by creating more complex language models. This allows you to build much more sophisticated applications, but it is also considerably more difficult to configure and develop.

A custom language model, represented by the `com.apple.speech.recognition.LanguageModel` class, has a list of zero or more words, phrases, or paths. For example, suppose that you want the system to handle commands such as "call Will" and "schedule a lunch with Brent next Tuesday" (perhaps with other names and days as well). Displaying the model in Backus-Naur Form (BNF) is one way to specify language models. Example 9-4 shows a BNF description of a relatively simple language model.

Example 9-4. A BNF description of a language model

```
<TopLM> = <call> <person> | schedule meeting with <person> |view today's
schedule;
<call> = call | phone| dial;
<person> = Will | Brent | Cynthia | Diane;
```

Building up a custom language model allows your application to mix and match names and phrases, rather than learning each phrase with each possible name and action.

If your application requires this sort of sophistication, investigate the installed documentation at */Developer/Research/JavaSpeechFramework/ Documentation/com/apple/speech/recognition/Model.html*. The use of this model precludes the use of the simpler API from the sample applications. It was left out of this book, largely because of the still-missing support for speech in JDK 1.4. For projects complex enough to require the sophistication of custom language models, you'll probably want to investigate a commercial package such as IBM's ViaVoice (*http://www.apple.com/macosx/ applications/viavoice/*).

## CHAPTER 10

QuickTime for Java

When Java first came out, multimedia APIs were relatively weak; scratchy 8-bit sound just doesn't cut it in today's world. Users had rich media on their desktops and laptops, and the Java world quickly scrambled to find a better media API. Unsurprisingly, Java turned to QuickTime, one of the oldest and most sophisticated media APIs available.

Apple has ported QuickTime to Windows and released a set of Java APIs that provide users who would have to write their own native wrappers an easier interface to QuickTime. The APIs are still relatively "C-like," but using them is much easier than writing your own bridge. Applications built using the QuickTime for Java technology are also cross-platform, as long as the only platforms you consider are Windows and Mac OS; Unix users are still out of luck when it comes to QuickTime. The examples in this chapter will run on Windows as well as on Mac OS X.

One of QuickTime's most interesting features is its sheer scope of available functionality. The rich range of supported media types can be overwhelming. This chapter explores the available range of media and demonstrates how to play that media back from within Java applications.

Getting Started

The QuickTime API has two basic components: the documentation, which was designed for you, and a set of Java classes, which are for your Java compiler. To make the most out of QuickTime, make sure you can access both.

Documentation

When you install Mac OS X and the included developer tools, QuickTime is installed by default. Therefore, you don't have to download separate archives when you start. Before diving into QuickTime's classes, browse the documentation, located at */Developer/Documentation/QuickTime/index.html*. As you can tell from the filename, this material is in HTML, which is simple to browse through and utilize. Figure 10-1 shows the initial index page with its content pane and table of contents.

Figure 10-1. QuickTime documentation

You'll notice that there are a lot of links to follow; you could probably spend several days reading through all the included documents. When browsing through the HTML, you'll quickly realize that QuickTime supports a broad range of rich APIs. Its complexity has been compared to a complete operating system. Of particular interest is the Java-specific information it links to on this first page, as shown in Figure 10-2.

 This chapter assumes that you are working with QuickTime for Java on the Mac OS X JDK 1.3.1 JVM. Currently, Quick-Time hasn't been brought up to speed for JDK 1.4; be sure to check *http://developer.apple.com/java/* for the latest information on QuickTime for Java and JDK 1.4.

QuickTime API

file://localhost/Developer/Documentation/QuickTime/Java/tp_java_digest.htm

New Docs
Function Index
Topic Index
Programming Summary

PDF Files | Glossary

QuickTime Road
Map

Fundamentals
Read Me First
QuickTime Overview
What's New in
QuickTime
Includes...
AppleScript
JavaScript
SMIL
QuickTime for Windows
Mac OS for QuickTime

Movie Toolbox
Fundamentals
New Features
Access Keys
Creating and Saving
Time and Space
Editing
Previews
Data Types
App-Defined Functions
Movie Controllers

Document: Done

QuickTime for Java

| Chapter Contents | Next |

Summary of QuickTime for Java

Since its introduction in 1991, QuickTime has evolved into the equivalent of five large multimedia toolkits, with an extensive API in the C language. It is designed to produce full-length movies, music, animated sprites, virtual reality, and 3D modeling. Besides its widespread use for delivering high-quality digital content over the Internet, QuickTime has become the core multimedia technology used in over 11,500 CD-ROM titles and hundreds of new DVD titles.

QuickTime for Java came about to meet developers' need for a way to get at QuickTime besides using C calls. The idea was to integrate the write-once, run-everywhere capabilities of Java with QuickTime's robust media architecture.

An early version of the QuickTime for Java technology was first demonstrated at the JavaOne conference in 1998. The current version is now available free to the Java community and other QuickTime developers at www.apple.com/quicktime/qtjava

This document summarizes the highlights of QuickTime for Java under the following headings:

- "The QuickTime for Java API" summarizes the principal programming elements of the Java API for QuickTime
- "Using QuickTime in Multimedia Production" presents several scenarios for using QuickTime for Java in the multimedia production space.
- "An Overview of QuickTime for Java" gives you basic facts about this software.
- "Integrating QuickTime with Java" discusses how the QuickTime for Java Application Framework works.
- "The QuickTime for Java Package Structure" describes the packages that make up QuickTime for Java.

Figure 10-2. QuickTime for Java documentation

Class Files

Once you've gotten the lay of the land, you'll want to locate the actual QuickTime classes and ensure that they are available on your compiler and runtime environment. Navigate to */System/Library/Java/Extensions/* and look for *QTJava.zip*. Then add this archive to your classpath, through either a script or the command line:

```
setenv CLASSPATH /System/Library/Java/Extensions/QTJava.zip:$CLASSPATH
```

This step will give you access to the APIs themselves, allowing you to code to your heart's content. Note that QuickTime presents an unusually "close to the metal" implementation that exposes a lot of C-based functionality. Put bluntly, it's a bit easier to shoot your application in the head with QuickTime for Java than with almost any other Java API.

The QuickTime API

The QuickTime API is large and complex, and the underlying API's original native heritage makes it especially hard for a Java developer to get a handle on it. Fortunately, the QuickTime for Java bindings help you write your application, but they can be difficult to understand without first examining the native layer.

Native Origins

QuickTime's architecture is based on the original Mac OS APIs, in which each API cluster was referred to as a "toolbox" or a "manager." This section looks at the overall architecture of QuickTime and walks through some of the fundamental building blocks. This book cannot explore every nuance of QuickTime, but this section should help you understand how all the pieces fit together.

A few basic packages provide the conceptual underpinnings for QuickTime: Movie Toolbox, Image Compression Manager, Image Decompressor Manager, and Component Manager. A set of predefined components provides much of the implementation. Figure 10-3 shows how these elements relate to an application that is playing a movie.

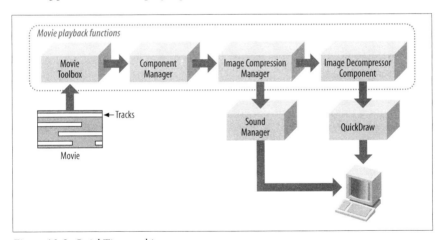

Figure 10-3. QuickTime architecture

The Movie Toolbox

A native application's primary interface to QuickTime is the Movie Toolbox. This API set lets you store, retrieve, and manipulate time-based data stored in QuickTime movies. A single movie may contain several types of data. For example, a movie that contains video information might include both video data and the sound data that accompanies that video.

The Movie Toolbox also provides functionality for editing movies. For example, editing functions shorten a movie by removing portions of the video and sound tracks, and other functions extend a movie by adding new data from other QuickTime movies.

The Image Compression Manager

Image data requires a large amount of storage space. Storing a single 640 × 480 pixel image in 32-bit color can require as much as 1.2 MB of disk space. Sequences of images, like those that might be contained in a QuickTime movie, demand substantially more storage than do single images. This is true even for sequences that consist of fairly small images because the movie consists of a large number of those images. Consequently, minimizing the storage requirements for image data is an important consideration for any application that works with images or sequences of images.

The Image Compression Manager provides a device-independent and driver-independent means of compressing and decompressing images and image sequences. It also contains a simple interface for implementing software and hardware image-compression algorithms. Images can be imported and exported easily from many formats. In most cases, applications use the Image Compression Manager indirectly by calling Movie Toolbox functions or displaying a compressed picture.

The Component Manager

QuickTime provides components as an abstraction so that every application doesn't need to know about all possible types of audio, visual, and storage devices. A component is essentially a library or plug-in registered by the Component Manager. The component's code can be available as a system-wide resource, or in a resource that is local to a particular application.

QuickTime provides a number of useful default components for application developers. These components provide essential services to your application and to the managers that comprise the QuickTime architecture. QuickTime uses the following Apple-defined components:

- Movie controller components, which allow applications to play movies by using a standard user interface

- Standard image-compression dialog components, which allow the user to specify the parameters for a compression operation through a dialog box or similar mechanism

- Image compressor components, which compress and decompress image data
- Sequence grabber components, which allow applications to preview and record video and sound data as QuickTime movies
- Video digitizer components, which allow applications to control video digitization by an external device
- Media data-exchange components, which allow applications to move various types of data in and out of a QuickTime movie
- Derived media handler components, which allow QuickTime to support new types of data in QuickTime movies
- Clock components, which provide timing services defined for Quick-Time applications
- Preview components, which the Movie Toolbox's standard file preview functions use to display and create visual previews for files
- Sequence grabber channel components, which manipulate captured data for a sequence grabber component
- Sequence grabber panel components, which allow sequence grabber components to obtain configuration information from the user for a particular sequence grabber channel component

Applications gain access to components by calling the Component Manager. Once an application connects to a component, it calls that component directly.

Atoms

QuickTime stores most of its data by using its own custom memory structures called *atoms*. Movies and each of their individual tracks are organized and stored as atoms, as are various media and data samples. In fact, this is the last step before actually writing a movie file to disk. In this way, many atoms, called *classic atoms* (or simply "atoms"), contain both data and references to other atoms.

Atoms that contain only data and not other atoms are called *leaf atoms*. QuickTime in particular uses both classic and leaf atoms to form hierarchies of data, treelike structures that represent complex media files. Quick-Time provides a complete API set for accessing and manipulating both types of atoms.

QuickTime for Java

To allow Java programmers access to QuickTime's native APIs, Apple provides bindings for the underlying QuickTime components. Fortunately, Apple's bindings between QuickTime and Java are more sophisticated than a simple API translation. In addition to providing simple APIs, QuickTime for Java provides an additional application framework to assist with integration into Java applications.

The quicktime.app package is the core of the QuickTime and Java binding set. The classes in this package present different kinds of media. The framework uses the interfaces in quicktime.app to abstract and express common functionality that exists between different QuickTime objects.

As such, the services that the QuickTime for Java application framework renders to the developer belong to the following categories:

- Integration of QuickTime with the Java runtime environment, which includes sharing display space between Java and QuickTime and passing events from Java into QuickTime
- A set of classes that provides services that simplify the authoring of QuickTime content and operation
- Creation of objects that present different forms of media, using QTFactory.makeDrawable( ) methods
- Various utilities (classes and methods) that deal with single images as well as groups of related images
- Spaces and controllers architecture, which allows you to deal with complex data-generation or presentation requirements
- Composition services that allow complex layering and blending of different image sources
- Timing services that let you schedule and control time-related activities
- Video and audio media capturing from external sources
- Exposure of the QuickTime visual effects architecture

Understanding the Java bindings

The QuickTime Java classes that represent media types are created from structures and data types from the standard QuickTime C language header files. These data types provide the QuickTime for Java API basic class structure. For example, the Movie data type in *Movies.h* becomes the Movie class in Java; functions in C become methods in Java; and capitalization and notation conventions are changed to match the Java language. However, there is a slight twist—most QuickTime C functions have in the method name the object being operated on (remember that C is not object-oriented), creating a more procedural approach. To translate this approach to an object-oriented Java environment, classes are created for each object, and methods are bound to that object.

For example, the QuickTime native function SetMovieGWorld logically translates (or is bound by) the Java method setGWorld( ) on the Movie class. Similarly, the QuickTime native function MCSetControllerPort logically translates (or is bound by) the Java method setPort( ) on the MovieController class.

The QuickTime for Java SDK provides a complete list of the QuickTime functions that QuickTime for Java binds. The supplied HTML documentation for these binding calls provides only brief descriptions, often little more than function names and parameter lists. Therefore, you'll often need to refer to the native documentation to understand the use of a given class or method, or even the general purpose of the API.

Supported Media Types

Supported media types for QuickTime include (but are not limited to):

- MPEG-4 (including streaming and QuickTime Movies)
- AAC Audio codec for QuickTime Movies
- MP3, including access to ID3v2 metadata
- Flash 5
- JFIF/JPEG/JPEG 2000
- Digital Video (DV)
- QuickDraw PICT
- QuickTime Image
- Photoshop (Versions 2.5 and 3.0)
- Silicon Graphics
- GIF
- BMP
- PNG
- Audio CD (import as AIFF)
- TGA
- TIFF

The SimplePlayer Application

As discussed in the last chapter, using these APIs is the best way to get a feel for them. To demonstrate QuickTime, look at the SimplePlayer example. This player can load and play a variety of media formats, including Quick-Time movies and MP3 audio files. Additionally, the application allows you to export files to other formats, demonstrating that facet of the QuickTime API. As they are put to use in SimplePlayer, try to recognize the key classes and methods from the last section.

The source for this application, shown in Example 10-1, is surprisingly concise. Much of this code is actually spent in setup and user interface. The actual QuickTime APIs used are fairly simple to understand.

Example 10-1. The SimplePlayer application

```
package com.wiverson.macosbook.quicktime;

import quicktime.std.movies.Movie;

import java.awt.event.*;
import quicktime.QTException;
import quicktime.io.QTFile;
import java.awt.FileDialog;
import java.awt.Frame;
import javax.swing.JButton;
import javax.swing.JLabel;
import javax.swing.JPanel;
import javax.swing.JDialog;

public class SimpleMoviePlayer
    extends javax.swing.JFrame
    implements quicktime.std.StdQTConstants,
               quicktime.Errors,
               quicktime.io.IOConstants
{
    public static void main(String args[])
    {
        try
        {
            // Required to initialize the QuickTime environment.
            // Performs checks to ensure QuickTime is installed and
            // also loads and sets up QuickTime.
            quicktime.QTSession.open();

            SimpleMoviePlayer myPlayer = new SimpleMoviePlayer("Simple Player");

            myPlayer.pack();
            myPlayer.show();
            myPlayer.toFront();
        } catch (Exception e)
```

Example 10-1. The SimplePlayer application (continued)

```
        {
            e.printStackTrace( );
            quicktime.QTSession.close( );
        }
    }


/* ------------------ User interface ----------------------------------- */

    JButton importButton = new JButton("Import Media...");
    JButton referenceButton = new JButton("Export Reference Media...");
    JButton exportButton = new JButton("Export Full Media...");
    JPanel commandPanel = new JPanel( );
    JLabel statusLabel = new JLabel("Ready.");

    // The QTCanvas is the "heavy lifter" QuickTime component
    // that does all the hard work for punching the QuickTime
    // viewer through and into the JFrame.
    quicktime.app.display.QTCanvas myQTCanvas;

    /* Creates the application user interface. You'll
     * notice that there is no reference to new user interface
     * options for QuickTime features - those are controlled by
     * the "punched through" QuickTime capabilities.
     */
    SimpleMoviePlayer(String title)
    {
        super(title);

        getContentPane( ).add(statusLabel, "North");

        importButton.addActionListener(new ActionListener( )
        {
            public void actionPerformed(java.awt.event.ActionEvent ae)
            {
                importMedia( );
            }
        });
        commandPanel.add(importButton);

        referenceButton.addActionListener(new ActionListener( )
        {
            public void actionPerformed(java.awt.event.ActionEvent ae)
            {
                makeReferenceMovie( );
            }
        });
        commandPanel.add(referenceButton);

        exportButton.addActionListener(new ActionListener( )
        {
            public void actionPerformed(java.awt.event.ActionEvent ae)
```

Example 10-1. The SimplePlayer application (continued)

```
            {
                exportMovie( );
            }
        });

        commandPanel.add(exportButton);

        this.getContentPane( ).add(commandPanel, "South");

        addWindowListener(new WindowAdapter( )
        {
            public void windowClosing(WindowEvent e)
            {
                // Go ahead and clean up the QuickTime layer
                quicktime.QTSession.close( );
                dispose( );
            }

            public void windowClosed(WindowEvent e)
            {
                System.exit(0);
            }
        });
    }


/* ----------------------- Importing Media ----------------------------- */

    public void importMedia( )
    {
        try
        {
            FileDialog myFileDialog =
            new FileDialog(this, "Choose Media to Import...", FileDialog.LOAD);

            myFileDialog.show( );

            if (myFileDialog.getFile( ) == null)
                return;

            QTFile importFile =
                new QTFile(myFileDialog.getDirectory() + myFileDialog.getFile(
));

            // You can import any supported media type into QuickTime using
            // the QTFactory.

            // QTFactory.makeDrawable( ) methods take a variety of inputs,
            // from URLs to an InputStream, and produce a usable media object.
            // The media object might represent a sound file (such as an MP3),
            // a picture (such as a GIF), or a full movie (such as a
            // QuickTime .mov)
```

Example 10-1. The SimplePlayer application (continued)

```
        quicktime.app.display.QTDrawable media = null;

        try
        {
            media = quicktime.app.QTFactory.makeDrawable(importFile);
        } catch (quicktime.QTException qtException)
        {
            // If not a user cancel, go ahead and report error
            if(qtException.getMessage( ).indexOf("cantFindHandler") > 0)
                qtException.printStackTrace( );
            else
            {
                java.awt.Toolkit.getDefaultToolkit().beep( );
                statusLabel.setText("Unable to open this file type.");
            }
        }

        if(media != null)
        {
            if (myQTCanvas == null)
            {
                myQTCanvas = new quicktime.app.display.QTCanvas( );
                this.getContentPane( ).add(myQTCanvas, "Center");
            }
            myQTCanvas.setClient(media, true);
            statusLabel.setText(importFile.getPath( ));

            // This resizes the UI. Note that the "preferred" size
            // for myQTCanvas has been changed to whatever works for
            // the player.
            pack( );
        }
    } catch (QTException err)
    {
        if (err.errorCode( ) == userCanceledErr) return;
        err.printStackTrace( );
    } catch (java.io.IOException ie)
    {}
}

/* ------------------------ Playing Movies ------------------------ */

public void displayMovie(Movie m) throws QTException
{
    // make a QTPlayer out of the Movie and set it as the
    // client of the QTCanvas

    quicktime.app.players.QTPlayer p =
      new quicktime.app.players.QTPlayer(
        new quicktime.std.movies.MovieController(m)
      );
```

Example 10-1. The SimplePlayer application (continued)

```
        if (myQTCanvas == null)
        {
            myQTCanvas = new quicktime.app.display.QTCanvas( );
            getContentPane( ).add(myQTCanvas, "Center");
        }

        myQTCanvas.setClient(p, true);
        pack( );
    }

/* ----------------------- QuickTime References ----------------------- */

    public void makeReferenceMovie( )
    {
        try
        {
            FileDialog rfd =
             new FileDialog(this, "Choose Movie to Reference...", FileDialog.
LOAD);
            rfd.show( );

            if (rfd.getFile( ) == null)
                return;

            QTFile movieFile = new QTFile(rfd.getDirectory() + rfd.getFile( ));

            FileDialog ofd =
             new FileDialog(this, "New Movie to create...", FileDialog.SAVE);

            ofd.show( );

            if (ofd.getFile( ) == null)
            {
                return;
            }

            makeReferenceMovie(movieFile, ofd.getDirectory() + ofd.getFile( ));
        } catch (QTException err)
        {
            if (err.errorCode( ) == userCanceledErr)
                return;
            err.printStackTrace( );
        }
    }

    //makes a new movie that references the data in an existing movie
    public void makeReferenceMovie(QTFile movieFile, String outputPath)
        throws QTException
    {
```

Example 10-1. The SimplePlayer application (continued)

```
      // Create the movie object from the original movie
      Movie theMovie = Movie.fromFile(quicktime.io.OpenMovieFile.
asRead(movieFile));

      displayMovie(theMovie);
      QTFile outputMovie = new QTFile(outputPath);

      //shortcut movies are movies that just contain a reference
      //to another movie.  It can begin to be complicated for users
      //to track which is which - you may wish to expose a flag
      //indicating handles to movies as opposed to flattened
      //movies in your user interface.

      //make a Data ref out of a URL that references the movie
      quicktime.std.movies.media.DataRef targetDataRef =
      new quicktime.std.movies.media.DataRef("file://" + movieFile.getPath());

      //make the very small short cut movie
      outputMovie.createShortcutMovieFile(
      kMoviePlayer, smSystemScript, createMovieFileDeleteCurFile,
targetDataRef);
    }


/* ----------------------- Exporting Movies ----------------------- */

    public void exportMovie()
    {
        try
        {

            FileDialog efd =
              new FileDialog(this, "Choose Movie to Export...", FileDialog.LOAD);

            efd.show();

            if (efd.getFile() == null)
                return;

            QTFile movieFile = new QTFile(efd.getDirectory() + efd.getFile());

            exportMovie(movieFile);
        } catch (QTException err)
        {
            err.printStackTrace();
        }
    }

    // export (to a movie) the incoming movie
    // user dialog allows user to customise media formats and
    // tracks that are exported
```

Example 10-1. The SimplePlayer application (continued)

```
public void exportMovie(QTFile movieFile) throws QTException
{
    // Create the movie object from the original movie
    Movie theMovie =
    Movie.fromFile(quicktime.io.OpenMovieFile.asRead(movieFile));

    displayMovie(theMovie);

    // we do this in a different thread because exporting can take some time
    // and the event thread should not be blocked for so long... but it tends
    // to really drag the UI anyways on Mac OS X for serious exporting.

    new Thread(
      new com.wiverson.macosbook.quicktime.SimpleMoviePlayer.Runner(
      theMovie, statusLabel)
    ).start( );
}

static class Runner implements Runnable
{
    Runner(Movie mov, JLabel inStatus)
    {
        theInputMovie = mov;
        status = inStatus;
    }

    Movie theInputMovie;
    JLabel status;

    public void run( )
    {

        try
        {
        // this determines both the exporter type, the resulting file type.
        // thus one could specify this to be AIFF and the resulting file will
        // be an AIFF file - in this case the result will be a movie.

            int exportType = kQTFileTypeMovie;

        //an application can alternatively configure exporter through setting
        //up the exporter in code to conform to the format appropriate

            FileDialog ofd =
        new FileDialog(new Frame( ), "Export Movie to...", FileDialog.SAVE);
            ofd.show( );
            if (ofd.getFile( ) == null)
                return;

            QTFile outFile = new QTFile(ofd.getDirectory() + ofd.getFile( ));
```

Example 10-1. The SimplePlayer application (continued)

```
                    // Create a movie exporter so we can customise its settings
                    // this could also be used in the convertToFile version, but
                    // if we don't have custom settings then we allow the convertToFile
                    // to create the exporter for us-based on the exportType we pass to it

                        quicktime.std.qtcomponents.MovieExporter theMovieExp =
                        new quicktime.std.qtcomponents.MovieExporter(exportType);

                    // Set export settings from the user.
                        theMovieExp.doUserDialog(
                    theInputMovie, null, 0, theInputMovie.getDuration( ));

                    //this returns a dupFNErr on windows and is also more work for
                    //the application create the output file but don't open it
                        outFile.createMovieFile(kMoviePlayer,
                        createMovieFileDeleteCurFile);

                        status.setText("Starting export...");
                        // do the export of the movie
                        theMovieExp.toFile(
                    outFile, theInputMovie, null, 0, theInputMovie.getDuration( ));
                        status.setText("Export complete.");
                    } catch (QTException e)
                    {
                        e.printStackTrace( );
                    }
                }
            }
        }
```

Imports and Startup

The class begins with a few basic QuickTime imports, including `quicktime. std.movies.Movie` (a core class that encapsulates a great deal of abstract media information). Then the `main( )` method merely sets the application up, initializing the QuickTime environment and then creating the user interface. The interest lies in the actual methods, as usual.

User Interface

The next chunk of code sets up the player's user interface, which has been kept simple so you can get to the good stuff. A few buttons are added to a window to let you select media types, and a few event listeners are created and attached. The most interesting portion of this code is the reference to `quicktime.app.display.QTCanvas`:

```
        // The QTCanvas is the "heavy lifter" QuickTime component
        // that does all the hard work for punching the QuickTime
```

```
// viewer through and into the JFrame.
quicktime.app.display.QTCanvas myQTCanvas;
```

This panel represents the QuickTime interface to media types. It's not actually added to the user interface until a user decides to load data, which you'll see in the next method, importMedia( ).

Importing Media

The importMedia( ) method lets you open any supported media type, not just a movie. Regardless of the format being loaded, it displays a standard file dialog box (configured by QuickTime), as shown in Figure 10-4.

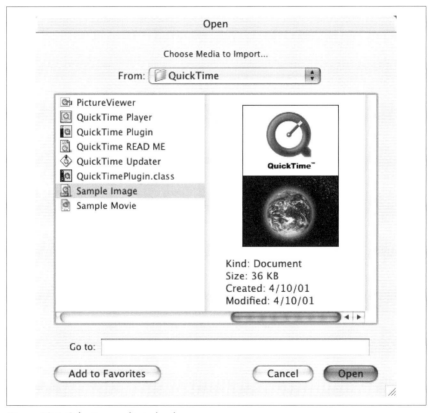

Figure 10-4. Selecting media to load

Assuming that the user selects a valid media file, the quicktime.app.display. QTCanvas object instance (discussed in the last section) is created and added to the Swing user interface, and the media file is set for that canvas (similar to a standard Java panel).

Look at the `quicktime.app.display.QTDrawable` object below. This object is the representation of a QuickTime data type. The media object might represent a sound file (such as an MP3), a picture (such as a GIF), or a full movie (such as a QuickTime *.mov* file). The `QTFactory` returns a playable `QTDrawable` media object when it's able to import from a URL successfully:

```
quicktime.app.display.QTDrawable media = null;

try
{
    media = quicktime.app.QTFactory.makeDrawable(importFile);
} catch (quicktime.QTException qtException)
{
    // If not a user cancel, go ahead and report error
    if(qtException.getMessage( ).indexOf("cantFindHandler") > 0)
        qtException.printStackTrace( );
    else
    {
        java.awt.Toolkit.getDefaultToolkit().beep( );
        statusLabel.setText("Unable to open this file type.");
    }
}

if(media != null)
{
    if (myQTCanvas == null)
    {
        myQTCanvas = new quicktime.app.display.QTCanvas( );
        this.getContentPane( ).add(myQTCanvas, "Center");
    }
    myQTCanvas.setClient(media, true);
    statusLabel.setText(importFile.getPath( ));

    // This resizes the UI. Note that the "preferred" size
    // for myQTCanvas has been changed to whatever works for
    // the player.
    pack( );
}
} catch (QTException err)
{
    if (err.errorCode( ) == userCanceledErr) return;
    err.printStackTrace( );
} catch (java.io.IOException ie)
{}
```

The complicated process of loading a file now becomes a matter of about 50 lines of code (including the user interface manipulation). This is one of the draws of the QuickTime APIs: they do a lot of the work for you, with minimal developer coding.

Playing a Movie

Once you've loaded the appropriate media types, playing them is simple. The displayMovie() method plays a QuickTime movie and is centered around the QTPlayer and QTCanvas objects:

```java
public void displayMovie(Movie m) throws QTException
{
    // make a QTPlayer out of the Movie and set it as the
    // client of the QTCanvas

    quicktime.app.players.QTPlayer p =
        new quicktime.app.players.QTPlayer(
            new quicktime.std.movies.MovieController(m)
        );

    if (myQTCanvas == null)
    {
        myQTCanvas = new quicktime.app.display.QTCanvas( );
        getContentPane( ).add(myQTCanvas, "Center");
    }

    myQTCanvas.setClient(p, true);
    pack( );
}
```

This method is largely a utility function, called when the current movie is changed. This method is called when the user loads another movie or changes the reference being used.

QuickTime References

QuickTime movies support the notion of *references* as well as direct data representations of media types. Imagine that you're editing a movie, and hours of video are stored on your hard drive. While you're working with the movie, you cut and paste several smaller movie pieces. It would be terribly inconvenient to copy hundreds of megabytes between files every time you select a section of video and then copy and paste; you'd have to watch your computer export the data, recompress it to fit into the rest of the stream, and then save the modified movie to disk again. This task would be very time consuming, as well as an inefficient use of your drive space.

A QuickTime reference, therefore, is an indirect way to point to a large media set without actually pointing to the entire set. It's very useful when you're editing a video or other large multimedia file. In fact, this player lets you create references for movies, which is accomplished programmatically through the makeReferenceMovie() methods. The first version, with no parameters, simply determines those parameters and calls the second overloaded version.

In the overloaded version of this method, the movie is loaded and played, and then a reference is created:

```
//make a Data ref out of a URL that references the movie
quicktime.std.movies.media.DataRef targetDataRef =
new quicktime.std.movies.media.DataRef("file://"  +
        movieFile.getPath( ));

//make the very small short cut movie
outputMovie.createShortcutMovieFile(
kMoviePlayer, smSystemScript,
    createMovieFileDeleteCurFile, targetDataRef);
}
```

Ultimately, the QuickTime API exports a movie as a reference rather than as a full copy. This is a fast operation—don't by shy about creating and using references this way.

Exporting Movies

The final portion of the application exports movies. This is the most complex part of the code, as quite a bit of work is involved in taking a movie and converting it into another format. First, the movie must be flattened. A *flattened* media file is self-contained, without references to other files on disk. This type of file is basically the converse of the references we just talked about—the flattened version is a single file with all of its movie content represented physically on disk (rather than with references to other files). Fortunately, the QuickTime API handles this task implicitly; you won't see any line of code like this:

```
theInputMovie.flatten( );
```

Instead, when you convert the movie to another format, the API handles this task transparently. This also happens automatically when you save the file out to disk, which is important for distribution of movies; you can't burn a reference of a movie onto a DVD, for example.

Flattening and exporting were handled in a separate thread. Unlike creating references, flattening takes a lot of time, especially when export formats are specified (for example, converting from one format of high-resolution video to another). While this separate thread still may not let a user do much other work, it at least keeps the player from "freezing" until the export is done, and even lets you create a nice process indicator for the user.

> Don't be too careless when flattening movies; the process is intensive and can take a lot of time. If you try to preempt the user and flatten movies with every edit, for example, you'll end up with a very unpleasant movie editing experience.

Running the Player

Once you've gotten the code entered, compiled, and ready to roll, fire up SimplePlayer. You should see the simple Swing interface, illustrated in Figure 10-5.

Figure 10-5. The Simple Player

Load up some QuickTime files (which have a *.mov* extension) and look at what the player can do. If you don't have any video available, you'll find some samples in */Applications (Mac OS 9)/iMovie/iMovie Tutorial/Media*. One is shown in the player in Figure 10-6.

Figure 10-6. Movie playback

As mentioned back in this section's introduction, SimplePlayer can also play back other media types, such as MP3 files. Figure 10-7 shows a little Johnny Cash blaring out of my Apple speakers. If you can play an audio or video format through your normal QuickTime player included with OS X, then you can play it with SimplePlayer.

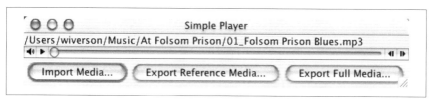

Figure 10-7. MP3 playback

Figure 10-8 demonstrates the player's export features, showing you the output file, as well as the export format and what encoding to use. You'll also see an "Options" button that you can select, and the resultant screen is shown in Figure 10-9. All these options are essentially "freebies"; the Quick-Time API handles them automatically, and you don't have to add any extra code to deal with them. In this way, users can adapt their multimedia to different outputs. For example, you could export a video clip in one format to support playback via the Web, or another for playback on a custom DVD.

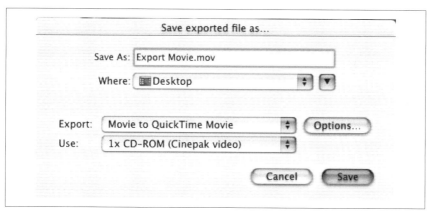

Figure 10-8. Export media

 While these options don't require extra code, they *do* require extra processing time. You may want to test them to see how they affect exporting video, but always be aware that advanced options can require extra time to execute.

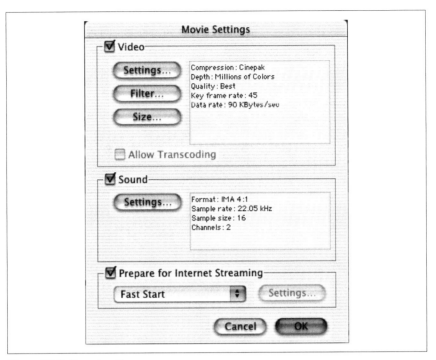

Figure 10-9. Export options

## CHAPTER 11

The Mac OS X Spelling Framework

Users (and developers) tend to be imperfect. In particular, most folks upon occasion miszpell a word or two. Because of this, integrated spellchecking is one of Mac OS X's most useful native APIs. Apple also makes available the Java Spelling Framework, a set of wrappers for the native spelling libraries included in your Mac OS X distribution. Like the Speech API and Quick-Time, these wrappers are part of the platform, and no special steps for using spelling are required beyond an extra download or two.

At its core, the Java Spelling Framework is refreshingly straightforward. It can be attached directly to a Swing text component to provide either interactive or real-time spellchecking. It can handle user interface complexity either automatically, or in a more programmatic fashion suitable for more sophisticated applications. It's easy to imagine using the Spelling API and the Java Servlet API to construct a web-based spellchecker for user-submitted text. You could aid users in searches, for example, by suggesting corrected spellings for misspelled words. You could even use this framework to build a fully featured GUI word processor. The possibilities are nearly limitless.

This chapter adds interactive and real-time spellcheck functionality to the SimpleEdit application constructed in Chapters 4 and 5. This functionality will give you a feel for the Spelling Framework and help you understand how it integrates into existing programs.

 If you've been browsing but haven't kept your code up to date with the examples, you'll need the example code from Chapter 4, along with the updates detailed in Chapter 5, to build the sample application in this chapter. You can also download this code online at the book's web site.

Getting Set Up

To get started, download the Spelling Framework from *ftp://ftp.apple.com/ developer/Sample_Code/Java/JavaSpellingFramework.sit*. Expanding the archive creates a folder called *JavaSpellingFramework* with the following contents:

```
build/
com/
doc/
Images/
Native/
JavaSpellingFramework.pbproj
ReadMe.txt
```

The *build* directory contains an example and is the target for other examples and compilation targets within the distribution. You'll find the source in the *com* directory, Javadoc for the source in the *doc* directory, and support files in the *Images* and *Native* directories. Project Builder uses the *.pbproj* file to assemble the project, and I'm sure you know what *ReadMe.txt* is all about.

Once you've expanded these files, build the project to create classes for use by your application. First, though, you might need to perform a few tweaks to get the code in the proper state for your platform.

Mac OS X 10.2

If you're running Mac OS X 10.2 or later, you'll need to take care of a few extra steps. First, rebuild the libraries to get them to work properly. Expand the *JavaSpellingFramework.sit* archive, and double-click on *JavaSpellingFramework.pbproj* to open the application in Project Builder. This will load up the entire framework, including its source files and images. In fact, the directory pane in Project Builder will look just like your Finder window, complete with all Spelling Framework directories and files, plus a few extras (the *.framework* files).

Once you open the project, navigate to the *JTxtCmpontDrvr.java* source file, as shown in Figure 11-1. You'll find this file in *Classes/com/apple/spell/ui*. Clicking on the file will open up the source in Project Builder. You should then navigate to line 230 or so, and uncomment lines 236 and 237:

```
if ((!ignoreWSIssue) && (!Character.isWhitespace(s.array[posOfChange])))
        return;
```

 Option-L in Project Builder is the shortcut to move to a specific line of code.

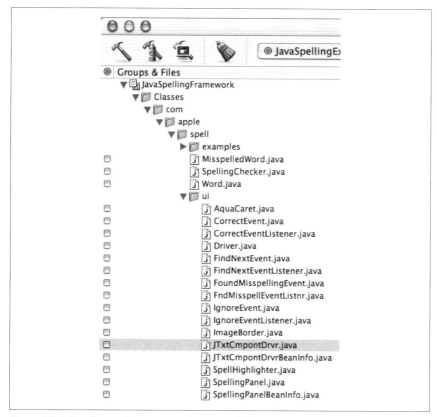

Figure 11-1. JtxtCmpontDrvr.java in Project Builder

You also need to change line 247:

```
while ((p0 < d.getLength())&& (!Character.isWhitespace(s.array[p1]))
                        && (p1 < d.getLength()))
    p1++;
```

The first change fixes a problem in which words are prematurely marked as errors, and the second change fixes an array-out-of-bounds error. By the time you read this, these errors may already be fixed in the code; just check it out in your own downloaded version. At this point, you're ready to build the framework.

Building the Framework

To compile the Spelling API, open the project in Project Builder (if you haven't already). Simply select "Build → Build...", as shown in Figure 11-2.

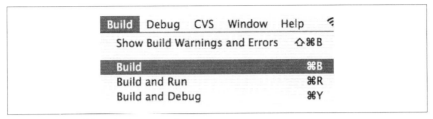

Figure 11-2. Building the framework

In my compilation, I received 10 warnings and no errors. You should expect similar results. If you do encounter errors, you may have introduced a typo when you made a change specified in the previous section. Check your changes and build again.

Once the build is successful, you will have libraries and samples in the target directory, *build*. Open this folder in the Finder, and you should see the generated files as shown in Figure 11-3.

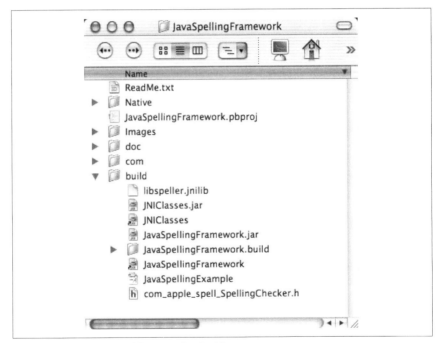

Figure 11-3. The spelling libraries after building

Setting Up the Java Environment

Now you need to ensure that your Java environment can access these libraries. The two files you should focus on are the native portion of the framework (packaged as a Java Native Interface library), *libspeller.jnilib*, and the Java classes, in *JavaSpellingFramework.jar*. Copy the *libspeller.jnilib* file to your *~/Library/Java/Extensions* directory (you'll need to create the *Java* and *Extensions* directories yourself), as shown in Figure 11-4.

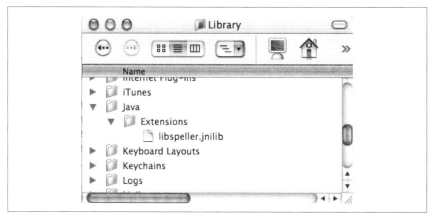

Figure 11-4. Installing the JNI Library

Now, as long as the *JavaSpellingFramework.jar* file is on your application's classpath, you'll be able to access the spelling functionality.

The Spelling API

The spelling kit offers several different layers of API. The selection of an API depends on the customization you wish to offer and the type of application you are building.

The com.apple.spell.SpellChecker class is the fundamental building block for spelling. This class contains several static methods that work with ordinary Java Strings. It lets you search for misspelled words, which are then returned as com.apple.spell.MisspelledWord objects. You can work with multiple languages, ask for suggestions, and add and remove words from the dictionary—all without worrying about the details of the underlying spellchecking engine. These classes do not, however, provide any sort of user interface.

The next layer of the API calls the method com.apple.spell.ui. JTextComponentDriver.checkSpelling(), passing in a javax.swing. JTextComponent to the method. This step invokes a standard spelling dialog (as shown in Figure 11-5). Alternatively, you can call com.apple.spell.ui. JTextComponentDriver.startRealtimeChecking() on a JTextComponent to get real-time spellchecking (in which spelling mistakes are underlined in red as the user enters incorrect words).

The third layer of the API registers event handlers to receive notifications when the com.apple.spell.ui.JTextComponentDriver class processes events such as finding a misspelled word or changing, correcting, or ignoring a word.

This design is attractive because it lets Swing applications add support for spellchecking. At the same time, less conventional applications can rely on the same underlying functionality to perform spellcheck with whatever custom user interface is desired.

Spelling in Action

Now that you have a basic understanding of the Spelling API, consider the actual code that uses it. As in previous chapters, this code should address any questions you might have and detail the use of spelling from a Java application.

User-Requested Spellchecking

You'll now add the ability to spellcheck the JTextArea of the SimpleEdit application created in Chapter 4. This modification allows the user to select "Spelling" from the "Tools" menu and run a spellcheck on SimpleEdit application text.

The plug-in mechanism adds this functionality, implementing the SimpleEditPlugin interface again. This makes interaction with SimpleEdit a piece of cake. Example 11-1 is the source code for this plug-in.

Example 11-1. A spellchecking plug-in

```
package com.wiverson.macosbook.spelling;

import com.wiverson.macosbook.SimpleEdit;

public class SpellCheckPlugin implements
    com.wiverson.macosbook.SimpleEditPlugin
{

    public SpellCheckPlugin( )
    {
    }

    public void doAction(SimpleEdit frame, java.awt.event.ActionEvent evt)
    {
        com.apple.spell.ui.JTxtCmpontDrvr mySpellchecker =
        new com.apple.spell.ui.JTxtCmpontDrvr( );
        mySpellchecker.checkSpelling(frame.getJTextArea( ));
    }
```

Example 11-1. A spellchecking plug-in (continued)

```
public String getAction( )
{
    return "Check Spelling...";
}

public void init(SimpleEdit frame)
{
}
```

}

There's very little to this code; no initialization is required, so only the doAction( ) method and a short getAction( ) method body need to be implemented. getAction( ) is self-explanatory, and doAction( ) just loads a text-area spellchecker and uses it to check spelling in the SimpleEdit text box.

To use this plug-in, make sure the *JavaSpellingFramework.jar* is on the classpath when you start the SimpleEdit application. Then launch the application, passing in the name of the plug-in as an argument. To launch from the command line, use a command like this:

```
java -cp .:JavaSpellingFramework.jar
    com.wiverson.macosbook.SimpleEdit
    com.wiverson.macosbook.spelling.SpellCheckPlugin
```

As shown in Figure 11-5, the spellchecking facility integrates seamlessly with the SimpleEdit application.

If more control over the modifications made by the spellchecker is needed, you can subclass the com.apple.spell.ui.JTxtCmpontDrvr class and override the methods handleFindNextEvent( ), handleFoundMisspellingEvent( ), handleIgnoreEvent( ), and handleCorrectEvent( ) for notification as the user interacts with the dialog.

Real-Time Spellchecking

As computers have gotten faster, the ability to perform real-time spellchecking in word processors has become increasingly popular. *Real-time spellchecking* simply means that the application checks spelling as you type without you having to make a specific request for this behavior. This feature is most commonly implemented by underlining misspelled words in red as the user types them. The spelling toolkit that Apple provides is powerful enough to support this feature, and you'll want to implement it in any word-processing applications you produce.

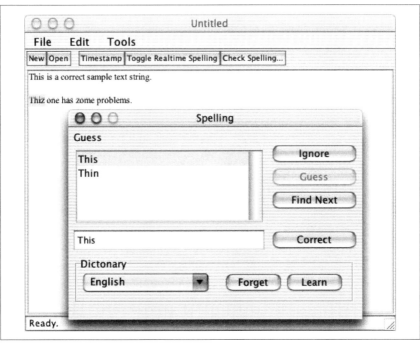

Figure 11-5. Interactive spellchecking

Use SimpleEdit's plug-in mechanism to add this functionality again, and the code turns out to be as simple as user-requested spell checking. Example 11-2 is the relevant plug-in code.

Example 11-2. Real-time spellchecking plug-in

```
package com.wiverson.macosbook.spelling;

import com.wiverson.macosbook.SimpleEdit;

public class RuntimeSpellPlugin implements
    com.wiverson.macosbook.SimpleEditPlugin
{

    public RuntimeSpellPlugin( )
    {
    }

    private boolean runtimespell = false;
    com.apple.spell.ui.JTxtCmpontDrvr mySpellchecker =
        new com.apple.spell.ui.JTxtCmpontDrvr( );

    public void doAction(SimpleEdit frame, java.awt.event.ActionEvent evt)
    {
```

Example 11-2. Real-time spellchecking plug-in (continued)

```
        if(!runtimespell)
        {
            mySpellchecker.startRealtimeChecking(frame.getJTextArea( ));
        } else
        {
            mySpellchecker.stopRealtimeChecking( );
        }
        runtimespell = !runtimespell;
    }

    public String getAction( )
    {
        return "Toggle Realtime Spelling";
    }

    public void init(SimpleEdit frame)
    {
    }
}
```

The doAction( ) method handles the important work. It merely has to start and stop the interactive spellchecker based upon the state of the runtimespell flag. This step lets the user turn real-time spellchecking on and off easily without adding complexity to your plug-in code.

As shown in Figure 11-6, words that the user types are now highlighted with a dotted red underscore. If the user Control-clicks (or, if using a two-button mouse, right-clicks) on a word, a pop-up menu with suggestions appears. It's a lot of functionality for such a minor addition.

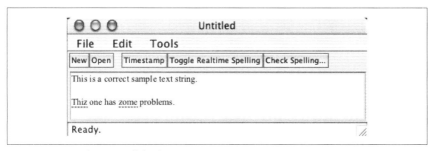

Figure 11-6. Real-time spellcheck

When you use the real-time spellcheck capability, new words that the user types are checked, but cut-and-pasted words are not, and words are not rechecked if the real-time checking is turned off and then back on. Fortunately, the Java source layer provided by Apple's toolkit controls this behavior, and you can customize it to add more functionality (for example, by integrating default language choices into your own preferences).

Custom Spellchecking

So far, you've dealt with spelling only in GUI applications. However, you might want to implement spellchecking in an application that doesn't use Swing controls or that operates at a lower level. In these cases, you should bypass the com.apple.spell.ui package and drop into the base spelling package, com.apple.spell. Here, you'll find several useful items that don't assume the existence of a user interface.

The com.apple.spell.SpellingChecker class provides lower-level access to the Mac OS X Spelling API. It's simple to use, as it's simply comprised of several static methods. The method signatures are shown here:

```
// Locates the first misspelled word in a String
MisspelledWord findMisspelledWordInString(String in, String language);

// Finds a misspelled word with an offset.
MisspelledWord findFirstMisspelledWord(String in, int startingAt, String langauge);

// Gives suggestions for a word, or use the method on MisspelledWord
String[] suggestGuessesForWord(String word, String language);

// Adds a custom word to the dictionary, useful for jargon.
boolean learnWord(String word, String language);

// Removes a custom word from the dictionary.
boolean forgetWord(String word, String language);
```

If you want to work with these APIs, first call SpellingChecker. getAvailableLanguages( ) to identify the installed languages on the system you're working with. Then the other static methods can be called; each is used by passing in a section of text and the preferred language to spell in.

These APIs work naturally with ordinary Java Strings. If you expect to deal with large quantities of text, develop a model in which spellchecking operates on another thread to avoid user interface deadlocks, passing in a paragraph or a fixed quantity of text to be checked.

Imagine using this API to provide a variety of interesting services, such as adding spellchecking capabilities to web applications via JSP or servlets—which would allow users of non–Mac OS X platforms to enjoy one of Mac OS X's most useful features. Familiarizing yourself with the Spelling API does more than just improve your Swing applications; it can make your programming more user-friendly.

## CHAPTER 12

Databases

The last few chapters have dealt largely with features specific to GUI applications. Speech, spelling, and QuickTime are generally used to provide rich desktop experiences. As you might expect, these applications are commonly packaged as standalone applications (detailed in Chapter 7), or at least as desktop applications delivered via the Web (detailed in Chapter 8).

However, sometimes an application needs to be controlled by, and staged on, a remote server. Online stores like Amazon.com come immediately to mind here—these applications cannot reside on a user's desktop. Additionally, speech and QuickTime become non-choices, as the remote application knows little (if anything) about the users visiting their web sites. These applications, when housed on remote servers, are called *web applications*. They are generally more complex than the applications discussed so far, both in development and packaging. They spread out over multiple servers in many cases, and involve the enterprise Java APIs. Of course, Mac OS X is still a great platform on which to develop these applications, and the next several chapters will explore this aspect of the Mac.

Once you move into the world of web applications, you'll begin to hear about databases. Like any good operating system, Mac OS X boasts several good database products, most notably from the open source suite of software. This chapter explains the basics of databases, and then takes a brief survey of popular databases for the Mac OS X platform.

Basic Concepts

A database, at its simplest, is an application that keeps track of data in a structured manner. By this definition, you could think of a spreadsheet as a type of database—you work with data in rows, columns, and tables. You input data, and then add functions to perform sums and other calculations on the data. In the Java world, however, a database typically refers to a relational database. A *relational database* also stores data in rows and columns, but locates them within larger data components called tables. Additionally, relational databases allow keys between these tables, building the relationships for which the database type is named.

SQL

When learning about relational databases, you'll hear the term *Structured Query Language* (SQL), which is the language you will use to access a relational database. SQL works with any relational database and underlies the many GUI tools you will see for working with these types of databases.

To solidify these concepts, look at some examples. Consider a simple database table, as defined in Table 12-1.

Table 12-1. A simple database table

ID	First	Last	Email
1	Will	Iverson	wiverson@ix.netcom.com
2	Bob	Smith	bob@bobsmith.com

Much like a spreadsheet, the data in the database is stored in columns (ID, First, Last, Email) and rows (in this case, two rows of data). The ID column is commonly used when working with relational databases. It generally provides a unique ID for each row, used by other tables that may need to reference that row.

 While an ID column is almost always used in relational databases, it is not required. Additionally, it sometimes exists but has a different name, such as row-id or identifier.

When communicating with a relational database, send SQL commands like:

```
SELECT ID, First, Last
  FROM SimpleTable
  WHERE ID=1
```

Essentially, the first line specifies the columns to select, the second line indicates which database table is desired, and the third line indicates a selection criterion. Using the sample data in Table 12-1 would return the first row of data. Here are several other simple SQL statements:

```
SELECT Email
  FROM SimpleTable
  WHERE Last = 'Smith'
```

```
SELECT First, Last
  FROM SimpleTable
 WHERE Email LIKE '%netcom.com'
 ORDER BY Last, First
```

The real strength of relational databases, however, lies in their ability to issue relational queries—in effect "stitching" together the data in two or more tables with a single query:

```
SELECT s.First, s.Last, p.PhoneNumber
  FROM SimpleTable s, PhoneNumberTable p
 WHERE p.PersonID = s.ID
   AND s.Last = 'Iverson'
```

For example, suppose you have a customers table and an orders table. You could issue a single query against both tables, asking for the most recent order for each customer:

```
SELECT c.first, c.last, o.description
  FROM customers c, orders o
 WHERE o.customerID = c.ID
 GROUP BY o.customerID
 HAVING MAX(o.orderDate)
```

An in-depth description of SQL is beyond the scope of this book, but it's a powerful, popular way to express data and queries against that data.

Having to learn another programming language (such as SQL) when you start working with Java can be daunting, but learning SQL is easier than writing your own database. SQL has also become an extremely popular language; even if you decide to switch to another programming language in the future, that new language will probably possess a mechanism for interacting with databases via SQL.

Mac OS X Databases

The rest of this chapter will walk through the installation of popular databases on the Mac OS X platform. Each database has pros and cons, and your decision to use a specific database will probably depend on its performance, functionality, and price. You should browse the O'Reilly library for more extensive coverage of these databases before making your final decision.

MySQL

MySQL is a popular, lightweight, open source relational database. Many developers support it, which makes it an ideal database on which to start the RDBMS learning process. Over the years, MySQL has evolved, adding an increasingly broad range of sophisticated features. Still, its most popular use is as a storage mechanism for dynamic web applications—specifically those built using open source languages such as Perl and PHP. It is also an extraordinarily solid database for small, JSP-based web applications.

Installation

Installing MySQL on Mac OS X is fairly straightforward. First download a distribution of MySQL. A prebuilt Mac OS X binary is available at *http://www.mysql.com/downloads/*.

 Currently, an ideal download is MySQL 3.23, which is the one you'll use here. You can get it at *http://www.mysql.com/downloads/mysql-3.23.html*.

Scrolling through the list, you'll notice versions available for Windows, Solaris, FreeBSD, and Mac OS X. The availability of a Windows version sometimes makes MySQL a better choice than PostgreSQL (discussed later in this chapter).

The specific version used here is MySQL 3.23.55 for Mac OS X 10.2. You might notice that the last revision number for MySQL is updated frequently. Be sure to stay on top of the release notes to look for bug fixes for problems you may have.

When you click on the download link (I grabbed the "Standard" version rather than the "Max" version) and select a mirror site, you'll end up with a *.tar.gz* file. Double-click on it, and assuming your StuffIt Expander is installed, the file will be expanded into a new folder called *mysql-3.23.55-apple-darwin6.1-powerpc*. Move this folder into a location you can remember. For the rest of this discussion, assume that the files are installed in */Developer/mysql-3.23*.

 The folder/directory name is shortened to make it easier to type, but the version number remains to ensure that you can easily remember which version you are using. Later, you may wish to test or upgrade to another version, and you'll want this version information to keep things straight.

Next, go to the Apple menu, select "System Preferences...", and click on "Users." Add a new user, name the user mysql (for both the full name and the short name), and select an icon for that user.

Don't forget to assign a password to the mysql user (and remember the password). You can also use the NetInfo Manager to create new users that won't be visible in login screens, without a home directory, etc. For more information on NetInfo, consult *Mac OS X for Unix Geeks* by Brian Jepson and Ernest E. Rothman (O'Reilly).

Once you've installed MySQL, you'll need to perform some additional steps to get it running on your system. Open up the terminal, and navigate to the *bin* directory of the folder where you placed your MySQL installation.

Issue the commands as shown here to complete the software portion of the installation:

```
[localhost:~] wiverson% cd /Developer/mysql-3.23
[localhost:/Developer/mysql-3.23] wiverson% ./scripts/mysql_install_db
```

Now, set the permissions for the various directories:

```
[localhost:/Developer/mysql-3.23] wiverson% sudo chown -R mysql ./data
[localhost:/Developer/mysql-3.23] wiverson% sudo chown -R mysql *
[localhost:/Developer/mysql-3.23] wiverson% sudo chown -R root ./bin/*
```

This code assumes you created the mysql user, so be sure it is created before attempting these steps.

Starting MySQL

Now launch the server:

```
[localhost:/Developer/mysql-3.23] wiverson% sudo ./bin/safe_mysqld &
```

 If you have already performed a sudo in the last five minutes or so, you'll be able to execute this command with the & to put it in the background. If a longer time period has elapsed since sudo-ing in, though, you may be prompted for an administrative password. If you're having trouble, open a new terminal and execute the command without the &, or execute a sudo ls to force a password check.

Next, set passwords for MySQL's default administrator account. Follow the steps shown here (replace the text "groovy" with your choice of password, but retain the quotation marks):

```
[localhost:/Developer/mysql-3.23.47] wiverson% sudo ./bin/mysqladmin -u root
-p password 'groovy'
[localhost:/Developer/mysql-3.23.47] wiverson% sudo ./bin/mysqladmin -u root
-h localhost -p password 'groovy'
```

Now test the connection to the database:

```
[localhost:/Developer/mysql-3.23.47] wiverson% ./bin/mysql --user root --
password
Enter password:
Reading table information for completion of table and column names
You can turn off this feature to get a quicker startup with -A

Welcome to the MySQL monitor.  Commands end with ; or \g.
Your MySQL connection id is 6 to server version: 3.23.54

Type 'help;' or '\h' for help. Type '\c' to clear the buffer.

mysql>
```

After being prompted for the administrator password, you should see a
MySQL status message go by that displays the database connection ID and
server version. At the mysql> prompt, enter the show databases; command:

```
mysql> show databases;
+----------+
| Database |
+----------+
| macjava  |
| mysql    |
| test     |
+----------+
3 rows in set (0.00 sec)

mysql>
```

You should see a formatted display listing the mysql and test databases.
Type exit at the prompt, and you'll return to the command shell.

Stopping MySQL

Shut down the database by entering the following command:

```
[localhost:/Developer/mysql-3.23.47] wiverson% ./bin/mysqladmin --user=root
--password shutdown
```

As you can see, most of the work around MySQL involves the mysqladmin
and mysql commands. You should play around and become familiar with
them, as they will be your mainstay in database work.

Creating a database

Now that you've gotten a handle on the basics, restart the database and get
back into the MySQL monitor shell by executing the commands shown here:

```
[localhost:/Developer/mysql-3.23.47] wiverson% sudo ./bin/safe_mysqld &
[localhost:/Developer/mysql-3.23.47] wiverson% ./bin/mysql --user root -
passwords
```

You'll be prompted again for a password. At the MySQL prompt, create a new database and user. Replace the text "special" with your own password, retaining the quotation marks:

```
mysql> create database macjava
Query OK, 1 row affected (0.00 sec)
mysql> grant all on macjava.* to javadev@localhost identified by "special";
Query OK, 0 rows affected (0.00 sec)
mysql> exit
```

Working with a database

Before issuing SQL commands to work with a database, log back in to the database:

```
[localhost:/Developer/mysql-3.23.47] wiverson% ./bin/mysql --user javadev --
password macjava
```

After entering your password again, you'll see the mysql> prompt. To start working with the macjava database, type the following command:

```
mysql> use macjava
Database changed
```

You're now all set to begin adding tables, columns, and data to the database. To test this code, enter some SQL as shown:

```
mysql> select now( );
+---------------------+
| now( )              |
+---------------------+
| 2003-01-05 00:02:34 |
+---------------------+
1 row in set (0.14 sec)

mysql>
```

 To learn how to create tables and add sample data, see the next chapter.

MySQL JDBC configuration

You can download the MySQL JDBC driver (now known as Connector/J) from *http://www.mysql.com/downloads/api-jdbc-stable.html* (follow the links to a local mirror). Make sure the resultant JAR file (*mysql-connector-java-2.0.14-bin.jar* in my case) is on your classpath.

If using Version 2.0.14 or later, you'll use com.mysql.jdbc.Driver as your driver class (prior releases used org.gjt.mm.mysql.Driver). The JDBC connection URL is in the form *jdbc:mysql://127.0.0.1/databasename*. Replace

127.0.0.1 with the hostname of your MySQL server, and you know what to do with *databasename*.

PostgreSQL

PostgreSQL is another popular open source database. Like MySQL, Postgre-SQL is free, easy to run, and great for development work. While it doesn't offer a native installation for the Windows platforms, it is a little heavier-duty than MySQL, so it often finds a place in open source production environments.

Installation

The easiest way to install PostgreSQL is to download a prebuilt package from *http://www.osxgnu.org/software/Database/postgresql/*. PostgreSQL prebuilt binaries for Mac OS X currently have some serious problems, though.

 As of February 2003, the latest posted version (7.1.3) was built with support for a command history in the interactive "psql" interpreter using the up and down keys, and it includes the JDBC drivers (in */usr/local/pgsql/share/java*). Unfortunately, this package is not currently compatible with Mac OS X 10.2.

Therefore, the other way to install PostgreSQL on Mac OS X is to download and install it from the source available at *http://www.postgres.org/*. Select a mirror location close to you, and then download the source for the database project. In this instance, you'll use the *postgres-7.2.3.tar.gz* release.

Create a new user in the "Users" System Preferences pane with the name "PostgreSQL User", the short name "postgres", and whatever password you want. Log out of Mac OS X, log back in as this user, and uncompress the *postgres-7.2.3.tar.gz* file in your *~/Documents* directory.

 As noted in the MySQL section, using NetInfo to create a user without a home directory is a good security practice.

Then open the Terminal and execute the commands shown here from the new PostgreSQL installation directory:

```
[localhost:~/Documents/postgresql-7.2.3] wiverson% cd src/include/port/
darwin
[localhost:include/port/darwin] wiverson% mv sem.h sem.orig.h
```

```
[localhost:include/port/darwin] wiverson% echo '#include <sys/sem.h>' > sem.
h
[localhost:include/port/darwin] wiverson% more sem.h
#include <sys/sem.h>
[localhost:include/port/darwin] wiverson% cd ../../../backend/port
```

This code fixes some issues in the *sem.h* file included with the distribution; these fixes are critical, so don't omit this step!

Next, comment out a few lines in the file *Makefile.in*, located in your installation's *src/backend/port* directory. If you have followed these instructions, the complete path to this file would be *~/Documents/postgresql-7.2.3/src/backend/ port/Makefile.in*. Use the # character to comment out the lines shown here:

```
...
#ifeq ($(PORTNAME), darwin)
#OBJS += darwin/SUBSYS.o
#endif
...
```

 The easiest way to do this from the command line is to use the pico text editor. You can search for this text and quickly find it using pico and the Control-W "Where is" shortcut.

Finally, after making these fixes, you can compile and install the database:

```
[localhost:src/backend/port] wiverson% cd ~/Documents/postgresql-7.2.3
[localhost:~/Documents/postgresql-7.2.3] wiverson% ./configure --mandir=/
usr/local/share/man --with-openssl=/usr/lib --enable-recode
creating cache ./config.cache
checking host system type... powerpc-apple-darwin6.3
checking which template to use... darwin
checking whether to build with locale support... no
checking whether to build with recode support... yes
checking whether to build with multibyte character support... no
checking whether NLS is wanted... no

...omitted for brevity...

linking ./src/include/port/darwin.h to src/include/pg_config_os.h
linking ./src/makefiles/Makefile.darwin to src/Makefile.port
linking ./src/backend/port/tas/dummy.s to src/backend/port/tas.s
[localhost:~/Documents/postgresql-7.2.3] wiverson% make
make -C doc all
gzip -d -c man.tar.gz | /usr/bin/tar xf -
for file in man1/*.1; do \
  mv $file $file.bak && \
  sed -e 's/\\fR(l)/\\fR(7)/' $file.bak >$file && \
  rm $file.bak || exit; \
done
/bin/sh ../config/mkinstalldirs man7
mkdir man7
```

```
for file in manl/*.l; do \
  sed -e '/^\.TH/s/"l"/"7"/' \
            -e 's/\\fR(l)/\\fR(7)/' \
      $file >man7/`basename $file | sed 's/.l$/.7/'` || exit; \
done
make -C src all
```

...omitted for brevity...

```
tsort: pl_comp.o
ranlib libplpgsql.a
gcc -traditional-cpp -g -O2 -Wall -Wmissing-prototypes -Wmissing-
declarations -Wno-error  -flat_namespace -bundle -undefined suppress pl_
gram.o pl_scan.o pl_handler.o pl_comp.o pl_exec.o pl_funcs.o    -o
libplpgsql.so.1.0
rm -f libplpgsql.so.1
ln -s libplpgsql.so.1.0 libplpgsql.so.1
rm -f libplpgsql.so
ln -s libplpgsql.so.1.0 libplpgsql.so
All of PostgreSQL successfully made. Ready to install.
[localhost:~/Documents/postgresql-7.2.3] wiverson% sudo make install
make -C doc install
gzip -d -c postgres.tar.gz | ( cd /usr/local/pgsql/doc/html && /usr/bin/tar
xf - )
for file in man1/*.1 man7/*.7 ; do \
  /bin/sh ../config/install-sh -c -m 644 $file /usr/local/share/man/$file ||
exit; \
done
make -C src install
```

...omitted for brevity...

```
Thank you for choosing PostgreSQL, the most advanced open source database
engine.

[localhost:~/Documents/postgresql-7.2.3] wiverson%
```

> Some of these commands can take time to execute (several
> minutes or more), and no user feedback will be provided.

You've now installed PostgreSQL on your system. When you're done, the resulting PostgreSQL installation is stored at *usr/local/pgsql*, with the relevant PostgreSQL commands available at *usr/local/pgsql/bin*.

Initializing PostgreSQL

Next, configure a test data set. Execute the following commands to initialize a database:

```
[localhost:local/pgsql/bin] wiverson% su - postgres
Password:
[localhost:~] postgres% mkdir ~/pgsql
[localhost:~] postgres% mkdir ~/pgsql/data
[localhost:~] postgres% cd /usr/local/pgsql/bin/
[localhost:local/pgsql/bin] postgres% ./initdb -D ~/pgsql/data
The files belonging to this database system will be owned by user
"postgres".
This user must also own the server process.

Fixing permissions on existing directory /Users/postgres/pgsql/data... ok
creating directory /Users/postgres/pgsql/data/base... ok
creating directory /Users/postgres/pgsql/data/global... ok
creating directory /Users/postgres/pgsql/data/pg_xlog... ok
creating directory /Users/postgres/pgsql/data/pg_clog... ok
creating template1 database in /Users/postgres/pgsql/data/base/1... ok
creating configuration files... ok
initializing pg_shadow... ok
enabling unlimited row size for system tables... ok
creating system views... ok
loading pg_description... ok
vacuuming database template1... ok
copying template1 to template0... ok

Success. You can now start the database server using:

    ./postmaster -D /Users/postgres/pgsql/data
or
    ./pg_ctl -D /Users/postgres/pgsql/data -l logfile start

[localhost:local/pgsql/bin] postgres% ./postmaster -D /Users/postgres/pgsql/
data
DEBUG:  database system was shut down at 2003-01-04 23:38:21 PST
DEBUG:  checkpoint record is at 0/1096F4
DEBUG:  redo record is at 0/1096F4; undo record is at 0/0; shutdown TRUE
DEBUG:  next transaction id: 89; next oid: 16556
DEBUG:  database system is ready
```

You're now running the PostgreSQL server, and any status information will be echoed to the console. Press Control-C in the terminal; this will cause PostgreSQL to shut down. If you haven't already, log out of the postgres user account and log back in with your regular account.

Starting PostgreSQL

Open a new Terminal window and execute the commands shown below to start PostgreSQL:

```
[localhost:/usr/local/pgsql] postgres% cd /usr/local/pgsql/
[localhost:/usr/local/pgsql] postgres% ./bin/postmaster -i -D ~/pgsql/data/
>& ~/pgsql/log &
[1] 10524
[localhost:/usr/local/pgsql] postgres%
```

The su - postgres command lets you masquerade as the postgres user (you'll need to enter the postgres user's password as well), so you don't have to constantly log out and log in as different users. When you execute the postmaster command, the server's output will be sent to the ~/*pgsql/log* file.

 PostgreSQL reports much of its information by using the STDERR output stream (not just STDOUT), and the >&~/pgsql/ log sequence tells the shell to redirect output to a file instead of to these output streams. The final & tells the shell that this process should be run in the background.

You can monitor the output of this file by executing the command tail -501f ~/pgsql/log:

```
[localhost:~] postgres% tail -501f ~/pgsql/log
DEBUG:  database system was shut down at 2003-01-04 23:42:58 PST
DEBUG:  checkpoint record is at 0/109734
DEBUG:  redo record is at 0/109734; undo record is at 0/0; shutdown TRUE
DEBUG:  next transaction id: 89; next oid: 16556
DEBUG:  database system is ready
```

Stopping PostgreSQL

You can shut the server down by executing the command ps to find the process ID (PID) of the postmaster process, which you can then terminate by issuing a kill *PID* command, where *PID* is the postmaster process ID:

```
[localhost:/usr/local/pgsql] postgres% ps | grep postmaster
10524 std  S       0:00.05 ./bin/postmaster -i -D /Users/postgres/pgsql/data/
10531 std  R+      0:00.00 grep postmaster
[localhost:/usr/local/pgsql] postgres% kill 10524
[localhost:/usr/local/pgsql] postgres%
```

Creating a database

Now you can work with PostgreSQL data as a user. Make sure the database is running as described above. As the postgres user, execute the /usr/local/ pgsql/bin/createuser command. Use your main account's short name from the "System Preferences → Accounts" dialog for the username, and allow database creation for new users.

Next, open a new Terminal window and execute the createdb command to create your own database. You'll want to supply your own database name, of course:

```
[localhost:/usr/local/pgsql] postgres% ./bin/createdb macjava
CREATE DATABASE
[localhost:/usr/local/pgsql] postgres%
```

Working with a database

Now you're ready to work with the psql program, an interactive SQL tool:

```
[localhost:/usr/local/pgsql] postgres% ./bin/psql macjava
Welcome to psql, the PostgreSQL interactive terminal.

Type:  \copyright for distribution terms
       \h for help with SQL commands
       \? for help on internal slash commands
       \g or terminate with semicolon to execute query
       \q to quit

macjava=#
```

Use the name of the database you just created. You can use this program to enter SQL commands that execute directly against the database:

```
macjava=# select now( );
              now
------------------------------
 2003-01-04 23:59:14.946273-08
(1 row)

macjava=#
```

When you're done working in the psql shell, enter \q and press return.

PostgreSQL JDBC configuration

To start working with PostgreSQL via JDBC, you will need the JDBC drivers available at *http://jdbc.postgresql.org/download.html* and the Postgres 7.2 JDBC 2 release (*pgjdbc2.jar*). To work with PostgreSQL, make sure that this file is on your classpath.

The driver name is org.postgresql.Driver, and the JDBC connection URL (which connects to the database you just created) is in the form *jdbc: postgresql://127.0.0.1/databasename*.

Oracle 9i

One important validation of Mac OS X has been its release of commercial database products for the platform. The database world still largely revolves around the folks at Oracle, so there is perhaps no more important database product for Mac OS X than a release of Oracle. Happily, it's now possible to download a developer version of Oracle 9*i* specifically tailored for use with Mac OS X 10.2 from *http://otn.oracle.com/software/products/oracle9i/content.html*. Click on the "Take a Survey" link to register, and you can then download the software. If you're connecting to an existing Oracle 9*i* instance, you'll just need the JDBC drivers; otherwise, download the entire database for installation on your platform.

Oracle 9i is a very complex product, so if you're just starting to work with SQL databases, it is not the easiest place to begin. Beginning with MySQL or PostgreSQL is much easier.

 To get an idea of how complex Oracle is, note that the Post-greSQL 7.1.2 release is a little over 5 MB, whereas Oracle 9i weighs 345 MB. While a release's size isn't always indicative of its productivity, it usually says something about the complexity of the software involved.

For more information on Oracle 9i, and for guidelines on adopting it for your application development, read the overview at O'Reilly's MacDev-Center.com: *http://www.macdevcenter.com/pub/a/mac/2002/11/12/oracle_part1.html*. You should also check out *Oracle in a Nutshell*, by Rick Greenwald and David Kreines, and *Java Programming with Oracle JDBC*, by Donald Bales (both from O'Reilly).

Next Steps

This chapter introduces you to SQL and helps you install two popular (and free) databases for Mac OS X. SQL is a rich language for working with very large data sets, and you are strongly encouraged to look at the following O'Reilly texts for more information:

- *Database Programming with JDBC and Java*, by George Reese
- *Managing & Using MySQL*, by George Reese, Randy Jay Yarger, and Tim King
- *SQL in a Nutshell*, by Kevin Kline
- *Practical PostgreSQL*, by John C. Worsley and Joshua D. Drake

The following chapter uses the MySQL database to build a simple web application.

## CHAPTER 13

Servlets, JSP, and Tomcat

Most users are familiar with HTML, and virtually everyone who owns a computer today is familiar with web browsers. The previous chapter introduced relational databases, but didn't discuss how to web-enable the information you're storing. This chapter covers that topic and provides a way for you to put a face on your web application. If you're already a web or J2EE developer, much of this material will be familiar, although you'll encounter several Mac OS X twists along the way. If you've never played in the enterprise Java space, this chapter should whet your appetite for Mac OS X and get you moving in the right direction.

This chapter assumes that you've installed a database (in particular, MySQL) and that you'd now like to present information to the end user. Two Java technologies are ideal for this task: JavaServer Pages (JSP) and Java servlets. JSP is a specification and technology that lets a developer create HTML pages with embedded bits of Java code. Servlets are a more code-oriented technology and are not based on HTML pages; however, they still simplify HTML generation, and are excellent for producing web-based user interfaces. This chapter details how to run these components in your Mac OS X environment.

Apache Tomcat

To run JSPs and servlets, you'll need a container that takes the output of these components and displays it to the user. The ideal choice for this task is the Tomcat web container. Tomcat is the Apache-sponsored, open source, official reference servlet container implementation of the Java servlet and JavaServer Pages technologies. Those of you who know this topic well can skip to the next section. For those of you who are new to Tomcat, a few words are in order.

A Brief History of Tomcat

Originally, simple web servers delivered static HTML documents to web browsers. An important legacy of this era can be found on every Mac OS X machine: the web-sharing feature under "System Preferences → Sharing → File & Web" is a full version of the famous Apache httpd, one of the original web servers. Apache is a robust, powerful, well-supported web server, but on its own, its capabilities for serving dynamic content are limited. A web page returned by Apache is (mostly) the static document on disk.

To address the increasing need for dynamic content, a number of technologies were developed for Apache. They were integrated into the server as plug-ins, and allowed Apache to add to its feature set. These plug-ins ranged from support for Perl-based CGI scripts to the ability to run C++-based extensions. Many extensions were limited, however. They often introduced additional overhead, many times disproportional to the amount of functionality added. A growing number of common tasks were also of interest, such as standardized mechanisms for connecting to a database and presenting dynamically generated documents.

Further down the web-container timeline, developers began to notice that Java had several advantages for these sorts of tasks. The Java runtime environment had many desirable features, the most significant of which were integrated support for a rich threading model, a rich exception model for handling failure states, and an existing API for connection to relational databases (referred to as JDBC). The threading model reduced the large overhead that CGI scripts were creating on Apache, and the core Java API simplified common tasks such as database access and content generation. However, the core Java API still did not integrate tightly with HTML, and forced developers to handle a lot of common networking tasks on their own.

At this point, the Java Servlet specification entered the scene. In many ways, this specification developed as a standard way to write Java-based plug-ins for web servers. Today, these servlets are typically installed in their own specialized server, called an application server or web container. A servlet is essentially a lump of Java code that takes in a request (usually via HTTP) and writes out a response (usually delivered by HTTP). Generally, users would form their response with an output stream, as in the following Java code:

```
out.print("<A HREF='..\\index.jsp'>");
out.print("<IMG SRC='images\\titlebar.gif'>");
out.println("</A>");
for(int i = 0; i < 5; i++)
    out.println(i + "<BR>");
```

As you can see, this API hides all the details of network connection and buffering output formation; the developer simply spits out HTML, and the web container converts it to a graphical interface. However, Java was still largely a developer language. Web designers wanted the same ability to produce dynamic content, and Java and servlets were too complex for the typical HTML designer.

Additionally, developers using servlets soon noticed that they spent significant amounts of time massaging their HTML to fit in Java source, which was a poor way to encourage a division of labor between the HTML web monkeys and the Java coders. This (and the growing popularity of a similar technology from Microsoft, ASP) led to the development of JavaServer Pages. In a very real sense, JSP is an inverted version of a servlet. The code above written as a JSP fragment would look like this:

```
<A HREF='..\index.jsp'>
<IMG SRC='images\titlebar.gif'>
</A>
<%
for(int i = 0; i < 5; i++) {
%>
<%= i %>
<BR>
<% } %>
```

Note that you are now writing HTML, with the Java code broken out into script sections identified by <% ... %> and <%= ... %>.

At first, the advantage of this JSP syntax over the servlet code may not be obvious. However, the advantages can be significant, especially if you are doing a lot of web design and interface creation. One of the most important differences is that most web developers (as well as web design tools, such as Macromedia's Dreamweaver MX) are comfortable working with the bits of escaped Java source in a JSP page, but there is no such thing as a visual layout tool for servlets.

The final piece of this puzzle, and history, is the entry of Tomcat. Tomcat is an open source version of the code that was originally part of Sun's Java Web Server Development Kit. It has now moved far beyond those initial pieces of code and become a rich, complex web container within which servlets and JSP pages can run.

Installing and Starting Tomcat

To get started with Tomcat, download the latest stable release of Tomcat, currently Version 4.1.8, located at *http://jakarta.apache.org/tomcat/*. Click on the *Binaries* link under the *Download* section to visit another section, which describes the meanings of various builds and a list of other Apache projects. Click on the *Tomcat* link under *Release Builds* to see a list of the current builds, with links determined by the mirrored site you prefer.

You could encounter a bug in some implementations of the default Mac OS X un-tarring utility, so err on the side of caution and download the ZIP version rather than a TAR distribution. These instructions download the file *http://www.rge.com/pub/infosystems/apache/jakarta/tomcat-4/binaries/tomcat-4.1.18.zip*. Make sure you know where on your system the downloaded file is, and then unzip the archive to create an expanded directory structure.

 If you use Internet Explorer and it automatically triggers StuffIt Expander, locate the folder where the archive was automatically expanded. This is your desktop by default, or a location specified in the "Preferences" dialog box.

Now move the properly unzipped directory structure into an appropriate location. The following directions assume that you have placed the resulting files into the directory */Developer/tomcat-4.1.18*.

Open up an instance of Terminal and issue the commands shown here:

```
[Localhost:~] wiverson% cd /Developer/tomcat-4.1.18/bin/
[Localhost:/Developer/tomcat-4.1.18/bin] wiverson% ls -l
total 392
-rwxr-xr-x  1 wiverson  admin  24659 Dec 19 14:49 bootstrap.jar
-rwxr-xr-x  1 wiverson  admin   7400 Dec 19 14:49 catalina.bat
-rwxr-xr-x  1 wiverson  admin   8618 Dec 19 14:49 catalina.sh
-rwxr-xr-x  1 wiverson  admin   9034 Dec 19 14:49 commons-daemon.jar
-rwxr-xr-x  1 wiverson  admin    511 Dec 19 14:49 cpappend.bat
-rwxr-xr-x  1 wiverson  admin   1284 Dec 19 14:49 digest.bat
-rwxr-xr-x  1 wiverson  admin    848 Dec 19 14:49 digest.sh
-rwxr-xr-x  1 wiverson  admin   2546 Dec 19 14:49 jasper.bat
-rwxr-xr-x  1 wiverson  admin   2833 Dec 19 14:49 jasper.sh
-rwxr-xr-x  1 wiverson  admin   1199 Dec 19 14:49 jspc.bat
-rwxr-xr-x  1 wiverson  admin    795 Dec 19 14:49 jspc.sh
-rwxr-xr-x  1 wiverson  admin   1942 Dec 19 14:49 setclasspath.bat
-rwxr-xr-x  1 wiverson  admin   1661 Dec 19 14:49 setclasspath.sh
-rwxr-xr-x  1 wiverson  admin   1215 Dec 19 14:49 shutdown.bat
-rwxr-xr-x  1 wiverson  admin    787 Dec 19 14:49 shutdown.sh
-rwxr-xr-x  1 wiverson  admin   1216 Dec 19 14:49 startup.bat
-rwxr-xr-x  1 wiverson  admin    788 Dec 19 14:49 startup.sh
-rwxr-xr-x  1 wiverson  admin  10593 Dec 19 14:49 tomcat-jni.jar
-rwxr-xr-x  1 wiverson  admin  65536 Dec 19 14:50 tomcat.exe
-rwxr-xr-x  1 wiverson  admin   2168 Dec 19 14:49 tool-wrapper.bat
-rwxr-xr-x  1 wiverson  admin   2484 Dec 19 14:49 tool-wrapper.sh
[Localhost:/Developer/tomcat-4.1.18/bin] wiverson%
```

Your directory listing should look similar to this output. Note that all of these files are already set to be executable.

 If you download a newer version of Tomcat, expect to see some minor differences, especially in the timestamps on these files.

Starting Tomcat

Next, use the *startup* script in the *bin* directory to fire up Tomcat:

```
[Localhost:/Developer/tomcat-4.1.18/bin] wiverson% env
    JAVA_HOME=/Library/Java/Home ./startup.sh
Using CATALINA_BASE:   /Developer/tomcat-4.1.18
Using CATALINA_HOME:   /Developer/tomcat-4.1.18
Using CATALINA_TMPDIR: /Developer/tomcat-4.1.18/temp
Using JAVA_HOME:       /Library/Java/Home
[Localhost:/Developer/tomcat-4.1.18/bin] wiverson% ps -a
  PID  TT  STAT     TIME COMMAND
  601 std  Ss     0:00.78 login -pf wiverson
  602 std  S      0:00.05 -tcsh (tcsh)
  616 std  R      0:04.13 /Library/Java/Home/bin/java
  619 std  R+     0:00.01 ps -a
[Localhost:/Developer/tomcat-4.1.18/bin] wiverson%
```

The JAVA_HOME environment variable is specified in this execution; Tomcat will not run without this variable set properly. Note the use of the ps -a command to see the started server.

> You may wish to set the JAVA_HOME environment variable in your shell profile, or in another generic script that you can use, before running Java programs. If you use this setting, you won't have to constantly set this variable.

If all is well, launch your browser and point it at the URL *http://localhost: 8080/*. Assuming Tomcat is running properly, you should see a cheery message like that illustrated in Figure 13-1.

Shutting Tomcat Down

Tomcat expects a specific signal to shut down in an orderly fashion. You can tell Tomcat to shut down cleanly by executing the following command:

```
[Localhost:/Developer/tomcat-4.1.18/bin] wiverson% env JAVA_HOME=/Library/
Java/Home ./shutdown.sh
```

This *shutdown* script ensures that Tomcat releases the resources it has tied up and stops all related processes.

> Because of the scripts used, it can be difficult to tell which particular Java process was used to launch Tomcat (either with a ps command or Mac OS X's ProcessViewer). Therefore, pay attention to which process ID is used to launch Tomcat (just in case you need to kill it manually).

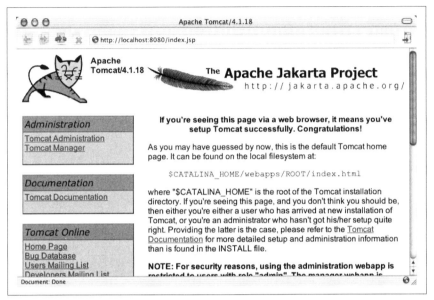

Figure 13-1. Tomcat success screen

Understanding JSP Compilation

Tomcat consists of two main architectural components: Catalina (a servlet container) and Jasper (a servlet that serves as the JSP compiler and default handler for JSP files).

When Catalina is launched, it waits for requests for resources in its *webapps* directory (or wherever the web content is located on your installation). If a request for a JSP is made, Catalina hands the request off to the servlet implementation of Jasper. If this is the first time the request is made, Jasper compiles the JSP into a Java source file, and then compiles this file by using the javac compiler in a binary Java class file. Finally, Jasper loads and executes this class file, returning the result. Future requests for the JSP page causes Jasper to compare the class file on disk to the JSP page on disk. If the timestamps don't match, Jasper recompiles the page dynamically and repeats the process.

It sounds a lot more complicated than it really is, but JSP compilation can make debugging JSP pages somewhat difficult. Because the original JSP is translated into Java source and then compiled into class files, the line numbers reported for errors sometimes correspond to the original JSP source. However, they usually map to the line numbers in the generated Java source. Be sure to fix bugs in the original JSP source, not in the Jasper-generated Java files.

Getting to Know Tomcat

Tomcat has a specific set of directories and configuration files, as shown in Figure 13-2. Take the time to become familiar with the various files and directories and to understand what goes where (and why). The next several subsections list important directories in this structure and their contents and usage.

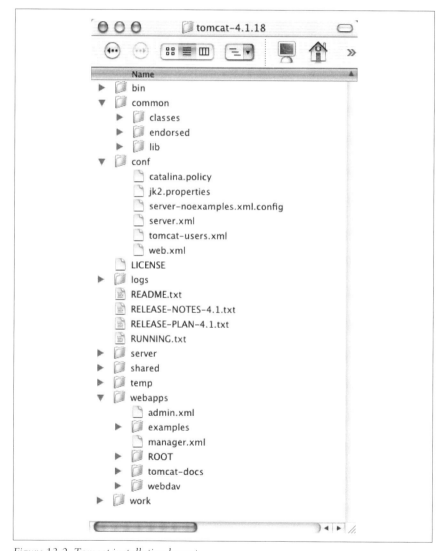

Figure 13-2. Tomcat installation layout

bin

The *bin* directory contains the scripts used to start and stop Tomcat, as well as scripts for the JSP precompiler (*jasper/jspc*). Under normal circumstances, you need only the *startup.sh* and *shutdown.sh* scripts.

common

The two subdirectories of the *common* directory contain code and libraries that are made available to all installed web applications. Place raw class files in the proper directories under the *common/classes/* directory. For example, if your class file is *MyNiftyObject.class* in the package `com.wiverson.utils`, the path to the class file is *common/classes/com/wiverson/utils/MyNiftyObject.class*.

JAR libraries can be placed inside the *common/lib/* directory. They will be added automatically to the classpath for all your web applications.

 Use this facility as sparingly as possible. Tomcat can be unpredictable when you have multiple versions of libraries in the *common* directories. If only one or two applications need a library or set of classes, consider placing those resources in the web application itself, rather than in the *common* subdirectories.

conf

Of most significant interest in this directory is a series of XML files that allow configuration of the Tomcat (Catalina) server. These files serve a function for Tomcat that is similar to the functions that the *httpd.conf* files serve for Apache.

server.xml

This file contains basic root configuration options for Tomcat. Try to use a text editor other than TextEdit for viewing and editing these files to avoid the line feed problems discussed in previous chapters.

The default connector point for the non-SSL channel is one of the most important values in this file. If you decide to use Tomcat instead of Apache to handle all your web services, change the value 8080 to 80 and use root access to bind to that port.

Pay special attention to the Context elements, which describe what content directories to serve and what the permissions are for those directories. For a production server, strip out the example contexts as well.

tomcat-users.xml

This file can manage users and roles for administration of the Tomcat server. In particular, if you wish to use the "manager" web application for remote administration, check the permissions listed here. As of this writing, the best (and only) place for documentation on this functionality is the official documentation on the Apache web site (*http://jakarta. apache.com/tomcat/*). However, I'm happy to report that O'Reilly's upcoming *Tomcat: The Definitive Guide* will clarify this topic once and for all.

web.xml

This file is pretty significant, as it configures the core component of Tomcat (Catalina) and binds the JSP compilation engine (Jasper) as a servlet. You can look here to add support for CGI scripts, set the default timeout for user sessions, and define file extension and MIME mappings, for example. This file, however, is beyond the scope of this book—visit the Tomcat web site for more information (and to inspect the file itself).

lib

This directory stores Java libraries used by the *jspc* tool (JSP compiler) and Tomcat. It has very little impact on normal web-based JSP application development.

logs

Not surprisingly, this is where Tomcat's log data is stored. When the system has problems, look here to see what's going on; you can often find useful nuggets of information about exceptions and other problems, as well as an access log.

server/lib

The two subdirectories under the *server/lib* directory contain code and libraries that are accessible to the server but not to your web applications (assuming you're using the *startup.sh* script). Unless you are working on Tomcat, you probably won't need or want to place files in these directories.

webapps

This directory contains the web applications that Tomcat is currently publishing to the Web. Each of these web applications typically corresponds to a standard directory layout.

You may see references to web application resource (WAR) files, which are essentially JAR files with additional semantics and structure for packaging web applications. If you decide to use a WAR or to create your own WAR files, drop them in this directory.

work

This directory is actually one of JSP's most important directories. It's where you put the intermediate files that handle a lot of the Tomcat work. The next section covers this topic in greater detail.

Database-Driven JSP Applications

This section outlines what is probably one of the most excruciatingly difficult ways to build a web application. There are lots of other, better ways to do it. If you are a web developer who is comfortable with talking to a relational database directly from JSP, I'd strongly recommend a commercial product such as Macromedia's Dreamweaver MX. If you're building database-driven Swing applications, look at some of the tools described in Chapter 2. If you're working on a larger site with several developers in different roles, consider using XML and XSLT, possibly in conjunction with Apache Cocoon (*http://xml.apache.org/cocoon*) and/or Struts (*http://jakarta. apache.org/struts*).

These disclaimers aside (hopefully delivering me from a thousand emails about what I am about to write), this application-building process is a very useful learning tool. Now let's discuss how to build and debug a simple JSP application.

The concept is to build a simple web application that executes simple SQL commands via a web browser using JSP. This section uses the MySQL database installation created in Chapter 12. The rest of this chapter assumes that you've installed MySQL as described and created the macjava database. See Chapter 12 for more details if you need a quick review.

Setting Up the Database

Before getting data to display with your web application, you need to put some data into the database. Save the contents of Example 13-1 as *init.sql* in your home directory (or somewhere you can easily locate).

Example 13-1. Setting up the database

```
USE macjava;

DROP TABLE IF EXISTS Contact;
DROP TABLE IF EXISTS Company;
CREATE TABLE Contact
(
    ID BIGINT UNSIGNED AUTO_INCREMENT NOT NULL PRIMARY KEY
);

ALTER TABLE Contact ADD firstName CHAR(50);    /* First name */
ALTER TABLE Contact ADD lastName CHAR(50);     /* Last name */

ALTER TABLE Contact ADD email CHAR(255) NOT NULL;/* email address */

ALTER TABLE Contact ADD companyID BIGINT NOT NULL;/* company worked for */
CREATE TABLE Company
(
    ID BIGINT UNSIGNED AUTO_INCREMENT NOT NULL PRIMARY KEY
);
ALTER TABLE Company ADD name CHAR(255);      /* Company public name */

INSERT INTO Company (ID, name) VALUES (1, "Big Dog Corp");
INSERT INTO Company (ID, name) VALUES (2, "Little Hampster Inc");

INSERT INTO Contact (ID, firstName, lastName, email, companyID)
    VALUES (1, "Biff", "Beefeater", "biff@null.com", 1);
INSERT INTO Contact (ID, firstName, lastName, email, companyID)
    VALUES (2, "Angry", "Master", "darkone@null.com", 1);
INSERT INTO Contact (ID, firstName, lastName, email, companyID)
    VALUES (3, "Smooth", "Slinker", "smooth@null.com", 2);
INSERT INTO Contact (ID, firstName, lastName, email, companyID)
    VALUES (4, "Glass", "Opal", "shatter@null.com", 2);
```

These commands describe how to set up two tables in MySQL and add a small amount of data to these tables. To actually add the data, execute the following command:

```
/Developer/mysql-3.23/bin/mysql --user javadev --password < ~/init.sql
```

 Note the use of the < directive to "pipe" the file into the mysql monitor.

Running this script should prompt you for the javadev user's password and then run silently. Any errors will be reported by line number. Note that the first two commands (DROP TABLE IF EXISTS) wipe out these tables and their data each time this script is run. This means that if you make a mistake, you can simply rerun the command to reenter the data, but *any* changes that are made later to the database will be destroyed without warning if this script is rerun.

Building the Web Application

The rest of this chapter shows how to build a web application from scratch. The process is time-consuming, but it should help you understand the different files and directories involved.

Start by creating a few supporting directories, as shown in Figure 13-3. Inside the *webapps* directory, create a directory called *jspdbtodo*. Inside that directory, create a directory called *WEB-INF*. Inside that directory, create another directory called *lib*. Remember that capitalization matters!

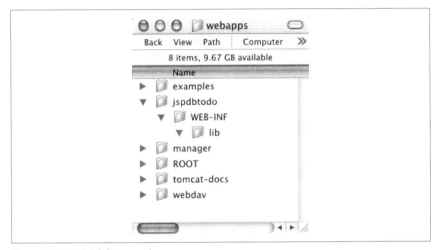

Figure 13-3. Initial directory layout

The *WEB-INF* directory is a special directory that is hidden to remote clients (such as web browsers) and lets you add protected resources specific to this application, such as configuration files that might store sensitive information (like passwords used to connect to a database). The *lib* directory inside *WEB-INF* contains JAR files that will automatically be added to this web application's classpath.

Creating your first JSP

Create a text file immediately inside the *jspdbtodo* directory called *index.jsp*. Enter the contents of this text file as shown in Example 13-2.

Example 13-2. A "Hello World" JSP page

```
<%@ page language="java" %>
<HTML>
<BODY>
Hello World! <BR>
<%= new java.util.Date().toString( ) %>
</BODY>
</HTML>
```

The first, slightly odd-looking tag is a page directive that tells Tomcat that the scripts in the page are Java. The page directive isn't strictly necessary, but is good form for adhering to the JSP specification.

Next, you'll notice what looks like a bit of Java code that creates a new java.util.Date object and converts it to a String, embedded within a <%= %> tag. This tag tells Tomcat to evaluate whatever code is placed inside as a String and to output the results of that expression to the page.

Experiment a bit and use your favorite browser to open this file directly from the filesystem (without it being translated by Tomcat). If you've installed things in the locations shown in this chapter, you should be able to simulate this effect by opening the URL *file:///Developer/tomcat-4.1.8/webapps/jspdbtodo/index.jsp* in your browser.

> The *file://* prefix tells your web browser to open a local file instead of using the HTTP protocol (denoted by the *http://* prefix to the URL).

Depending on your browser, you may get a timeout, see the "Hello World!" test but no date and time, or see "Hello World!" and the page's raw JSP scripts. Your browser gets the information directly from the disk and attempts to parse it, but browsers don't understand JSP pages. For this reason, your results are unpredictable and often inconsistent. What you need, of course, is for a web container to translate this page into standard HTML, which your browser can understand.

Try to view the same page rendered through the JSP engine. Make sure that Tomcat is running, and go to *http://localhost:8080/jspdbtodo/index.jsp*. This time, you should see "Hello World!" and the current date and time, as shown in Figure 13-4.

Debugging JSP pages

Now that you've gotten started with JSP, you need to learn how to figure out what's happening when things go wrong. Using the Terminal, cd to the

Figure 13-4. Hello World in a JSP

work directory inside your Tomcat installation. You should see a series of directories that correspond to the JSP you were just working with. Inside these directories, you'll see two files: *index$jsp.java* and *index$jsp.class*. These are also shown in the Finder, as seen in Figure 13-5.

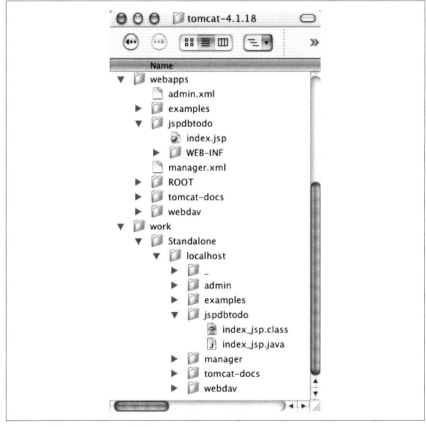

Figure 13-5. A JSP's compiled files

As mentioned earlier, when you first view a JSP using Tomcat, it will automatically translate the JSP into a Java servlet source file (the *index$jsp.java* file) using Jasper, and then use the javac compiler included with the Mac OS X JDK to compile that Java source file into the corresponding *index$jsp.class* file. This class file will be loaded and executed, and if the JSP is then modified, the corresponding source files will be regenerated.

When a problem arises, you will get an exception and stack trace that correspond to this Java source file, not your original JSP. Open the corresponding Java source to find the offending line.

Try to "break" your JSP—don't terminate a String, or put gibberish inside the <% ... %> tags. Watch and see what happens, and take note of the displayed error message. Look at the *.java* source generated by your *.jsp* file, and try to understand the relationship between the different errors you get and the different places where files are generated. If the JSP precompiler reports an error, you'll get an error notification with a line number that corresponds to the original JSP file; however, runtime errors are reported against the Java source file.

Talking to the Database

After covering the basics of JSP, you're ready to write a JSP that accesses your MySQL database. As described in the last chapter, the Connector/J JDBC driver is perfect for using Java to talk to a MySQL database.

Copy the JDBC driver JAR file, *mysql-connector-java-2.0.14-bin.jar*, to your web application's *WEB-INF/lib* directory, as shown in Figure 13-6. This will make the driver available to your web application.

Figure 13-6. Installing the MySQL JDBC driver

Next, alongside the "Hello World" *index.jsp* file, add a new file called *test. jsp* with the code shown in Example 13-3 (using the proper password for the javadev MySQL user instead of "special", of course).

Example 13-3. A database-driven JSP

```
<%@ page language="java" import="java.sql.*" %>
<HTML>
<BODY>
<%
    Driver myDriver = null;
    Connection myConnection = null;
    String SQLstatement = "select now()";
    try
    {
        String jdbcURL = "jdbc:mysql://127.0.0.1/macjava";
        String jdbcUsername = "javadev";
        String jdbcPassword = "special";
        myDriver =
                (Driver)Class.forName("com.mysql.jdbc.Driver").newInstance();
        myConnection =
          DriverManager.getConnection(
            jdbcURL, jdbcUsername, jdbcPassword);

        PreparedStatement myStatement;
        ResultSet myResults;

        myStatement = myConnection.prepareStatement(SQLstatement);
        myResults = myStatement.executeQuery();

        while(myResults.next())
        {
            %>
            <%= myResults.getString(1) %>
            <%
        }

    } catch (Exception e)
    {
        %>
        <%= e.getMessage() %>
        <%
        e.printStackTrace();
        System.out.println(SQLstatement);
        return;
    } finally
    {
        try
        {
            myConnection.close();
        } catch (Exception e)
```

Example 13-3. A database-driven JSP (continued)

```
       { /* Silent failure */}
    }
%>
</BODY>
</HTML>
```

Before going any further, note that this situation is probably the worst possible case for using JSP. There is virtually no HTML—all you have done here is put a bunch of Java code in a tiny bit of HTML. Also, most of this code accesses the database directly, which is another violation of good coding principles. In a more realistic application, you would probably write helper Java classes to access the database, and make these classes available through JSP tag libraries. Then you could access the tag libraries from an HTML interface using JSP. However, that scenario is beyond the scope of this book, and has little to do with Mac OS X. Try to follow along, but understand that this example of using JSP on Mac OS X is not necessarily the ideal guide for great Java coding practices.

That said, it works, and it's pretty easy to understand. Ironically, the output is virtually identical to the previous JSP except that the current date and time are retrieved from the database instead of the Java runtime. This JSP is also a great way to test that everything is installed properly—that your JSPs are compiled properly, that the connection with the database works, and so forth.

Retrieving Data

This section builds two pages that talk to the database. The first lets users view a list of companies within the database. Clicking on a company name tunnels you down into a detail page, which shows all contacts for that company.

For a real project, you would factor out all of the logic into JavaBeans, or break it out into custom tags. This project, however, will make a very simple set of JSP pages. You shouldn't duplicate our database connection logic, however, so you'll actually create four pages:

- *company.jsp*, the page that users will first visit
- *contact.jsp*, a detail page that shows a list of contacts for a given company
- *header.jsp*, which contains the database connection logic
- *footer.jsp*, which contains cleanup code for the database connection

Place all four files directly in the web application directory itself. When you're done, the directory structure will look like Figure 13-7.

Figure 13-7. Database web application layout

The *index.jsp* page and the *test.jsp* page are left over from the earlier examples.

Enter the text shown in Example 13-4 and save it as *header.jsp*. You'll note that the code is apparently a snippet of Java source inside a set of brackets. You'll also notice that the variable SQLstatement is used but never declared or initialized—the subpages will handle that step. The try block is incomplete; it will be closed off in the *footer.jsp* file. Also, the myResults variable is initialized but never used.

Example 13-4. Opening a database connection

```
<%
    Driver myDriver = null;
    Connection myConnection = null;
    try
    {
        String jdbcURL = "jdbc:mysql://localhost/macjava";
        String jdbcUsername = "javadev";
        String jdbcPassword = "special";
        myDriver =
                (Driver)Class.forName("org.gjt.mm.mysql.Driver").newInstance( );
        myConnection = DriverManager.getConnection(jdbcURL,
                jdbcUsername, jdbcPassword);
```

Example 13-4. Opening a database connection (continued)

```
        PreparedStatement myStatement;
        ResultSet myResults;

        myStatement = myConnection.prepareStatement(SQLstatement);
        myResults = myStatement.executeQuery( );
%>
```

Next, create the corresponding *footer.jsp* file with the contents shown in Example 13-5.

Example 13-5. Closing the database connection

```
<%
} catch (Exception e)
    {
        %>
        <%= e.getMessage( ) %>
        <%
        e.printStackTrace( );
        System.out.println(SQLstatement);
        return;
    } finally
    {
        try
        {
            myConnection.close( );
        } catch (Exception e)
        { /* Silent failure */}
    }
%>
```

Here, you'll do some basic error handling and cleanup. You'll notice that a catch and finally match the try block from *header.jsp*.

A key point here is that you can't use the *header.jsp* and *footer.jsp* without being aware of the expectations (for example, an input SQLstatement variable) and the outcome (a ResultSet object declared as myResults). This sort of variable management can be used for a variety of JSP tricks, not the least of which is the enforcement of compile-time rules about your pages. In essence, then, these two components are hardcoded to depend on each other, as well as on certain aspects of pages that will include them. Take care to document these requirements so other developers don't misuse these components.

Now create the *company.jsp* file shown in Example 13-6.

Example 13-6. JSP for listing companies

```
<%@ page language="java" import="java.sql.*" %>
<HTML>
<BODY>
<% String SQLstatement = "select ID, name from Company"; %>
<%@ include file="header.jsp" %>

<H1>Company List Report</H1>

<TABLE border="1" cellpadding="3" width="50%">
<% while(myResults.next())
        {
        %>
        <TR>
            <TD>

        <%= myResults.getString("ID") %>
            </TD><TD>
            <A HREF="contact.jsp?companyID=<%=myResults.getString("ID") %>">
        <%= myResults.getString("name") %>
        </A>
            </TD>
        </TR>
        <%
        }
%>
</TABLE>

<%@ include file="footer.jsp" %>
</BODY>
</HTML>
```

This page is starting to look more like normal HTML. It still has a bit of Java in it, but nowhere near as much as the prior *test.jsp* example. Most heavy lifting is done in the include files (*header.jsp* and *footer.jsp*). You'll notice that the SQLstatement variable is initialized here, and that the myResults object is used to iterate over the resulting data. The resulting data is massaged into a HTML TABLE, and links are created to the *contact.jsp* subpage with the specified company ID value appended as a parameter.

Create the final detail page, *contact.jsp*, as detailed in Example 13-7.

Example 13-7. The company detail page

```
<%@ page language="java" import="java.sql.*" %>
<HTML>
<BODY>
<%
long companyID = new Long(request.getParameter("companyID")).longValue();
```

Example 13-7. The company detail page (continued)

```
String SQLstatement = "select firstName, lastName, email, companyID from Contact
where companyID = " + companyID; %>
<%@ include file="header.jsp" %>

<H1>Contact List for Company</H1>

<TABLE border="1" cellpadding="3" width="50%">
<% while(myResults.next())
    {
        %>
        <TR>
            <TD>
            <%= myResults.getString("firstName") %>
            </TD><TD>
            <%= myResults.getString("lastName") %>
            </TD><TD>
            <%= myResults.getString("email") %>
            </TD><TD>
        </TR>
        <%
    }
%>
</TABLE>
<BR><BR>
<A HREF="company.jsp">Return to Company List</A>

<%@ include file="footer.jsp" %>
</BODY>
</HTML>
```

This page is similar to the previous *company.jsp* page. The SQLstatement is initialized against the incoming company ID. A link provided at the bottom of the page lets users bounce back to the opening page.

 This sort of JSP application is created visually by integrating the database functionality into Macromedia Dreamweaver MX. Everything built here, and significantly more, could be constructed via drag and drop and by setting options visually—but that wouldn't be half as fun, right?

You'll quickly see several different aspects to the development of web applications: tracking user input in the form of links and forms, retrieving data, formatting the results for different browsers or devices, handling multiple languages, allowing user defined layouts, and so on. Designing web applications and user interfaces can quickly become complicated. Having a clear idea of what JSP and Tomcat let you do is the first step in getting a handle on these programming topics.

Reviewing the Application

Look at the final arrangement of the files on disk. As shown in Figure 13-7, you've got several files in your web directory. Visiting the *http://localhost: 8080/jspdbtodo/company.jsp* URL displays the output shown in Figure 13-8.

Figure 13-8. Company HTML page

Clicking the links on this page take you to a detail page that provides information on the company's contacts, as shown in Figure 13-9.

Figure 13-9. Contact HTML page

It's easy to imagine building a web application with tremendous additional functionality, such as search or the ability to add contacts.

Frontending Tomcat with Apache

Mac OS X includes a default installation of the popular, effective web server Apache. In fact, the "personal web sharing" functionality of Mac OS X, available from the Network control panel, merely provides a nice graphical user interface on top of the Apache web server.

Figure 13-10 illustrates the browser and servers installed to handle a Java-based n-tier web application. Apache receives requests from the client browser for dynamically generated application content and then forwards them to the Java application server, which can then build a response from the SQL database. Apache handles client-browser requests for static content (such as images or large downloadable files) directly.

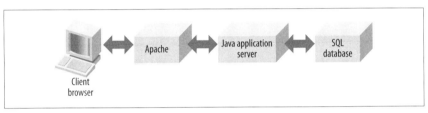

Figure 13-10. Four-tier application

To get Tomcat 4.0.4 and Apache to talk to each other, either download and build the source for the connector yourself or download a prebuilt binary. Fortunately, Chad Thompson has already provided instructions on how to do this at O'Reilly's macdevcenter.com, available at *http://www. macdevcenter.com/pub/a/mac/2002/08/20/tomcat_integration.html.*

Next Steps

Now that you've seen how to build simple web applications that generate web pages, you can learn more about JSP, SQL, Tomcat, and MySQL by consulting the following texts:

- *MySQL Cookbook*, by Paul DuBois (O'Reilly)
- *JavaServer Pages*, by Hans Bergsten (O'Reilly)
- *Java Servlet Programming*, by Jason Hunter (O'Reilly)
- *Tomcat: The Definitive Guide*, by Jason Brittain and Ian Darwin (O'Reilly)

The next two chapters look at how to install and work with Enterprise Java-Beans and JBoss to build more complex web applications, and how to use web services to integrate different web-based systems.

## CHAPTER 14

EJB and JBoss

Once you move into the world of web applications, you'll find tasks that aren't well suited for servlets and especially for JSPs. In particular, the most complicated business processes in enterprise Java are not easily coded up in a JavaServer Page. Dealing with complicated financial transactions, for example, isn't something that fits well into a page of mostly HTML, or even into a servlet that is geared toward a request/response model. Instead, you need technology that provides security, transactions, and a strong server-side component model.

Enterprise JavaBeans (EJB) refers to a specification that builds these types of server-side components. These components are installed into a J2EE application server. By writing Java components that conform to this specification, you take advantage of the application server's sophisticated functionality as well as a known set of interfaces.

The specific functionality offered by a particular J2EE application server varies, but generally the use of EJB features prominently in J2EE applications. In the last chapter, you saw a simpler form of a web application based on JSP pages, servlets, and often a database and some helper classes. J2EE applications are a bit more complex, often having three, four, or more application tiers and involving five, six, or even ten different Java APIs. In these more complex cases, you need a J2EE application server instead of (or in addition to) a simple web container like Tomcat.

This chapter shows you how to install JBoss, a popular open source J2EE application server. Like Tomcat, JBoss runs smoothly on Mac OS X and offers enterprise-level services for Apple's newest platform. It also examines some basic examples that come with JBoss to give you a feel for how EJBs function on Mac OS X. Like the last chapter, EJB aficionados can skim the chapter looking for Mac OS X specifics, while newbies can learn enough about EJB to get started in J2EE development.

It's far beyond the scope of this text to describe EJB application development, design, and architecture. Instead, this chapter will help you get JBoss
installed and a sample application installed and working. For a more thorough investigation of EJB, consult O'Reilly's *Enterprise JavaBeans* by Richard Monson-Haefel.

JBoss

Although numerous commercial J2EE server offerings are available, few of
them (as of this writing) have releases built specifically for Mac OS X. Many
have Linux and Unix versions of their products, but Mac OS X offerings
remain sparse. This situation is expected to change as Mac OS X gains
momentum, but for now it creates a problem for enterprise Java developers.
To deal with this problem, you need to obtain a server that can be built from
source, and therefore optimized for Mac OS X. Since commercial offerings
don't make source available, JBoss quickly rises to the top of the heap.
Freely available and completely open source, JBoss works beautifully on
Mac OS X. This chapter will show you how to get it running.

Downloading a Release

You can download releases of JBoss from *http://www.jboss.org/*. The release
used here is 3.0.4, which uses the default JBoss web server.

> Some releases of JBoss are bundled with the Tomcat web
> server, which functions as detailed in the last chapter. You
> are welcome to use that release, and it works well on Mac
> OS X. However, this chapter assumes the "pure" JBoss
> release.

You should download the *JBoss-3.0.4.zip* file, weighing in at 28.7 MB. This
release of JBoss includes a web (HTTP) server, a JSP and servlet container,
and support for EJB, CMP 2.0, RMI, IIOP, Clustering, JTS, and JMX.

Installation

Assuming you've downloaded the *JBoss-3.0.4.zip* file into your home directory (~), execute the commands below to expand the JBoss distribution:

```
[Localhost:~] wiverson% ls -l jboss-3.0.4.zip
-rw-r--r--  1 wiverson  staff  28711934 Nov 20 16:33 jboss-3.0.4.zip

[Localhost:~] wiverson% sudo mkdir /usr/local/jboss
```

Acronym Frenzy

Lest all the acronyms overwhelm you, here is a brief rundown of some of the common ones in J2EE:

- CMP: Container Managed Persistence, a feature of EJB that allows persisting data to a database
- EJB: Enterprise JavaBeans
- IIOP: Internet Inter-Orb Protocol, a more traditional protocol for communication over distributed architectures
- J2EE: Java 2 Enterprise Edition
- JMX: Java Management Extensions, an API that allows other Java applications to interface with a J2EE server programmatically through a standard set of coding paradigms
- JSP: JavaServer Pages
- JTS: Java Transaction Service, the Java API for handling transactions, committals, and rollbacks of database communication
- RMI: Remote Method Invocation, which allows remote components to be interacted with as if they were local objects

```
[Localhost:~] wiverson% sudo chown wiverson:staff /usr/local/jboss

[Localhost:~] wiverson% cd /usr/local/jboss

[Localhost:/usr/local/jboss] wiverson% cp ~/jboss-3.0.4.zip .

[Localhost:/usr/local/jboss] wiverson% unzip jboss-3.0.4.zip
Archive:  jboss-3.0.4.zip
   creating: jboss-3.0.4/
   creating: jboss-3.0.4/bin/
   creating: jboss-3.0.4/client/
   creating: jboss-3.0.4/docs/
   creating: jboss-3.0.4/docs/dtd/
   creating: jboss-3.0.4/docs/examples/
   creating: jboss-3.0.4/docs/examples/jca/
   creating: jboss-3.0.4/lib/
   creating: jboss-3.0.4/server/

   ...
   omitted for brevity
   ...
  inflating: jboss-3.0.4/docs/tests/overview-frame.html
  inflating: jboss-3.0.4/docs/tests/overview-summary.html
  inflating: jboss-3.0.4/docs/tests/stylesheet.css

[Localhost:/usr/local/jboss] wiverson% cd /usr/local/jboss/jboss-3.0.4
```

```
[Localhost:local/jboss/jboss-3.0.4] wiverson% mv ./* ../

[Localhost:local/jboss/jboss-3.0.4] wiverson% cd ..

[Localhost:/usr/local/jboss] wiverson% rmdir jboss-3.0.4

[Localhost:/usr/local/jboss] wiverson% ls
bin           docs              lib
client        jboss-3.0.4.zip server
```

You'll need to replace the bolded username (wiverson) with the username you want to run JBoss as. This name could be a special user account you created just for this purpose, or your own user account. When you are done, you'll have a complete JBoss installation in the *usr/local/jboss/* directory.

 Using NetInfo to create a "homeless" user is a good way to protect JBoss user accounts. (Refer to O'Reilly's *Mac OS X for Unix Geeks* for more information.)

Starting JBoss

To start JBoss, simply enter the following command:

```
[Localhost:/usr/local/jboss] wiverson%  /usr/local/jboss/bin/run.sh
=========================================================================
===

  JBoss Bootstrap Environment

  JBOSS_HOME: /usr/local/jboss

  JAVA: java

  JAVA_OPTS:  -Dprogram.name=run.sh

  CLASSPATH: /usr/local/jboss/bin/run.jar:/lib/tools.jar


=========================================================================
===

18:09:09,910 INFO  [Server] JBoss Release: JBoss-3.0.4 CVSTag=JBoss_3_0_4
18:09:10,091 INFO  [Server] Home Dir: /usr/local/jboss
18:09:10,093 INFO  [Server] Home URL: file:/usr/local/jboss/
18:09:10,096 INFO  [Server] Library URL: file:/usr/local/jboss/lib/
18:09:10,105 INFO  [Server] Patch URL: null
18:09:10,107 INFO  [Server] Server Name: default
...
omitted for brevity
...
```

```
18:09:53,489 INFO  [jbossweb] Started WebApplicationContext[/jmx-
console,file:/usr/local/jboss/server/default/deploy/jmx-console.war/]
18:09:53,706 INFO  [jbossweb] successfully deployed file:/usr/local/jboss/
server/default/deploy/jmx-console.war/ to /jmx-console
18:09:53,709 INFO  [MainDeployer] Deployed package: file:/usr/local/jboss/
server/default/deploy/jmx-console.war/
18:09:53,719 INFO  [URLDeploymentScanner] Started
18:09:53,721 INFO  [MainDeployer] Deployed package: file:/usr/local/jboss/
server/default/conf/jboss-service.xml
18:09:53,838 INFO  [Server] JBoss (MX MicroKernel) [3.0.4 Date:200211021607]
Started in 0m:43s:637ms
```

After a lot of messages scroll past, you will see a status message along the
lines of:

```
[Server] JBoss (MX MicroKernel) [3.0.4 Date:200211021607] Started in 0m:22s:
871ms
```

This indicates that JBoss is now running. To verify that it is working properly, open the administrative console at *http://localhost:8080/jmx-console/*.
You should see something similar to Figure 14-1.

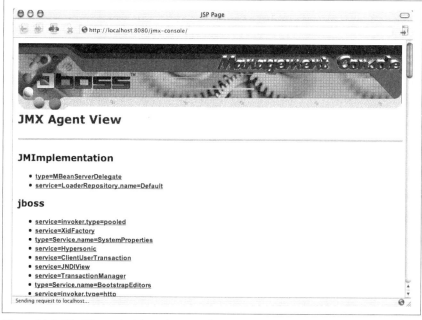

Figure 14-1. The JBoss administrative console

JBoss ships with three different configurations: "minimal," "default," and "all." These configurations are stored in the directory */usr/local/jboss/server/*. When you start up the server with the default *run.sh* command, you imply that you wish to use the */usr/local/jboss/server/default* directory as your server directory.

This is particularly relevant if you want to deploy JBoss with the absolute minimal server configuration. In that event, copy the minimal configuration directory, and then add library and configuration data to support your application as you add functionality.

Getting Started with J2EE

When starting a new application or development environment, first build the proverbial "Hello World" example. This step is instructional when working with J2EE, as it was for JSP in Chapter 13.

"Hello World" in J2EE

Start by building the simplest of all possible web applications: a "Hello World" JSP file. You created a similar JSP in the last chapter, but deploying a JSP as part of a J2EE application is different from deploying a JSP as a simpler web application. You will get a feel for these differences by working through these basic steps.

Create a file called *index.jsp*, with the contents shown in Example 14-1.

Example 14-1. A Hello World JSP

```
<HTML>
    <HEAD>
        <TITLE>Test</TITLE>
    </HEAD>
    <BODY>
    Hello World!<BR>
    <%= new java.util.Date().toString( ) %>
    </BODY>
</HTML>
```

To deploy this file, create a WAR file. A WAR is just a ZIP file with a specific encoding, and in this case you can get away with not creating a *web.xml* file or any other supporting configuration or property files. Copy the *index.jsp* file to the */usr/local/jboss/server/default/deploy* directory, and then issue the following command:

```
[Localhost:~/Documents] wiverson% ls index.jsp
index.jsp
```

```
[Localhost:~/Documents] wiverson% zip test.war index.jsp
  adding: index.jsp (deflated 19%)

[Localhost:~/Documents] wiverson% mv test.war /usr/local/jboss/server/
default/deploy/

[Localhost:~/Documents] wiverson%
```

This command creates the needed WAR file and places it in JBoss's deployment directory (*/usr/local/jboss/server/default/deploy*). Any WAR or EAR (another type of archive specifically used for J2EE applications) file in this directory is automatically deployed by the JBoss application server without any further user intervention.

The JBoss terminal will notify you that the application has been deployed with the following message:

```
18:30:29,809 INFO  [MainDeployer] Starting deployment of package: file:/usr/
local/jboss/server/default/deploy/test.war
18:30:30,412 INFO  [jbossweb] Registered jboss.web:
Jetty=0,JBossWebApplicationContext=2,context=/test
18:30:30,618 INFO  [jbossweb] Extract jar:file:/usr/local/jboss/server/
default/tmp/deploy/server/default/deploy
/test.war/58.test.war!/ to /tmp/Jetty_0_0_0_0_8080__test/webapp
18:30:31,609 INFO  [jbossweb] Started WebApplicationContext[/test,jar:file:/
usr/local/jboss/server/default/tmp
/deploy/server/default/deploy/test.war/58.test.war!/]
18:30:31,760 INFO  [jbossweb] Internal Error: File /WEB-INF/web.xml not
found
18:30:31,774 INFO  [jbossweb] successfully deployed file:/usr/local/jboss/
server/default/tmp/deploy/server/default/deploy
/test.war/58.test.war to /test
18:30:31,777 INFO  [MainDeployer] Deployed package: file:/usr/local/jboss/
server/default/deploy/test.war
```

You can open a web browser to view *http://localhost:8080/test/* and see the phrase "Hello World!" and the current time displayed. Your output should be similar to that in Figure 14-2.

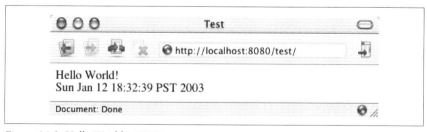

Figure 14-2. Hello World in J2EE

The JBoss Template Project

As you move beyond "Hello World" and into more complicated applications, you'll find that J2EE is a pretty complex environment. Trying to get all the configuration files, property files, source, images, HTML pages, classes, and JAR files into the right place can be a daunting task.

To help with this process, JBoss 3.0 has a default template for working with J2EE applications, available at *http://www.jboss.org/docs/#free-30x*. This template application is ideal to start working on, especially for EJB development, as it walks through the development and deployment of a minimal EJB application.

Dependencies

The template project uses the open source tools shown in Table 14-1 in addition to JBoss, which you should download before working with the template project.

Table 14-1. Supplemental tools required for the JBoss template project

Project	Version required	Version used	Available from
Ant	1.4.1+	1.5.1	*http://jakarta.apache.org/ant*
XDoclet	1.1.2+	1.1.2	*http://www.sf.net/projects/xdoclet*

You should already have Ant set up if you followed the instructions back in Chapter 2. I put my installation in */usr/local/ant*, and I made sure that I included its *bin* directory in my path. I placed XDoclet in the *~/xdoclet-1.1.2* directory.

The template directory structure

Download and uncompress the default template to a directory of choice; this case assumes that you've installed it in your home directory. You should end up with the directory structure shown in Figure 14-3.

In this case, you'll deal with only the *template* directory. Copy this directory to your working environment and rename it. You should use the cp command in the Terminal, not the Finder, to copy the *template* directory (the Finder won't copy files that start with .). This example assumes that you've copied the contents of the template to *~/ejbproject*:

```
[Localhost:~/JBoss.3.0TemplateAndExamples] wiverson% ls
cmp2        template     transaction
```

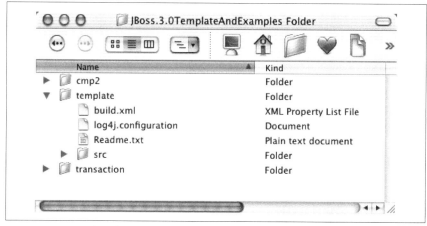

Figure 14-3. Template directory structure

```
[Localhost:~/JBoss.3.0TemplateAndExamples] wiverson% cp -r template ~/
ejbproject/

[Localhost:~/ JBoss.3.0TemplateAndExamples] wiverson% cd ~/ejbproject/

[Localhost:~/ejbproject] wiverson% ls
Readme.txt          build.xml            src
build               log4j.configuration  template

[Localhost:~/ejbproject] wiverson% ls -a
.                       .ant.properties.example   log4j.configuration
..                      Readme.txt                src
.DS_Store               build                     template
.ant.properties         build.xml
```

Now cd to the *~/ejbproject* directory and execute an ls -l command. You should see an *.ant.properties.example* file in the directory listing. If not, you didn't copy the template fully.

The Mac OS X Finder doesn't display files that begin with a period, and won't copy them unless you copy the enclosing folder. For this reason, you should get used to copying and listing directories with the Terminal application, at least when developing applications.

Make a copy of this file called *.ant.properties* (note the period at the start of the filename). Update the file to point to your own JBoss configuration. Example 14-2 shows how the configuration is set up on my system.

Example 14-2. Ant properties for the template project

```
# ATTENTION: this is an example file how to overwrite settings
# in this project Please rename it to ".ant.properties" and adjust
# the settings to your needs
# Set the path to the runtime JBoss directory containing the
# JBoss application server
# ATTENTION: the one containing directories like "bin", "client", "server" etc.
jboss.home= /usr/local/jboss
# Set the configuration name that must have a corresponding directory under
# <jboss.home>/server
jboss.configuration=default
# Set the path to the root directory of the XDoclet distribution (see
# http://www.sf.net/projects/xdoclet)
xdoclet.home=/Users/wiverson/xdoclet-1.1.2/
# Set this to "true" when you want to force the rebuild of the Xdoclet
# generated files (see XDoclet's <ejbdoclet> attribute "force")
xdoclet.force=false
# Set the EJB version you want to use (1.1 or 2.0, see XDoclet's
# <ejbdoclet> attribute "ejbspec")
ejb.version=2.0
# Set the JBoss version you want to use (2.4, 3.0 etc., see XDoclet's
# <jboss> attribute "version")
jboss.version=3.0
# Set the DB type mapping (Hypersonic SQL, PostgreSQL etc., see XDoclet's
# <jboss > attribute "typemapping")
type.mapping=Hypersonic SQL
# Set the DataSource name your are going to use
# (java:/DefaultDS etc., see XDoclet's <jboss> attribute "datasource")
datasource.name=java:/DefaultDS
# Uncomment this and adjust the path to point directly to JAR file
# containing the servlet classes
# Attention: By uncommenting this line you start the creation of a WAR file
servlet-lib.path= /usr/local/jboss/server/default/lib /javax.servlet.jar
```

 If you are familiar with JBoss, remember that you can also modify these properties through JBoss's *build.xml* file or an individual project's *build.xml* file. However, doing so presumes that the next developer will know to look in the build file, and is generally not a good idea. Stick to the properties files for a consistent build environment.

Next, look at the directory structure of the project's *src* folder, which is where all the interesting action occurs. Your structure should look like Figure 14-4.

Here is some information on this structure's most important files:

build.xml
    This file tells Ant how to build the J2EE application.

Name	Kind
build.xml	XML Property List File
log4j.configuration	Document
Readme.txt	Plain text document
▼ src	Folder
▼ etc	Folder
▼ bin	Folder
lcp.bat	Document
run-client.bat	Document
run-client.sh	Document
jndi.properties	Document
▼ WEB-INF	Folder
jboss-web.xml	XML Property List File
web-client.xml	XML Property List File
▼ main	Folder
▼ client	Folder
▼ test	Folder
▼ client	Folder
TestClient.java	Java Source File
▼ ejb	Folder
▼ test	Folder
▼ entity	Folder
TestBMPEntityBean.java	Java Source File
TestEntityBean.java	Java Source File
▼ interfaces	Folder
AbstractData.java	Java Source File
InvalidValueException.java	Java Source File
ServiceUnavailableException.java	Java Source File
▼ message	Folder
TestMessageDrivenBean.java	Java Source File
▼ session	Folder
SequenceGeneratorBean.java	Java Source File
TestSessionBean.java	Java Source File
▼ servlet	Folder
▼ web	Folder
index.jsp	Java Server Page File

Figure 14-4. Source tree for the template project

etc/bin

This directory contains the *run-client.sh* file, which executes a test Java client. Ant copies this file to the *build/bin* directory and updates it when you execute a build.

etc/WEB-INF

This directory contains the base configuration XML files for your application. Ant copies files in this directory into the deployable WAR file when you execute a build.

---

main/client/test/client/TestClient.java
This source is a very simple command-line test program. It is used to test the TestSession EJB.

main/ejb/test/entity/TestBMPEntityBean.java
main/ejb/test/entity/TestEntityBean.java
These two beans are examples of entity EJBs. Entity EJBs represent persistent data, such as user accounts and purchase orders. Typically, this data is stored in a database, although other storage mechanisms are possible. Each entity is uniquely identifiable by a number, or *key*. Entity EJBs fall into one of two categories: bean-managed persistence (BMP), for which the code for the EJB is responsible for saving and loading any persistent data, and container-managed persistence (CMP), for which the hosting server (or container) is responsible for managing, saving, and loading any persistent data.

main/ejb/test/interfaces
The contents of this directory are utility classes. You can inspect them at your leisure, but this chapter doesn't cover them.

main/ejb/test/message/TestMessageDrivenBean.java
This class is an example of a message-driven EJB. One of the newest aspects of the EJB specification, these EJBs represent asynchronous messages.

main/ejb/test/session/SequenceGeneratorBean.java
This class is an example of a session EJB that returns a new sequence number for a given named sequence. It's as much an example and tutorial as anything.

main/ejb/test/session/TestSessionBean.java
This Java class is an example of a minimal session EJB. Client/server sessions use session EJBs to perform nonpersistent operations. A session EJB might be used to handle simple calculations or other runtime utilities, but wouldn't represent something valuable and persistent such as a purchase order. A session EJB could retain some state across calls, but might expire or otherwise disappear.

web/index.jsp
This file is a simple web user interface to the TestSessionBean EJB.

Building from the template application

Now build the application. Execute the commands shown here:

```
[Localhost:~/ejbproject] wiverson% /usr/local/ant/bin/ant
Buildfile: build.xml

check-environment:
```

```
check-jboss:
...
omitted for brevity
...

create-client:
     [echo] JBoss Home on Unix: /usr/local/jboss
     [echo] Java Home on Unix: /System/Library/Frameworks/JavaVM.framework/
Versions/1.3.1/Home

main:

BUILD SUCCESSFUL
Total time: 26 seconds
```

When it's done, a "BUILD SUCCESSFUL" message will appear. You can verify that the build process worked by opening the URL *http://localhost: 8080/web-client/*. You should see the output shown in Figure 14-5.

Figure 14-5. Output from sample application

 The default generated web client path is named *web-client*, and the name is hardcoded in the *build.xml* file. You can change this name in the *build.xml* file itself by changing the JBoss configuration to point to a different path, or by copying and changing the name of the WAR file after it's generated by the default *build.xml* file. The best way to change it is through the *.ant.properties* file, that's not currently an option. For now, the best way to change the context of the deployed web client is to change the references to web-client in the *build.xml* file.

After the running the build for the first time, you will see a *build* directory next to the *src* directory in your project's directory structure. This is where the output of your build is placed, although files are also placed in the JBoss deployment directory automatically. Like the *src* directory, this area is worth exploring.

build/bin

This directory contains the final script files used to run the command-line Java client.

build/classes

This directory contains the compiled classes (both your source files and any autogenerated Java classes).

build/deploy

This directory contains the files that are deployed automatically to your JBoss 3.0 distribution. It's a bit redundant (these files are located both here and in the JBoss *deploy* directory), but it is a good way to verify which files are published during the build process.

build/generate

This directory contains all the Java source files generated by XDoclet. This directory is important, as stack trace information may point to line numbers of source files in it, or compilation errors in XDoclet generated source.

build/META-INF

This directory contains the deployment descriptors generated by XDoclet.

build/war

This directory contains files used to construct the deployed WAR(s).

Adding functionality to the template

Normally, the development of EJB-based applications is complicated. This text will not teach you EJB application development and architecture, but it will show you how to add a simple bit of functionality to this template.

Now add another method to the TestSessionBean session bean and invoke that method from a client. Open the file *~/ejbproject/src/main/ejb/test/session/ TestSessionBean.java* and add the method shown here:

```
/**
 * @ejb:interface-method view-type="remote"
 **/
public String getCurrentTimestamp( )
{
    return new java.util.Date().toString( );
}
```

You'll notice the special comments at the start of the listing. These comments are an XDoclet command that tells the build system to generate the proper wrapper code to make this method visible to the remote client.

For more on XDoclet, check out the online documentation at *http://xdoclet.sourceforge.net*.

Next, create a new *clock.jsp* file as shown in Example 14-3. Place this JSP in the template's */web* directory, alongside */web/index.jsp*.

Example 14-3. The clock JSP

```
<%@ page session="false"
   isThreadSafe="true"
   isErrorPage="false"
   import="javax.naming.*, test.interfaces.*"
%>
<HTML><HEAD><TITLE>EJB Clock</TITLE></HEAD>
<BODY>
<h4>World's Most Complex Clock</h4>
<p>The current server time is: </p>
<p><%
   try {
      Context myContext = new InitialContext( );
      TestSessionHome myHome = (TestSessionHome) myContext.lookup(
         "java:comp/env/ejb/webtest/TestSession"
      );
      TestSession mySession = myHome.create( );
      %>
<%= mySession.getCurrentTimestamp( ) %>
      <%
   }
   catch( Exception e ) {
      out.println( "Caught exception: " + e.getMessage( ) );
      e.printStackTrace( );
   }
%>
</BODY>
</HTML>
```

Now open the Terminal, cd to the *~/ejbproject* directory, and execute */usr/local/ant/bin/ant*. These steps will recompile the TestSessionBean, generate the proper client files, copy over *clock.jsp*, and rebuild and deploy a new WAR file into JBoss.

As long as you place EJBs, JSPs, and other resources alongside like components in the template project, no special steps are required to include new components in the build process.

JBoss automatically detects and redeploys the new WAR file (you will see this in the JBoss log if you are watching). You should now be able to open your web browser to the URL *http://localhost:8080/web-client/clock.jsp* and see the new clock in action, as shown in Figure 14-6.

Figure 14-6. The clock JSP

Pushing the Envelope

EJB is a popular architecture for building web applications, but it suffers from one significant liability: EJBs are accessible only from Java applications. While it is possible to use some arcane CORBA techniques in conjunction with RMI/IIOP to get to EJBs from non-Java programs, it is rarely worth the trouble. However, EJBs often expose functionality that you may want to make available to non-Java clients.

The next chapter shows how to build web services that are accessible by other, non-Java, systems, including Apple's proprietary scripting language, AppleScript. This lesson will round out your enterprise development skills on Mac OS X, and probably make you all the rage at the water cooler as well.

CHAPTER 15

Web Services

Depending on who you talk to, web services are as simple as a set of remote interfaces for an application or as complex as a complete reinvention of the Internet. As is generally the case, the truth lies somewhere in between. As you write enterprise applications, you will find that you often want to expose them to non-Java clients. This chapter details how to take on this task, at least within the context of web services. It examines both simple and complex applications of web services, and gives you a good idea of how to get started in this area of programming.

On the simple end of the spectrum, you can create a web service by providing an application programming interface (API) that is exposed as a set of remote procedure calls (RPC) over the Internet. An example of this is a wholesale business that wishes to provide a set of programmatic interfaces for merchants to verify (in real time) the current inventory of a product, and then order products that are in stock.

At the other end of the spectrum, web services can describe a complete framework for reworking the Internet itself, where HTML and hyperlinks are replaced by a complex system of registries, portable objects, XML-based interfaces to sites with dynamic discovery, or complex and hyper-intelligent models for business-to-business transactions. Obviously this view is a bit extreme, and best avoided for the sake of time, space, and general sanity.

This chapter looks at web services as an RPC mechanism. In particular, it focuses on one of RPC's simplest mechanisms, XML-RPC, and describes the differences between XML-RPC and its more sophisticated cousin, SOAP.

RPC

The core of all web services is the ability for code on different machines to interact. There are as many protocols, APIs, and solutions available for this task as there are developers, but remote procedure calls are probably the most traditional approach to the problem.

RPC Basics

A brief discussion of the remote procedure call (RPC) is in order. Object-oriented developers work with code such as that shown here:

```
Window myWindow = new Window( );
myWindow.setTitle("Hello");
```

You'll notice that the details of how to actually set a window title are completely hidden from the developer. Not just obvious details (such as the code for drawing the graphics) are hidden here, but runtime details (such as how the methods are bound to the object or how memory is allocated) are abstracted away. The details are typically a combination of runtime code, compilers, linkers, and other tools.

Is RPC a Reality?

The idea that a local object is as easily accessible as a remote object has never been verified, which makes a lot of the hype surrounding RPC irrelevant for client applications. Except in highly controlled production server environments, networks tend to be available in a spotty fashion, and the introduction of wireless devices makes it just that much worse. In the long run, perhaps in my lifetime, I'll see networks that are fast and reliable enough for me to trust as much as a local resource, but probably not. This is partly why asynchronous messaging is so important—but then again, writing both the user interface and the actual code for asynchronous RPC-based applications, including web services, is also complicated.

The basic idea behind RPC is that a developer ought to be able to work with a remote object as naturally as with a local object:

```
Window myWindow = RemoteWindowServer.getWindow( );
myWindow.setTitle("Hello");
```

In this example, a window is created and runs on a remote server, and all the standard interfaces that one would expect are now available, except now the actual drawing of the window occurs on the remote server. The details of how the text string "Hello" is sent across the network are abstracted away from the developer.

Java and RPC

Remote Method Invocation (RMI) is the built-in Java implementation of an RPC mechanism. RMI works well, but it requires some setup and configuration, and, perhaps most importantly, it's a very Java-specific way of performing RPC. The code that you write and expose as RMI services is readily accessible only from another Java application.

Recently, CORBA was positioned as the next big thing in RPC mechanisms, but it suffered from its complexity. In particular, a strong emphasis was placed on making CORBA a superset of several different languages, including C++ and other languages such as Pascal. CORBA bindings are included in the standard JDK distribution, but they have never seen the kind of popularity that its supporters would like.

XML-RPC

.In 1998, Userland (*http://www.userland.com*) began working with Microsoft on a standard mechanism for RPC. This mechanism worked across systems via TCP/IP, and was called XML-RPC. The XML in XML-RPC is actually a commentary on the implementation of the protocol itself; developers using XML-RPC client libraries should be familiar with the general XML-RPC format (much as a HTTP/HTML developer should be familiar with the basic HTTP formats). However, it's possible to use XML-RPC without ever having to worry about the underlying XML messages.

One of the most popular implementations of XML-RPC was the so-called Helma XML-RPC libraries, which have since been donated to the Apache Software Foundation as Apache XML-RPC. Like all Apache libraries and projects, Apache XML-RPC is free, open source, and runs well on Mac OS X.

Before using web services on Mac OS X, I'll show you a simple XML-RPC server and client implemented with Apache XML-RPC.

Installation and Setup

This example builds on material taught earlier in the book, which created a web services server and a graphical client.

The *xmlrpc-1.1.jar* file contains the Apache XML-RPC libraries. This file is available from *http://xml.apache.org/xmlrpc/* under the download binaries section (*http://xml.apache.org/dist/xmlrpc/release/v1.1/xmlrpc-1.1.zip* as of this writing). Once you have this file, set up the directory structure shown in Figure 15-1. You'll notice that the XML-RPC JAR file was placed in the *lib* directory. It is then referenced in the *build.xml* file shown in Example 15-1.

Figure 15-1. XML-RPC example directory structure

Example 15-1. XML-RPC build file

```
<project default="compile" basedir=".">
    <property name="src" location="src"/>
    <property name="build" location="build"/>

    <target name="compile">
        <javac
            srcdir="${src}"
            destdir="${build}"
            classpath="lib/xmlrpc-1.1.jar"
        />
    </target>
</project>
```

You'll use the `SimpleEdit` and `SimpleEditPlugin` classes developed in Chapter 4 for your client-side graphical user interface.

The remaining files, *XmlRpcAsynchClientPlugin.java*, *XmlRpcClientTest-Plugin.java*, and *XmlRpcMiniServer.java*, will be added in the next few sections.

XML-RPC Basics

Figure 15-2 illustrates the basic model for working with XML-RPC (and SOAP). Server APIs and client libraries hide the complexity required to make method calls across different systems. In the case of Apache XML-RPC, you'll use the built-in web server to handle your server needs. Once you create a web server (using the class org.apache.xmlrpc.XmlRpcServer), you'll just pass in an ordinary Java object to handle the incoming requests. You will not need to interact with complex interfaces or APIs; you'll just write ordinary Java application code.

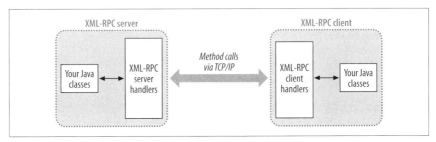

Figure 15-2. Web Services development model

Clients, however, require slightly more preparation. You can make a remote call *synchronously*, in which the execution of that thread stops until a response is returned, or *asynchronously*, in which you pass an event notification handler that is called when the remote method call completes. The advantage of asynchronous execution is that control returns to your application immediately; the Apache XML-RPC libraries automatically create a new thread for the remote communication and let your application know (via the handler) when a result has been returned. Either way, you'll want to use the class org.apache.xmlrpc.XmlRpcClient for the actual request.

If you decide to support asynchronous clients, implement the interface org.apache.xmlrpc.AsyncCallback, which has only two methods: handleError( ), which lets you know something went wrong, and handleResult( ), which tells you that a request returned properly.

A Simple XML-RPC Application

The following subsections detail the process of building up an XML-RPC application. The Apache XML-RPC framework handles much of the complexity involved in this process, leaving you to implement application-specific functionality. This means that you get to focus on your business logic, rather than the intricacies of HTTP, XML, sockets, and network programming.

XML-RPC servers

The code shown in Example 15-2 demonstrates a simple XML-RPC server. Note that this server is written to be launched from the Terminal.

Example 15-2. XML-RPC mini-server

```
package com.wiverson.macosbook.webservices;

public class XmlRpcMiniServer extends org.apache.xmlrpc.XmlRpcServer
{

    public static void main(String[] args)
    {
        System.out.print("Launching...");
        try
        {
            org.apache.xmlrpc.WebServer myWebServer =
            new org.apache.xmlrpc.WebServer(9000);
            myWebServer.addHandler("MiniServer ", new MiniServer());
            myWebServer.start();
        } catch (java.io.IOException e)
        {
            e.printStackTrace();
        }
        System.out.println("ready.");
    }

    public static class MiniServer
    {
        public String now()
        {
            synchronized(this)
            {
                try
                {
                    this.wait(5000);
                } catch (java.lang.InterruptedException e)
                {}
            }
            return new java.util.Date().toString();
        }

        public String add (String a, String b)
        {
            return "" + (new Integer(a)).intValue() + (new Integer(b)).intValue();
        }
    }
}
```

You'll notice that this code is surprisingly sparse. It creates a server (assigned to port 9000) and then defines a simple Java class (MiniServer) with only two methods.

The first method, MiniServer.now(), returns the current date and time as a String (although a this.wait() method causes it to take a few extra seconds to execute). The second method, MiniServer.add( ), takes two Strings, converts them to integers, and then returns the result as a String.

This class is then instantiated and has a handler attached to it through the addHandler( ) method. This method makes the object available for remote access by an XML-RPC client. Finally, start( ) does just what you would expect—it gets the server to listen for XML-RPC requests.

When you build and run the code, you won't see much—just a notice of when the server is ready to accept communication:

```
[Luthien:~/xmlrpc] wiverson% /usr/local/ant/bin/ant
Buildfile: build.xml

compile:

BUILD SUCCESSFUL
Total time: 5 seconds
[Luthien:~/xmlrpc] wiverson% java -classpath ./lib/xmlrpc-1.1.jar:./build
com.wiverson.macosbook.webservices.XmlRpcMiniServer
Launching...ready.
```

Assuming that you've placed the *xmlrpc-1.1.jar* file somewhere on the JVM classpath, you can verify that the server is running with a simple command line in a new Terminal window:

```
[Luthien:~/xmlrpc] wiverson% java -classpath ./lib/xmlrpc-1.1.jar org.
apache.xmlrpc.XmlRpcClient http://localhost:9000/ MiniServer.add 1 2
3
```

 The XML-RPC JAR must be on your command-line classpath (through the CLASSPATH environment variable or the -cp argument to java) for clients, in addition to being in the classpath of the JVM running the XML-RPC server. Since running the example probably will involve two Terminal windows, it might require setting the classpath in both windows before running any code.

You've now created a server that provides a programmatic API (in this case, the two methods now( ) and add( )), which is available over a network.

Synchronous XML-RPC clients

Next, add the ability to talk to this XML-RPC server to a Java application. Again, you'll build on the SimpleEdit application developed in Chapter 4, starting with a synchronous client call to the XML-RPC service.

Synchronous refers to the fact that the application waits for the remote method to return before continuing program execution. For normal, local method calls, this behavior is usually acceptable, as most operations can be completed very rapidly. However, as this exercise demonstrates, it can have undesirable side effects if the application's user interface is waiting for a remote method to complete (this is also referred to as being *blocked*). Still, the model is much easier and more deterministic. You always know what is going on in your application because it proceeds linearly, method invocation by method invocation, until all requests have been serviced and responded to.

Example 15-3 illustrates a simple XML-RPC client, which implements both a command-line version of the client and a SimpleEditPlugin.

Example 15-3. A synchronous XML-RPC client

```
package com.wiverson.macosbook.webservices;

public class XmlRpcClientTestPlugin
    implements com.wiverson.macosbook.SimpleEditPlugin
{

    public XmlRpcClientTestPlugin( )
    {
    }

    public static void main(String[] args)
    {
        System.out.print("Calling synch...");
        System.out.println(new XmlRpcClientTestPlugin().callRemote( ));
    }

    public String callRemote( )
    {
        try
        {
            org.apache.xmlrpc.XmlRpcClient xmlrpc =
            new org.apache.xmlrpc.XmlRpcClient
                ("http://localhost:9000/MiniServer");
            java.util.Vector params = new java.util.Vector( );
            return (String) xmlrpc.execute("MiniServer.now", params);
        } catch (java.net.MalformedURLException e1)
        {
            e1.printStackTrace( );
        } catch (java.io.IOException e2)
        {
            e2.printStackTrace( );
        }catch (org.apache.xmlrpc.XmlRpcException e3)
        {
            e3.printStackTrace( );
        }
        return "Unable to connect.";
    }
```

Example 15-3. A synchronous XML-RPC client (continued)

```
public void doAction(com.wiverson.macosbook.SimpleEdit frame,
    java.awt.event.ActionEvent evt)
{
    frame.appendDocumentText(this.callRemote( ));
}

public String getAction( )
{
    return "Test Synchronous XML-RPC";
}

public void init(com.wiverson.macosbook.SimpleEdit frame)
{
}
}
```

The actual web services work occurs in the callRemote( ) method. In this case, you make the remote invocation with the org.apache.xmlrpc. XmlRpcClient class. Specify the remote server's address and the object you wish to communicate with, and then call the execute( ) method to make the remote call. Using this class from the command line is straightforward:

```
[Luthien:~/xmlrpc] wiverson% java -classpath ./lib/xmlrpc-1.1.jar:./build
com.wiverson.macosbook.webservices.XmlRpcClientTestPlugin
Calling synch...Sun Jan 12 21:03:36 PST 2003
```

When running this application, you'll notice that the application appears to freeze after the "Calling synch..." is echoed to the screen and before the result is written out.

Similarly, you can launch the SimpleEdit application to see the interface (as shown in Figure 15-3):

```
[Luthien:~/xmlrpc] wiverson% java -classpath ./lib/xmlrpc-1.1.jar:./build
com.wiverson.macosbook.SimpleEdit com.wiverson.macosbook.webservices.
XmlRpcClientTestPlugin
```

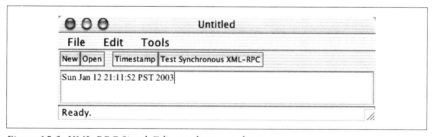

Figure 15-3. XML-RPC SimpleEdit synchronous client

You will notice that the SimpleEdit program appears to have locked up when accessing the remote service (keeping in mind the delay introduced in the server to simulate a poor network). The solution is to use asynchronous client services.

Asynchronous XML-RPC clients

This section builds a version of the client that takes advantage of the built-in support for asynchronous remote method calls. In effect, the code says "Call this remote method and keep track of the call for me. Let me know when something happens, but in the meantime I'll continue working." Simply put, it takes care of the multithreading for you, leaving you to write a simple handler that receives the notifications. This is shown in Example 15-4.

Example 15-4. An asynchronous XML-RPC client

```
package com.wiverson.macosbook.webservices;

public class XmlRpcAsynchClientPlugin
    implements com.wiverson.macosbook.SimpleEditPlugin
{
    public XmlRpcAsynchClientPlugin( )
    {
    }

    public static void main(String[] args)
    {
        System.out.print("Calling asynch...");
        new XmlRpcAsynchClientPlugin( ).callRemote(null);
        System.out.println("ok...");
    }

    public void callRemote(com.wiverson.macosbook.SimpleEdit frame)
    {
        try
        {
            org.apache.xmlrpc.XmlRpcClient xmlrpc =
            new org.apache.xmlrpc.XmlRpcClient
                ("http://localhost:9000/MiniServer");
            java.util.Vector params = new java.util.Vector( );
            AsynchTimeHandler myAsynchTimeHandler = new AsynchTimeHandler(frame);
            xmlrpc.executeAsync("MiniServer.now", params, myAsynchTimeHandler);
        } catch (java.net.MalformedURLException e1)
        {
            e1.printStackTrace( );
        } catch (java.io.IOException e2)
        {
            e2.printStackTrace( );
        }
    }
}
```

Example 15-4. An asynchronous XML-RPC client (continued)

```java
public void doAction(com.wiverson.macosbook.SimpleEdit frame,
    java.awt.event.ActionEvent evt)
{
    this.callRemote(frame);
}

public String getAction( )
{
    return "Test Async XML-RPC";
}

public void init(com.wiverson.macosbook.SimpleEdit frame)
{
}

public class AsynchTimeHandler implements org.apache.xmlrpc.AsyncCallback
{
    public AsynchTimeHandler(com.wiverson.macosbook.SimpleEdit frame)
    {
        myFrame = frame;
    }

    private com.wiverson.macosbook.SimpleEdit myFrame = null;

    public void handleError(Exception e, java.net.URL uRL, String str)
    {
        e.printStackTrace( );
    }

    public void handleResult(Object obj, java.net.URL uRL, String str)
    {
        if(myFrame != null)
            myFrame.appendDocumentText((String) obj);
        else
            System.out.println((String) obj);
    }
}
}
```

As you can see, this code is a bit more sophisticated than its synchronous counterpart. Most importantly, there is an additional inner class, AsynchTimeHandler, to actually process the result returned by the remote method. This inner class implements the interface org.apache.xmlrpc. AsyncCallback, with the two methods handleError( ) and handleResult( ) supporting either failures or successful completion.

Accessing XML-RPC Services from AppleScript

In the folder */Applications/AppleScript*, you'll find a tool called Script Editor (shown in Figure 15-4) that is used to work with Apple's proprietary Apple-Script language. AppleScript is Apple's standard language for handling interapplication scripting, with a long heritage on the Mac OS platform. If you're coming from a Unix background, you might be used to stringing together multiple applications with shell scripts. It may be useful to think of AppleScript as a way to create shell scripts that hook together graphical applications.

Figure 15-4. AppleScript Script Editor

A full introduction to AppleScript is beyond the scope of this book, but it is useful to know that you can connect AppleScript to Java applications via XML-RPC. Example 15-5 shows how to connect to the XML-RPC server you created earlier using AppleScript.

Example 15-5. An XML-RPC client in AppleScript

```
script MiniServer

    on now( )
        tell application "http://localhost:9000/"
            return call xmlrpc {method name:"MiniServer.now"}
        end tell
    end now

    on add(s1, s2)
        tell application "http://localhost:9000/"
            return call xmlrpc
            {
                method name:"MiniServer.add", parameters:{s1, s2}
            }
        end tell
    end add

end script

display dialog MiniServer's add(1, 2)
display dialog MiniServer's now( )
```

Running the script causes AppleScript to display two dialogs, as shown in Figures 15-5 and 15-6.

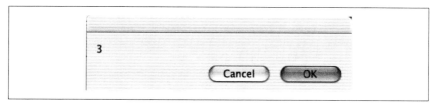

Figure 15-5. AppleScript and the XML-RPC addition functionality

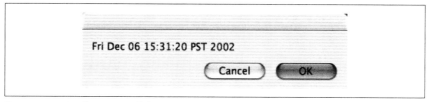

Figure 15-6. AppleScript and the XML-RPC "now" functionality

For more information on building applications with AppleScript, visit *http://www.macdevcenter.com* for some excellent introductory articles.

SOAP

The Simple Object Access Protocol (SOAP) is a more complex RPC mechanism than XML-RPC, but both share a common basis (an underlying protocol based on XML and HTTP) and conceptual model. SOAP adds many features to RPC, including explicit support for asynchronous message delivery via the Simple Mail Transport Protocol (SMTP), the basis for delivery of Internet email.

The use of SOAP versus XML-RPC depends largely on the eventual target use of your application and who or what you're communicating with. Generally, the simplicity of XML-RPC has led to widespread adoption, whereas the overall sophistication and capabilities of SOAP have led to broader adoption in the enterprise (not to mention the explicit endorsement of SOAP by entities such as Microsoft and IBM).

This chapter looks at Apache Axis 1.0, an open source implementation of the SOAP 1.1 specification providing both server and client capabilities.

Obtaining Axis

You can download Apache Axis 1.0 from *http://xml.apache.org/axis/*. The download used here is Release 1.0 from *http://xml.apache.org/axis/releases.html*.

Installation

The rest of this chapter assumes that you are working with JBoss, installed as described in Chapter 14.

 The process of installing Axis under Tomcat is similar to installation under JBoss. For complete instructions, refer to *http://cvs.apache.org/viewcvs.cgi/~checkout~/xml-axis/java/docs/install.html*.

SOAP requires a servlet (or, sometimes, several servlets) to receive requests, and then respond to those requests, via HTTP. Using a servlet lets you avoid dealing with network sockets manually, which is always a hassle.

Axis comes prepackaged with a WAR directory, ready to install in a web container or application server.

If you decide to install Axis manually or on another system later, the core libraries are in the following JAR files:

axis-1_0/lib/axis.jar
axis-1_0/lib/jaxrpc.jar
axis-1_0/lib/saaj.jar
axis-1_0/lib/commons-logging.jar
axis-1_0/lib/commons-dicovery.jar
axis-1_0/lib/wsdl4j.jar

While you can set up Axis to expose any Java class as a web service, one of its best features is its ability to expose Java Web Service files with little (or no) developer intervention.

What is JWS?

A Java Web Service (JWS) file is an ordinary Java source file with a different extension (*.jws*), placed in a specific directory exposed as part of a web application. When a request is made for a JWS file, Axis compiles the file as if it were a Java file, adding additional wrappers to make the objects and methods within available to the remote caller. In this way, it operates much like a JSP file, but instead of providing HTML documents to web browsers, JWS files provide web services.

One of JWS's key advantages is that it is a much easier development model than a traditional edit/compile cycle, like JSPs or servlets. Instead of packaging your files as a WAR file and then deploying them, you can work directly on the files in a deployment directory, with Axis handling compilation (and recompilation) as requests come in from clients, all due to the *.jws* extension.

Copying the files

To facilitate using JWS files, install Axis in JBoss not as a sealed WAR, but as a directory that you can deploy directly, as shown below:

```
[Luthien:~/Public/xml-axis-10] wiverson% ls
README              lib                 samples             xmls
docs                release-notes.html  webapps

[Luthien:~/Public/xml-axis-10] wiverson% cd webapps/axis/

[Luthien:xml-axis-10/webapps/axis] wiverson% mkdir /usr/local/jboss/server/
default/deploy/axis.war

[Luthien:xml-axis-10/webapps/axis] wiverson% cp -r * /usr/local/jboss/
server/default/deploy/axis.war
```

To support the dynamic compilation of JWS files with JBoss, add the servlet library to the Axis web application's *WEB-INF/lib* directory:

```
[Luthien:xml-axis-10/webapps/axis] wiverson% cd /usr/local/jboss/server/
default/lib/

[Luthien:server/default/lib] wiverson% cp javax.servlet.jar ../deploy/axis.
war/WEB-INF/lib/
```

If JBoss isn't already running, start it now. You can verify that Axis is properly installed by viewing the default Axis management page at *http:// localhost:8080/axis/*. If everything is working properly, you'll see the configuration page shown in Figure 15-7.

Figure 15-7. Axis configuration

SOAP Basics

SOAP is a direct descendent of XML-RPC, proposed by some of the same vendors that originally worked on XML-RPC. It's been positioned as the enterprise version of web services, adding functionality such as support for more complex objects, namespaces, and envelopes. It is also associated with related technologies such as the Web Services Description Language (WSDL). This topic is beyond the scope of this text, however. If you're interested in these advanced features of SOAP, consult O'Reilly's *Java Web Services*, by David Chappell and Tyler Jewell.

For your purposes here, SOAP is just another RPC mechanism, similar to XML-RPC. There are significant differences in the protocols used to communicate between systems and the implementation libraries, but the conceptual model is the same as the one shown in Figure 15-2.

Server application development is most easily handled via JWS files, described above. Client development is similar to that of XML-RPC, with a slightly different set of classes. An `org.apache.axis.client.Service` object binds to a specific remote server, and an `org.apache.axis.client.Call` object executes a remote method. This section creates a *.jws* file for your server and uses these client APIs to retrieve the methods' results.

Building a SOAP Web Service

The web service you'll build for Axis is much like the one you built for XML-RPC. Add a file called *SimpleWebService.jws* to the */usr/local/jboss/server/ default/deploy/axis.war* directory with the contents shown in Example 15-6.

Example 15-6. A simple web service

```
public class SimpleWebService
{

    public SimpleWebService( )
    {
    }

    public int add(int a, int b)
    {
        return a + b;
    }

    public String now( )
    {
        return new java.util.Date().toString( );
    }

    public String slownow( )
    {
        synchronized(this)
        {
            try
            {
                this.wait(5000);
            } catch (java.lang.InterruptedException e)
            {}
        }
        return new java.util.Date().toString( );
    }

}
```

You'll notice that the JWS appears to be an ordinary Java class. Axis offers other mechanisms for handling SOAP requests that provide more control, but for many services, the JWS mechanism is more than adequate.

Accessing a SOAP Web Service from Java

The easiest way to talk to the web service is directly from your browser's address bar. As shown in Figure 15-8, you can simply request a web service via an HTML request, like *http://localhost:8080/axis/SimpleWebService. jws?method=now*.

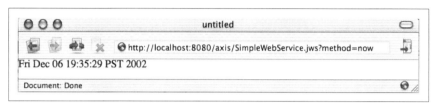

Figure 15-8. The "now" function via an HTTP GET request

You can also send parameters via the request parameters of a URL, such as *http://localhost:8080/axis/SimpleWebService.jws?method=add&a=1&b=2*. In this example, the parameter names provided on the URL (a and b) aren't significant. However, for more complex web services they are important, as they associate values with specific parameters in code. Figure 15-9 shows the results of this request.

Figure 15-9. The "add" functionality via an HTTP GET request

Example 15-7 shows how to access SOAP via Java. SOAP is more complex than XML-RPC, and therefore requires a bit more setup and configuration. It also affords a great deal more sophistication, however, and if your application requires very specific details about the methods invoked and how they are interacted with, it can be well worth the extra work.

Example 15-7. Accessing SOAP services

```
package com.wiverson.macosbook.webservices;

import org.apache.axis.client.Call;
import org.apache.axis.client.Service;
import javax.xml.namespace.QName;
import com.wiverson.macosbook.SimpleEdit;

public class SOAPClientPlugin implements
```

Example 15-7. Accessing SOAP services (continued)

```
    com.wiverson.macosbook.SimpleEditPlugin
{
    public SOAPClientPlugin( )
    {
    }

    public void doAction(SimpleEdit frame, java.awt.event.ActionEvent evt)
    {
        frame.appendDocumentText(this.remoteCall( ));
    }

    public String getAction( )
    {
        return "SOAP Client";
    }

    public void init(SimpleEdit frame)
    {
    }

    public static void main(String[] args)
    {
        System.out.println(new SOAPClientPlugin().remoteCall( ));
    }

    public String remoteCall( )
    {
        try
        {
            String webserviceLocation =
            "http://localhost:8080/axis/SimpleWebService.jws";

            Service service = new Service( );
            Call call    = (Call) service.createCall( );

            call.setTargetEndpointAddress(new java.net.URL(webserviceLocation));

            return (String) call.invoke("now", null);

        } catch (Exception e)
        {
            System.err.println(e.toString( ));
        }
        return "Unable to connect.";

    }

}
```

Accessing a SOAP Web Service from AppleScript

SOAP might be more complex than XML-RPC, but a SOAP client is built into AppleScript as well, as shown in Figure 15-10.

Figure 15-10. Scripting a SOAP client

Example 15-8 shows a client similar to the one you built earlier to access the XML-RPC service. However, more detail is required (in particular, extra parameter information) for SOAP interaction. It may seem a bit odd that the AppleScript client enforces this extra detail (when the browser's HTTP GET was able to invoke the service without it), but that's the nature of SOAP—it's an evolving set of standards.

Example 15-8. Scripting a SOAP client

```
script SoapServer

    on now( )
        tell application "http://localhost:8080/axis/SimpleWebService.jws"
            return call soap {method name:"now"}
        end tell
```

Example 15-8. Scripting a SOAP client (continued)

```
end now

on add(s1, s2)
    tell application "http://localhost:8080/axis/SimpleWebService.jws"
        return call soap {method name:"add", parameters:{a:s1 as integer, b:
s2 as integer}}
    end tell
end add

end script

display dialog SoapServer's now( )
display dialog SoapServer's add(1, 2)
```

Additional Reading

Web services are fairly new and still developing. O'Reilly dedicates an entire section of their web site to this area, found at *http://webservices.oreilly.com*, and it's wise to watch web service developments closely. You may also benefit from monitoring sites such as *http://www.w3.org* and *http://www.xml.org* for information on the status of various proposed standards.

Final Thoughts

In one volume, you've walked from "Hello World" through desktop application development, web applications, enterprise application development, and finally web services. You've looked at how to build applications that are custom-tailored to the Mac OS X platform and how to maintain cross-platform compatibility.

In many ways, this book represents an eclectic overview of the Java application development world. Perhaps one of the book's most interesting and impressive aspects is that it shows you how to build all of these applications on a single operating system. Such an elegant operating system, combining the best of a modern graphical operating system and solid Unix underpinnings, deserves excellent applications.

> "When I am working on a problem I never think about beauty. I only think about how to solve the problem. But when I have finished, if the solution is not beautiful, I know it is wrong."
>
> ——Buckminster Fuller (1895-1983)

Index

We'd like to hear your suggestions for improving our indexes. Send email to *index@oreilly.com*.

CurrentJDK directory, 8
cursor, hiding in full screen display, 114
custom spellchecking, 186

D

Darwin, 2
database-driven JSP
    applications, 210–222
    building web application, 212–222
    creating first JSP, 212
    database connections, 217–220
    debugging JSP pages, 213
    retrieving data, 217–221
    reviewing the application, 222
    talking to the database, 215–217
    setting up the database, 210–212
databases, 187–200
    Dreamweaver connection, setting
        up, 31
    Java Database Connectivity (see
        JDBC)
    Mac OS X, 189–200
    MySQL, 189–194
    PostgreSQL, 194–199
    relational, 188
    Structured Query Language
        (SQL), 188
    queries involving multiple
        tables, 189
dates, creating java.util.Date object and
    converting to String, 213
debugging JSP pages, 213
delivering applications (see
    web-delivered applications)
dependencies
    JBoss template project, 231
    JNI and, 83
deployment
    applets, 126–128
    build/deploy directory (J2EE
        application), 237
deployment descriptors generated by
    XDoclet, 237
desktop shell integration, Apple
    extensions, 64
    Finder integration, 64
Developer Tools CD, 26

/Developer/Applications directory
    IconComposer application, 103
    MRJAppBuilder tool, 120
dialogs
    Quit handler for Finder
        integration, 76–79
    spoken, 141
    TalkingAlertJDialog class
        (example), 147
    TalkingJDialog class, 145–147
    triggered by menu callbacks, 65
dictation services on Mac OS X, 141
dictionaries, 107
    CFBundle dictionary keys, 107
    CFBundleDocumentTypes dictionary
        keys, 108
    Java dictionary keys, 109
        Arguments, 110
        ClassPath, 109
        JVMVersion, 110
        MainClass, 109
        VMOptions, 110
        WorkingDirectory, 110
    Properties dictionary keys, 110–113
        apple.awt.brushMetalLook, 112
        com.apple.hwaccel, 111
        com.apple.hwexclude, 111
        com.apple.macos.smallTabs, 111
        com.apple.macos.use-file-dialog-
            packages, 111
        com.apple.macos.useScreenMenu
            Bar, 111
        com.apple.macosx.AntiAliased-
            GraphicsOn, 112
        com.apple.macosx.AntiAliased-
            TextOn, 112
        com.apple.mrj.application.apple.
            menu.about.name, 112
        com.apple.mrj.application.grow-
            box.intrudes, 112
        com.apple.mrj.application.live-
            resize, 112
digital signatures
    JAR files for JNLP-based
        applications, 134
    jarsigner tool, using with Java Web
        Start code, 136

event handling
Finder integration
Open and Preferences
handlers, 75
registering handlers with
FinderIntegration class, 74
Swing GUI application, 58
event notification handler, in
asynchronous remote
calls, 244
exit( ) (System), 134
exporting movies from QuickTime
application, 173, 175
flattening media files, 173
Extensions folder, 7
extensions to Java (Apple), 63–86
comparison to other vendors, 63
Mac OS X Finder (see Finder)

F

fade effect when changing screen
resolutions, 114
file dialogs, icons displayed in, 116
file encoding, 89–92
Java, Unicode, and UTF, 91
Unicode, 90
file extensions supported by an
application, 109
file I/O (see input/output)
file:// prefix, 213
file separators, 93
getting for different systems, 35
FileDialog class, showing application
packages as files, 111
files
identifying types of in property list
dictionaries, 107
opening (Finder handlers for), 118
Finder, 64–79
application bundles, display of, 102
application recognition, 118
desktop integration, 64
files beginning with dot (.), 232
icons displayed in, 116
icons for, in Resources folder, 103
ingegration support class
"About" dialog box, 74
integration plug-in, 65–68

integration support class, 68–79
Open and Preferences
handlers, 75
"Quit" dialog, 76–79
registering handlers, 74
"Open" file handlers, 118
FinderIntegration class, 68–79
registering handlers, 74
FinderIntegrationPlugin class, 66
FinderIntegrationPlugin.java file, 65
flattened media files, 173
floating-point font metrics, 113
fonts
Aqua GUI, 41
floating-point metrics, 113
footer.jsp file, 218, 219
Foundation and Application Kit
frameworks in Cocoa, Java
APIs for, 11
freeware commercial software, 25
JavaBrowser, 29
JBuilder IDE, 25
Project Builder, 26–29
full screen display (JDK 1.4), 114
apple.awt.fakefullscreen
property, 114
apple.awt.fullscreencaptureall-
displays property, 114
apple.awt.fullscreenhidecursor
property, 114
apple.awt.fullscreenusefade
property, 114
functionality, adding to JBoss
template, 237–239
functions in C, becoming methods in
Java, 160

G

Gecko HTML rendering engine, 127
generate directory (J2EE
application), 237
getAction( ), 62, 183
getAvailableLanguages( )
(SpellChecker), 186
getProperties( ) (System), 35
getResource( ), 134
global properties files, 39

R

real-time spellchecking, 183–185
Recognizer class, 143
redirect output to a file
(PostgreSQL), 198
references, QuickTime movies, 172
relational databases, 188
accessing with SQL, 188
queries involving multiple
tables, 189
(see also databases; JDBC)
Remote Method Invocation (see RMI)
remote procedure calls (see RPC)
rendering via Java 2D, 113
apple.awt.antialiasing property, 113
apple.awt.fractionalmetrics
property, 113
apple.awt.interpolation
property, 113
apple.awt.rendering property, 113
apple.awt.textantialiasing
property, 113
resizing control, intruding into AWT
frames, 112
resizing windows (live), 112
resource files (see WAR files)
resource files, testing for cross-platform
compatibility, 95
Resources folder, 116
Finder, icons for, 103
icns file, 117
Resources/Java directory
JAR or class files (Java), 103
referenced with $JAVAROOT
variable, 109
Rhapsody, 2
RMI (Remote Method Invocation), 226,
242
over IIOP, 11
roles, management in tomcat-users.xml
file, 209
"root" location (Mac OS X), 6
RPC (remote procedure calls), 240,
240–242
basics of, 241
Java and, 242
SOAP, 253–260
Apache Axis
implementation, 253–255

basics, 255
(see also SOAP)
XML-RPC, 242–252
installation and setup, 242
simple application
(example), 244–250
run-client.sh file, 234

S

scopes, actions on menu bars, 44
screen resolutions, fade effect when
changing, 114
Script Editor tool (for AppleScript), 251
SDK (Software Development Kit)
MRJ, download site, 15
secure sandbox
for applets, 123
requirements for JNLP-delivered
applications in, 134
security
creating users without home
directories using NetInfo, 191,
194
java.policy file, 128
sem.h file, fixes for, 194
separator characters in directory or file
paths, 93
sequence grabber components
(QuickTime), 159
SequenceGeneratorBean.java file, 235
server/lib directory (Tomcat), 209
server.xml (Tomcat configuration
file), 208
servlet container (see Tomcat)
servlets, 202
Jasper (in Tomcat), 206
JavaServer Pages (JSP) and, 203
JSP, translation into by Tomcat, 215
SOAP requirement of, 253
session EJBs, 235
TestSessionBean.java (example), 235
adding method to, 237
web user interface to, 235
setLanguageModel( ) (Recognizer), 143
setupMenu( ), 59
shells
tcsh, 17
tsch, creating, 19
show( ), 59

About the Author

Will Iverson, principal consultant for Cascade Technology Group (*http://www.cascadetg.com*), has been working in the computer and information technology field professionally since 1990. His diverse background includes developing statistical applications for use in analyzing data from the NASA Space Shuttle, acting as the Java & Runtimes Product Manager for Apple Computer, and managing developer relations for Symantec's Internet Tools group (the creators of VisualCafé).

Colophon

Our look is the result of reader comments, our own experimentation, and feedback from distribution channels. Distinctive covers complement our distinctive approach to technical topics, breathing personality and life into potentially dry subjects.

The animal on the cover of *Mac OS X for Java Geeks* is a striped hyena (*Hyaena hyaena*). This nomadic species is native to the arid savanna, thorny bush, and stony deserts of northern and eastern Africa, the Middle East, India, and southern Asia. Striped hyenas have long coarse fur and are sandy-gray in color; they feature black spots on their legs, dark stripes running down their backs, and a heavy mane over their neck and shoulders. When threatened, their manes stand up, causing the hyena to appear much larger than their average weight of 100 pounds. Adults grow to nearly four feet long, not including their foot-long tails. These hyenas have pointed ears, a short muzzle, powerful jaws, and sharp teeth. While they resemble dogs both physically and socially (they sniff one another in greeting), hyenas belong to an entirely different animal family. Unlike the larger spotted hyena, striped hyenas do not "laugh"—verbal communication is in the form of short soft growls.

Striped hyenas are primarily nocturnal, preferring to sleep in caves or shaded outcroppings during the hot desert days. Small family groups may exist in these dens, but striped hyenas are not territorial; they rest and eat in the same areas for a short period of time before moving on. At night, they emerge to solitarily scavenge for carrion and other leftovers, even eating the bones from carcasses with no meat remaining on them. They supplement this diet by preying on small animals such as rodents, reptiles, and birds. As humans move into more and more of their habitat, it's become increasingly common for spotted hyenas to rely on garbage dumps and crops (they are particularly fond of fruit) for food. Human hunters are the largest threat to the striped hyena: some people believe that the organs and other parts of the hyena have medicinal value. Striped hyenas are listed as an endangered species, and populations in northern Africa are critically threatened.

Emily Quill was the production editor and proofreader for *Mac OS X for Java Geeks*. Ann Schirmer was the copyeditor. Philip Dangler, Claire Cloutier, and Jane Ellin provided quality control. Philip Dangler and Genevieve d'Entremont provided production assistance. Ellen Troutman-Zaig wrote the index.

Hanna Dyer designed the cover of this book, based on a series design by Edie Freedman. The cover image is a 19th-century engraving from the Dover Pictorial Archive. Emma Colby produced the cover layout with Quark-XPress 4.1, using Adobe's ITC Garamond font.

Bret Kerr designed the interior layout, based on a series design by David Futato. This book was converted to FrameMaker 5.5.6 by Andrew Savikas with a format conversion tool created by Erik Ray, Jason McIntosh, Neil Walls, and Mike Sierra that uses Perl and XML technologies. The text font is Linotype Birka; the heading font is Adobe Myriad Condensed; and the code font is LucasFont's TheSans Mono Condensed. The illustrations that appear in the book were produced by Robert Romano and Jessamyn Read using Macromedia FreeHand 9 and Adobe Photoshop 6. The tip and warning icons were drawn by Christopher Bing. This colophon was written by Philip Dangler.

Other Titles Available from O'Reilly

Java

Java Performance Tuning, 2nd Edition

By Jack Shirazi
2nd Edition January 2003
588 pages, ISBN 0-596-00377-3

Significantly revised and expanded, this second edition not only covers Java 1.4, but adds new coverage of JDBC, NIO, Servlets, EJB and JavaServer Pages. The book remains a valuable resource for teaching developers how to create a tuning strategy, how to use profiling tools to understand a program's behavior, and how to avoid performance penalties from inefficient code, making them more efficient and effective. The result is code that's robust, maintainable and fast!

Java Security, 2nd Edition

By Scott Oaks
2nd Edition May 2001
618 pages, ISBN 0-596-00157-6

The second edition focuses on the platform features of Java that provide security—the class loader, bytecode verifier, and security manager—and recent additions to Java that enhance this security model: digital signatures, security providers, and the access controller. The book covers in depth the security model of Java 2, version 1.3, including the two new security APIs: JAAS and JSSE.

Java Database Best Practices

By George Reese
1st Edition June 2003
304 pages, ISBN 0-596-00522-9

Java Database Best Practices rescues developers from having to slog through books on each of the various APIs before they figure out which method to use! This guide introduces each of the dominant APIs, explores the methodology and design components that use those APIs, and then offers practices most appropriate for different types and makes of databases, and different types of applications.

Java RMI

By William Grosso
1st Edition November 2001
576 pages, ISBN 1-56592-452-5

Enterprise Java developers, especially those working with Enterprise JavaBeans, and Jini, need to understand RMI technology in order to write today's complex, distributed applications. O'Reilly's Java RMI thoroughly explores and explains this powerful but often overlooked technology. Included is a wealth of real-world examples that developers can implement and customize.

Java Data Objects

By David Jordan & Craig Russell
1st Edition April 2003
384 pages, ISBN 0-596-00276-9

This book, written by the JDO Specification Lead and one of the key contributors to the JDO Specification, is the definitive work on the JDO API. It gives you a thorough introduction to JDO, starting with a simple application that demonstrates many of JDO's capabilities. It shows you how to make classes persistent, how JDO maps persistent classes to the database, how to configure JDO at runtime, how to perform transactions, and how to make queries.

Java Swing, 2nd Edition

By Marc Loy, Robert Eckstein, David Wood, James Elliott & Brian Cole
2nd Edition November 2002
1278 pages, ISBN 0-596-00408-7

This second edition of Java Swing thoroughly covers all the features available in Java 2 SDK 1.3 and 1.4. More than simply a reference, this new edition takes a practical approach. It is a book by developers for developers, with hundreds of useful examples, from beginning level to advanced, covering every component available in Swing. Whether you're a seasoned Java developer or just trying to find out what Java can do, you'll find Java Swing, 2nd edition an indispensable guide.

O'REILLY®

To order: 800-998-9938 • order@oreilly.com • www.oreilly.com
Online editions of most O'Reilly titles are available by subscription at safari.oreilly.com
Also available at most retail and online bookstores.

Java

Java Extreme Programming Cookbook
By Eric M. Burke & Brian M. Coyner
1st Edition March 2003
288 pages, ISBN0-596-00387-0

Brimming with over 100 "recipes" for getting down to business and actually doing XP, the *Java Extreme Programming Cookbook* doesn't try to "sell" you on XP; it succinctly documents the most important features of popular open source tools for XP in Java—including Ant, Junit, HttpUnit, Cactus, Tomcat, XDoclet—and then digs right in, providing recipes for implementing the tools in real-world environments.

Java Enterprise Best Practices
By The O'Reilly Java Authors, edited by Robert Eckstein
1st Edition December 2002
288 pages, ISBN 0-596-00384-6

This book is for intermediate and advanced Java developers, the ones who have been around the block enough times to understand just how complex—and unruly—an enterprise system can get. Each chapter in this collection contains several rules that provide insight into the "best practices" for creating and maintaining projects using the Java Enterprise APIs. Written by the world's leading Java experts, this book covers JDBC, RMI/-CORBA, Servlets, JavaServer Pages and custom tag libraries, XML, Internationalization, JavaMail, Enterprise JavaBeans, and performance tuning.

Java Cookbook
By Ian Darwin
1st Edition June 2001
882 pages, ISBN 0-59600-170-3

This book offers Java developers short, focused pieces of code that are easy to incorporate into other programs. The idea is to focus on things that are useful, tricky, or both. The book's code segments cover all of the dominant APIs and many specialized APIs and should serve as a great "jumping-off place" for Java developers who want to get started in areas outside their specialization.

Learning Java, 2nd Edition
By Pat Niemeyer & Jonathan Knudsen
2nd Edition June 2002
832 pages, ISBN 0-596-00285-8

This new edition of *Learning Java* comprehensively addresses important topics such as web applications, servlets, and XML. It provides full coverage of all Java 1.4 language features including assertions and exception chaining as well as new APIs such as regular expressions and NIO, the new I/O package. New Swing features and components are described along with updated coverage of the JavaBeans component architecture using the open source NetBeans IDE the latest information about Applets and the Java Plug-in for all major browsers.

Mac OS X for Java Geeks
By Will Iverson
1st Edition April 2003 (est.)
304 pages (est.), ISBN 0-596-00400-1

Mac OS X for Java Geeks delivers a complete and detailed look at the OS X platform for Java development. Based on the new 1.4 JDK and the 10.2 release of Mac OS X from Apple Computer, this is the most thorough guide available for both new and experienced Java developers who want to create cross-platform applications that take advantage of Mac OS X's unique functionality.

Java Management Extensions
By J. Steven Perry
1st Edition June 2002
312 pages, ISBN 0-596-00245-9

Java Management Extensions is a practical, hands-on guide to using the JMX APIs. This one-of-a-kind book is a complete treatment of the JMX architecture (both the instrumentation level and the agent level), and it's loaded with real-world examples for implementing Management Extensions. It also contains useful information at the higher level about JMX (the "big picture") to help technical managers and architects who are evaluating various application management approaches and are considering JMX.

O'REILLY®
To order: 800-998-9938 • order@oreilly.com • www.oreilly.com
Online editions of most O'Reilly titles are available by subscription at safari.oreilly.com
Also available at most retail and online bookstores.

Java

Java Servlet Programming, 2nd Edition
By Jason Hunter with
William Crawford
2nd Edition April 2001
780 pages, ISBN 0-596-00040-5

The second edition of this popular book has been completely
updated to add the new features of the Java Servlet
API Version 2.2, and new chapters on servlet security and advanced communication. In addition to
complete coverage of the 2.2 specification, we have
included bonus material on the new 2.3 version of
the specification.

Java & XML, 2nd Edition
By Brett McLaughlin
2nd Edition September 2001
528 pages, ISBN 0-596-000197-5

New chapters on Advanced SAX,
Advanced DOM, SOAP, and data
binding, as well as new examples
throughout, bring the second
edition of *Java & XML* thoroughly up to date.
Except for a concise introduction to XML basics,
the book focuses entirely on using XML from Java
applications. It's a worthy companion for Java
developers working with XML or involved in messaging, web services, or the new peer-to-peer move-
ment.

JavaServer Pages, 2nd Edition
By Hans Bergsten
2nd Edition August 2002
712 pages, ISBN 0-596-00317-X

Filled with useful examples and
the depth, clarity, and attention
to detail that made the first edition so popular with web devel-
opers, *JavaServer Pages*, 2nd Edition is completely
revised and updated to cover the substantial
changes in the 1.2 version of the JSP specifications,
and includes coverage of the new JSTL Tag
libraries—an eagerly anticipated standard set of
JSP elements for the tasks needed in most JSP
applications, as well as thorough coverage of Custom Tag Libraries.

J2EE Design Patterns
By William C.R. Crawford
& Jonathan Kaplan
1st Edition July 2003 (est.)
352 pages (est.), ISBN 0-596-00427-3

Crawford and Kaplan's *J2EE
Design Patterns* takes a different
approach than just simply pre-
senting another catalog of design patterns. The
authors broaden the scope by discussing ways to
choose design patterns when building an enterprise application from scratch, looking closely at
the real world tradeoffs that Java developers must
weigh when architecting their applications. They
also extend design patterns into areas not covered
in other books, presenting original patterns for
data modeling, transaction/process modeling, and
interoperability. This design pattern book breaks
the mold.

Enterprise JavaBeans, 3rd Edition
By Richard Monson-Haefel
3rd Edition September 2001
592 pages, ISBN 0-596-00226-2

Enterprise JavaBeans has been
thoroughly updated for the new
EJB Specification. Important
changes in Version 2.0 include a
completely new CMP (container-managed persistence) model that allows for much more complex
business function modeling; local interfaces that
will significantly improve performance of EJB
applications; and the "message driven bean," an
entirely new kind of Java bean based on asynchronous messaging and the Java Message Service.

Java Message Service
By Richard Monson-Haefel &
David Chappell
1st Edition December 2000
238 pages, ISBN 0-596-00068-5

This book is a thorough introduction to Java Message Service
(JMS) from Sun Microsystems. It
shows how to build applications using the point-
to-point and publish-and-subscribe models; use
features like transactions and durable subscriptions
to make applications reliable; and use messaging
within Enterprise JavaBeans. It also introduces a
new EJB type, the MessageDrivenBean, that is part
of EJB 2.0, and discusses integration of messaging
into J2EE.

O'REILLY®
To order: *800-998-9938* • *order@oreilly.com* • *www.oreilly.com*
Online editions of most O'Reilly titles are available by subscription at *safari.oreilly.com*
Also available at most retail and online bookstores.

Java

Java and SOAP

By Robert Englander
1st Edition May 2002
276 pages, ISBN 0-596-00175-4

Java and SOAP provides Java
developers with an in-depth look
at SOAP (the Simple Object
Access Protocol). Of course, it
covers the basics: what SOAP is, why it's soared to
a spot on the Buzzwords' Top Ten list, and what its
features and capabilities are. And it shows you how
to work with some of the more common Java APIs
in the SOAP world: Apache SOAP and GLUE.

Ant: The Definitive Guide

By Eric M. Burke & Jesse E. Tilly
1st Edition May 2002
288 pages, ISBN 0-596-00184-3

Ant is the premier build-man-
agement tool for Java environments. Ant is part of Jakarta, the
Apache Software Foundation's
open source Java project repository. Ant is written
entirely in Java, and is platform independent.
Using XML, a Java developer describes the modules involved in a build, and the dependencies
between those modules. Ant then does the rest,
compiling components as necessary in order to
build the application.

Java & XML Data Binding

By Brett McLaughlin
1st Edition May 2002
214 pages, ISBN 0-596-00278-5

This new title provides an in-
depth technical look at XML
Data Binding. The book offers
complete documentation of all
features in both the Sun Microsystems JAXB API
and popular open source alternative implementations (Enhydra Zeus, Exolabs Castor and Quick).
It also gets into significant detail about when data
binding is appropriate to use, and provides numerous practical examples of using data binding in
applications.

NetBeans: The Definitive Guide

By Tim Boudreau, Jesse Glick,
Simeon Greene, Vaughn Spurlin &
Jack Woehr
1st Edition October 2002
696 pages, ISBN 0-596-00280-7

O'Reilly's NetBeans: The Definitive
Guide is the authoritative reference
for understanding and using the NetBeans Integrated Development Environment for creating new
software with Java. Through a detailed tutorial, the
book explains the capabilities of the NetBeans
IDE, and compares it with competing software
such as Borland's JBuilder. Then the authors go
further, covering ways to expand NetBeans' basic
capabilities by writing new modules for adding
languages, new kinds of file storage, and collabora-
tive capabilities, etc.

Programming Jakarta Struts

By Chuck Cavaness
1st Edition November 2002
462 pages, ISBN 0-596-00328-5

O'Reilly's Programming Jakarta
Struts was written by Chuck
Cavaness after his internet company decided to adopt the
framework, then spent months really figuring out
how to use it to its fullest potential. Readers will
benefit from the real-world, "this is how to do it"
approach Cavaness takes to developing complex
enterprise applications using Struts, and his focus
on the 1.1 version of the Framework makes this the
most up-to-date book available.

Java NIO

By Ron Hitchens
1st Edition August 2002
312 pages, ISBN 0-596-00288-2

Java NIO explores the new I/O
capabilities of version 1.4 in
detail and shows you how to put
these features to work to greatly
improve the efficiency of the Java code you write.
This compact volume examines the typical chal-
lenges that Java programmers face with I/O and
shows you how to take advantage of the capabilities of the new I/O features. You'll learn how to put
these tools to work using examples of common,
real-world I/O problems and see how the new features have a direct impact on responsiveness, scala-
bility, and reliability.

Macintosh Developers

Learning Cocoa with Objective-C, 2nd Edition

By James Duncan Davidson & Apple Computer, Inc.
2nd Edition September 2002
384 pages, ISBN 0-596-00301-3

Based on the Jaguar release of Mac OS X 10.2, this new edition of *Learning Cocoa* covers the latest updates to the Cocoa frameworks, including examples that use the Address Book and Universal Access APIs. Also included with this edition is a handy quick reference card, charting Cocoa's Foundation and AppKit frameworks, along with an Appendix that includes a listing of resources essential to any Cocoa developer—beginning or advanced. This is the "must-have" book for people who want to develop applications for Mac OS X, and is the only book approved and reviewed by Apple engineers.

Learning Carbon

By Apple Computer, Inc.
1st Edition May 2001
368 pages, ISBN 0-596-00161-4

Get up to speed quickly on creating Mac OS X applications with Carbon. You'll learn the fundamentals and key concepts of Carbon programming as you design and build a complete application under the book's guidance. Written by insiders at Apple Computer, *Learning Carbon* provides information you can't get anywhere else, giving you a head start in the Mac OS X application development market.

Mac OS X Hacks

By Rael Dornfest & Kevin Hemenway
1st Edition March 2003
430 pages, ISBN 0-596-00460-5

Mac OS X Hacks reflects the real-world know how and experience of those well steeped in Unix history and expertise, sharing their no-nonsense, sometimes quick-and-dirty solutions to administering and taking full advantage of everything a Unix desktop has to offer: Web, Mail, and FTP serving, security services, SSH, Perl and shell scripting, compiling, configuring, scheduling, networking, and hacking.

Cocoa in a Nutshell

By Mike Beam
1st Edition May 2003
600 pages, ISBN 0-596-00462-1

Aside from material that Apple includes with its Developer Tools, very little documentation exists to cover Cocoa's Objective-C Frameworks—vital tools for anyone interested in developing applications for Mac OS X. This new title provides a complete overview of Cocoa's object classes with a series of chapters in the first half of the book, and a quick reference to Cocoa's Foundation and Application Kit (AppKit) classes in the second half.

Cocoa Design Patterns

By Erik M. Buck
1st Edition August 2003 (est.)
384 pages (est.), ISBN 0-596-00430-3

As more users "switch" from Unix and Windows to the Mac, programmers need to stay ahead of the curve and develop their applications using Apple's Cocoa frameworks. This book illustrates the core design patterns of Cocoa programming, and transfers knowledge about the structure and rationale of Cocoa; something that isn't covered in any other book in print. The book explains the essential patterns of objects that are used in Cocoa, and describes problems solved by Cocoa and the consequences of each solution.

Mac OS X for Unix Geeks

By Brian Jepson & Ernest E. Rothman
1st Edition September 2002
216 pages, 0-596-00356-0

If you're one of the many Unix developers drawn to Mac OS X for its BSD core, you'll find yourself in surprisingly unfamiliar territory. Even if you're an experienced Mac user, Mac OS X is unlike earlier Macs, and it's radically different from the Unix you've used before, too. Their new book is your guide to figuring out the BSD Unix system and Mac-specific components that are making your life difficult and to help ease you into the Unix inside Mac OS X.

x

O'REILLY®

To order: 800-998-9938 • order@oreilly.com • www.oreilly.com
Online editions of most O'Reilly titles are available by subscription at safari.oreilly.com
Also available at most retail and online bookstores.

Macintosh Developers

AppleScript in a Nutshell

By Bruce W. Perry
1st Edition June 2001
528 pages, ISBN 1-56592-841-5

AppleScript in a Nutshell is the first complete reference to Apple-Script, the popular programming language that gives both power users and sophisticated enterprise customers the important ability to automate repetitive tasks and customize applications. *AppleScript in a Nutshell* is a high-end handbook at a low-end price—an essential desktop reference that puts the full power of this user-friendly programming language in every AppleScript user's hands.

Building Cocoa Applications: A Step-by-Step Guide

By Simson Garfinkel & Mike Mahoney
1st Edition May 2002
648 pages, ISBN 0-596-00235-1

Building Cocoa Applications is a step-by-step guide to developing applications for Apple's Mac OS X. It describes, in an engaging tutorial fashion, how to build substantial, object-oriented applications using Cocoa. The primary audience for this book is C programmers who want to learn quickly how to use Cocoa to build significant Mac OS X applications. The book takes the reader from basic Cocoa functions through the most advanced and powerful facilities.

REALbasic: The Definitive Guide, 2nd Edition

By Matt Neuburg
2nd Edition September 2001
752 pages, ISBN 0-596-00177-0

Design astonishingly fast, full-fledged Mac applications with REALbasic! Even if you're a beginning programmer, this book will teach you the essential concepts for programming every aspect of REALbasic. It's a vital reference for the expanding legion of developers who are discovering the power and flexibility of REALbasic. Now covers REALbasic 3, so you can generate your project for Mac OS 8/9, Mac OS X, and Windows.

O'REILLY®

To order: *800-998-9938* • *order@oreilly.com* • *www.oreilly.com*
Online editions of most O'Reilly titles are available by subscription at *safari.oreilly.com*
Also available at most retail and online bookstores.

How to stay in touch with O'Reilly

1. Visit our award-winning web site

http://www.oreilly.com/

★ "Top 100 Sites on the Web"—PC Magazine
★ CIO Magazine's Web Business 50 Awards

Our web site contains a library of comprehensive product information (including book excerpts and tables of contents), downloadable software, background articles, interviews with technology leaders, links to relevant sites, book cover art, and more. File us in your bookmarks or favorites!

2. Join our email mailing lists

Sign up to get email announcements of new books and conferences, special offers, and O'Reilly Network technology newsletters at:

http://elists.oreilly.com

It's easy to customize your free elists subscription so you'll get exactly the O'Reilly news you want.

3. Get examples from our books

To find example files for a book, go to:

http://www.oreilly.com/catalog

select the book, and follow the "Examples" link.

4. Work with us

Check out our web site for current employment opportunites:

http://jobs.oreilly.com/

5. Register your book

Register your book at:

http://register.oreilly.com

6. Contact us

O'Reilly & Associates, Inc.
1005 Gravenstein Hwy North
Sebastopol, CA 95472 USA
TEL: 707-827-7000 or 800-998-9938
        (6am to 5pm PST)
FAX: 707-829-0104

order@oreilly.com
For answers to problems regarding your order or our products. To place a book order online visit:

http://www.oreilly.com/order_new/

catalog@oreilly.com
To request a copy of our latest catalog.

booktech@oreilly.com
For book content technical questions or corrections.

corporate@oreilly.com
For educational, library, government, and corporate sales.

proposals@oreilly.com
To submit new book proposals to our editors and product managers.

international@oreilly.com
For information about our international distributors or translation queries. For a list of our distributors outside of North America check out:

http://international.oreilly.com/distributors.html

adoption@oreilly.com
For information about academic use of O'Reilly books, visit:

http://academic.oreilly.com

O'REILLY®

To order: 800-998-9938 • *order@oreilly.com* • *www.oreilly.com*
Online editions of most O'Reilly titles are available by subscription at *safari.oreilly.com*
Also available at most retail and online bookstores.

Notes